ACHIEVING PRICE STABILITY

A Symposium Sponsored by
The Federal Reserve Bank of Kansas City

Jackson Hole, Wyoming
August 29 - 31, 1996

Contents

*The articles in this publication can be obtained in electronic form from the Federal Reserve Bank of Kansas City's web site. This service contains a wide array of information and data from the bank's Economic Research, Public Affairs, Financial Services, Bank Supervision, and Community Affairs departments. The web site is located at **http://www.kc.frb.org**.*

Foreword

Central banks throughout the world have come to recognize the importance of price stability to the long-run health and prosperity of their economies. While countries and their central banks are embracing price stability as a primary long-term goal for monetary policy, they are adopting a variety of strategies to achieve it. Some banks, for example, have adopted explicit inflation targets. In other cases, institutional structures such as currency boards and monetary union have been suggested as vehicles for achieving and maintaining price stability.

To gain a better understanding of how central banks can best reduce inflation and what policies and operating procedures should be implemented to maintain price stability, the Federal Reserve Bank of Kansas City sponsored a symposium entitled "Achieving Price Stability," held at Jackson Hole, Wyoming, on August 29-31, 1996. A distinguished group of central bankers, academics, and financial market representatives shared their views and research results on this important monetary policy issue.

The papers, commentary, and discussions at the symposium were substantive and informative. Accordingly, we gratefully acknowledge the outstanding contributions of all who participated. Also, special thanks go to members of the Bank's Research Division who helped plan and implement the program, especially to Thomas E. Davis, Senior Vice President and Director of Research. Dr. Davis, who will retire early in 1997, has provided exemplary leadership in ensuring the substance and timeliness of topics throughout the Bank's series of Jackson Hole conferences since the early 1980s.

We hope these proceedings will contribute to a better understanding of how central banks can best achieve and maintain price stability. As recognized by all conference participants, price stability is monetary policy's major contribution toward maximizing long-run economic growth and, ultimately, raising standards of living.

Thomas M. Hoenig
President
Federal Reserve Bank of Kansas City

Symposium Summary

George A. Kahn

Central banks throughout the world are moving to adopt long-run price stability as their primary goal. Whether operating with multiple short-run goals or legislative mandates for price stability, virtually all central banks have recognized the desirability of achieving price stability over time. Countries with moderate to high inflation are adopting policies to reduce inflation, and countries with low inflation are adopting policies to achieve and maintain price stability.

To better understand how central banks can best reduce inflation and what policies and operating procedures should be implemented to maintain price stability, the Federal Reserve Bank of Kansas City sponsored a symposium entitled "Achieving Price Stability," held at Jackson Hole, Wyoming, on August 29-31, 1996. The symposium brought together a distinguished group of central bankers, academics, and financial market representatives. Participants at the symposium agreed that low or zero inflation is the appropriate long-run goal for monetary policy. They disagreed, however, about whether a little inflation should be tolerated and what strategies should be adopted to achieve and maintain price stability.

Defining price stability

Symposium participants accepted Paul Volcker's and Alan Greenspan's conceptual definition that price stability obtains when people do not consider inflation a factor in their decisions. Participants disagreed, however, about operational definitions of price stability. While a wide range of people advocated price stability as the primary long-run goal of monetary policy, they interpreted the term *price stability* differently.

Stanley Fischer suggested the long-run goal of monetary policy should be defined as inflation of about 2 percent, on average, with a range of 1 to 3 percent per year.[1] One reason he felt the goal should be a low, positive inflation rate is that measured inflation overstates actual inflation. This view was widely accepted. As Alan Greenspan emphasized in opening comments at the symposium, the mismeasurement of inflation results, in part, from inadequately accounting for improvements in the quality of goods and services over time.[2] Mismeasurement also results from an inability to account for the continual introduction of new goods and services, especially those produced from "intellectual insight, as distinct from physical effort." Estimates of the upward bias in the consumer price index range from about 0.5 percent to 2 percent in the United States and average about 0.5 percent in Canada and the United Kingdom (Fischer, Freedman).

Another reason given for targeting a low, but positive, inflation rate is that a little inflation might "grease the wheels" of the economy and monetary policy. Fischer and Lawrence Summers emphasized two ways a little inflation might have lubricating properties. First, they said a little inflation would allow employers to lower real wages without cutting nominal wages.[3] The premise of the argument is that nominal wages are downwardly rigid. And, without a mechanism for lowering real wages in times of economic stress, employers would have to resort to laying off workers.

Second, Fischer and Summers said a little inflation lubricates monetary policy by making it possible for central banks to occasionally engineer negative real interest rates. Negative real rates, it is argued, are sometimes helpful in stimulating an economy out of recession. With positive inflation, central banks can push short-term nominal interest rates below the rate of inflation. Such a policy action would be impossible without some inflation since nominal interest rates cannot fall below zero. This argument has gained relevance in light of the recent recession in Japan, where historically low nominal interest rates appeared inadequate to foster economic recovery in the presence of zero or negative inflation.

Many participants at the symposium disagreed with the view that a little inflation greases the wheels of the economy. Some participants thought the evidence on nominal wage rigidity—which comes largely from historical data drawn from periods of moderate inflation—did not necessarily apply to a prospective environment of price stability. Such evidence was at best considered inconclusive (Feldstein, Freedman). In addition, many participants thought the negative real interest rate argument ignored the influence of monetary policy on other asset values, such as equity prices and the exchange rate (Feldstein). Moreover, they attributed the problems in Japan, not to a lack of monetary policy potency, but rather to the delayed actions of the Bank of Japan in lowering rates (McCallum).

Another issue discussed at the symposium was whether price stability should be defined in terms of the inflation rate or as a path for the level of prices. Under the first definition, a shock to the inflation rate would be followed by a gradual return of inflation to the rate associated with price stability. In the process, the price level would drift randomly over time. Under the second definition, a shock to the inflation rate would force the central bank to move inflation, for a period of time, above or below the level associated with price stability (and in some cases causing actual deflation). As a result, the price level would eventually return to its original path. The advantage of such a pre-determined path for the price level is that it would reduce uncertainty about the level of prices far into the future. The disadvantage, according to conventional wisdom, is that it would require greater variability in the inflation rate, with central banks having to offset positive shocks to inflation with negative shocks and vice versa (Fischer, Mullins).

Most participants at the symposium thought price stability should be defined in terms of the inflation rate, not the price level. However,

Lars Svensson put forward a technical argument suggesting that, contrary to conventional wisdom, achieving a pre-determined path for the price level could result in lower inflation variability. Some symposium participants were skeptical about the validity of this result in practice. Most participants felt that, at least for now, monetary policy should be aimed at achieving a low and stable inflation rate. Later, after further research, central bankers could reconsider the benefits and costs of stabilizing the price level.

Reducing inflation

Given that inflation in many countries is above the rate consistent with both conceptual and practical definitions of price stability, a key topic at the symposium was how central banks should reduce inflation. Following a discussion of conceptual issues, central bankers who had successfully reduced inflation in their countries described their experiences.

Symposium participants agreed reducing inflation was desirable because "inflation is economically and socially costly" (Fischer). One major cost is the uncertainty inflation creates about future prices. Another cost stems from the interaction of inflation with the tax code. For example, looking at the interaction of capital income tax rules and inflation, Martin Feldstein concluded the economic costs of inflation in the United States were surprisingly large. Specifically, he estimated the annual cost of an inflation rate of 2 percent rather than zero was 1 percent of GDP. Thus, permanently lowering inflation by two percentage points would generate an extra 1 percent of GDP each year. While not everyone agreed with Feldstein's surprisingly large estimates, everyone did agree there were significant benefits from reducing inflation and, therefore, inflation should be reduced over time.

With the desirability of reducing inflation clearly established, Mervyn King provided a conceptual framework for analyzing how central banks should reduce inflation over time. In particular, he examined how fast central banks should reduce inflation and how accommodating they should be in response to temporary economic shocks. He argued the best policy would combine explicit inflation targets with a discretionary approach to economic shocks. On the issue of the speed of disinflation, King advocated a gradual timetable, with inflation targets consistently set below the public's inflation expectations and steadily falling. On the issue of the appropriate response to shocks, King recommended that central banks at least partially accommodate temporary inflation shocks such as those stemming from increases in food and energy prices. However, he also suggested that until central banks establish their inflation-fighting credibility in the eyes of the public, they need to be particularly cautious in accommodating shocks, especially at the beginning of the disinflationary process.

Throughout his discussion, King emphasized the role of learning by central banks and the public. Monetary policy procedures evolve over time as central banks learn, and the public's expectations about monetary policy change only gradually.[4] It is therefore important for central banks to communicate what they learn to the public and for disinflationary policies to be transparent. Policymakers should make clear through their public statements and their actions what their inflation objective is, how they will respond to temporary shocks, and how they think the economy behaves.

The approach to disinflation that King advocated is a deliberate one, under which policymakers would try to make steady progress, year by year, toward price stability. An alternative approach is an opportunistic strategy, under which policymakers would try to keep an already low inflation rate low while waiting for an unexpected recession or favorable supply shock to ratchet the inflation rate down over time. Donald Kohn argued that an opportunistic strategy might enable central banks to reach price stability without deliberately slowing economic growth or reducing the level of economic activity. While Kohn said opportunistic disinflation was a strategy worth considering, he emphasized it was not the official policy of the Federal Reserve.

King had reservations about the opportunistic strategy. He suggested such a policy ran the risk of being interpreted as targeting an unemployment rate below the rate consistent with stable inflation. As a result, such a policy might reduce central bank credibility and thereby increase the output loss associated with disinflation. Other participants at the symposium (Freedman, Svensson) also had reservations about opportunistic disinflation, and the issue was left unresolved.[5]

Turning to the unique problems associated with a legacy of high inflation, Rudiger Dornbusch examined how countries with high inflation could best move toward price stability. He divided the problem into two parts—how to get out of extreme inflation (over 15 percent per *month*) and how to reduce moderate inflation (15 percent or less per *year*). To reduce extreme inflation, he recommended a complete change of regime, in which the government budget could not be financed by the central bank and in which the central bank would tie its currency to that of another country. Better yet, Dornbusch suggested, countries with extreme inflation should simply replace their local currency with that of a neighboring country with low and stable inflation, such as the United States or Germany.

To reduce moderate inflation, Dornbusch recommended the effort be viewed as one of several economic problems to be solved, and that a time frame of five or more years be adopted. For countries with a legacy of high inflation, too zealous an approach to reducing a moderate inflation risks "super-high" real interest rates, an overvalued currency, severe recession, and banking system problems. While concern for reducing moderate inflation is clearly appropriate, it must be balanced with a concern for economic growth.

Following the discussion of conceptual issues involved in reducing inflation, a panel of three central bankers discussed how they had reduced inflation in their countries. Donald Brash emphasized the comprehensive nature of reform in New Zealand and the use of explicit inflation targets to reduce inflation. Jacob Frenkel described the role of the exchange rate against the dollar in Israel's transition to moderate inflation and the use of inflation targets as a transparent guide to low inflation. Finally, Josef Tosovsky reviewed the Czech

Republic's rapid transition from a command economy to a market-oriented economy in which the nominal exchange rate was used as the anchor for stabilization policy.

At a luncheon address, Domingo Cavallo continued the discussion of practical experiences by describing the approach used in Argentina. Among other reforms, Argentina put in place a new monetary system which transformed the central bank into a virtual currency board. As such, the central bank permitted holders of pesos to exchange, at any time, one peso for one U.S. dollar. At the same time, all indexation clauses were prohibited. The results were striking. Inflation fell from 1,344 percent in 1990 to 1.6 percent in 1995 and to 0 percent from June 1995 to June 1996.

Maintaining price stability

After considering conceptual and practical issues in reducing inflation, the discussion turned to strategies for maintaining price stability. A variety of strategies were proposed, but all shared at least one common feature. All the strategies allowed monetary policy some capacity to accommodate shocks while still maintaining long-run price stability.

John Taylor began the discussion by reviewing various explanations for why price stability had not been maintained in the past. In his view, the most compelling explanation was the rise of economic theories in the 1960s suggesting a long-run tradeoff between inflation and output. These theories provided the intellectual basis for policymakers to pursue monetary policies biased toward higher inflation. When combined with unrealistically low estimates of the "full-employment unemployment rate" and energy price shocks, these policies inevitably produced higher inflation. Only after the economics profession began incorporating more realistic theories of expectations formation into models of inflation did policymakers move toward lowering and stabilizing inflation. The superior performance of the U.S. economy since the early 1980s has made it clear, in retrospect, that disinflation was the correct policy to pursue after the inflationary 1970s.

Looking to the future, specifically at policies for maintaining price stability once it has been achieved, Taylor advocated the flexible use of a policy rule. In particular, he recommended a rule incorporating a short-run tradeoff between inflation and output but not a long-run tradeoff. Taylor's preferred rule, which sets (along with various other parameters) a long-run target for inflation consistent with price stability, would guide policymakers in adjusting short-term interest rates in response to deviations of real GDP from potential and inflation from target.[6] Thus, if an output shock raised real GDP above potential, policymakers would raise short-term interest rates. Likewise, if inflation came in above target, policymakers would raise rates. While the rule would allow policymakers to counter adverse short-run shocks to supply and demand, adherence to the rule would nevertheless maintain long-run price stability.

In commenting on Taylor's presentation, David Mullins disagreed somewhat with Taylor's view on what went wrong in the 1970s, but generally agreed with Taylor on how to respond to shocks once price stability has been achieved. Arguing that the economics profession had less influence on policy than Taylor asserted, Mullins put relatively less weight on misguided economic theory and relatively more weight on adverse price shocks in explaining why price stability had not been maintained in the past. On the broader issue of how monetary policy should respond to shocks, Mullins emphasized the need to stay focused on the long-run goal of maintaining price stability.

Turning to monetary policy implementation, Charles Freedman reviewed from a practitioner's perspective a wide range of issues involved in maintaining price stability. Within the framework of explicit inflation targets, Freedman described (among other things) the role of inflation forecasts in conducting policy, the appropriate response of policy instruments to changes in forecast inflation, and the importance of transparency and communication. Central to his analysis were the effect central bank credibility has on the response of financial markets and inflation expectations to monetary policy actions, and the effect that monetary policy actions have on central bank credibility. The more credible the central bank's commitment is to price stability, the more flexible monetary policy can be in responding to shocks.

In responding to a deviation of inflation from target, monetary policy actions that return inflation quickly to target build credibility. However, they might also lead to undesirable volatility in output, interest rates, and exchange rates. A more gradual return of inflation to target smooths fluctuations in output and financial market variables but risks damaging central bank credibility and entrenching inflation expectations. Freedman said that empirical studies for Canada suggested the optimal time horizon for returning inflation to target was six to eight quarters. To minimize any harmful effects on credibility of such a gradual approach, the Bank of Canada has explicitly explained the approach in its statements to the public.

In commenting on Freedman's paper, Otmar Issing and Donald Kohn both expressed reservations about the use of explicit inflation targets. Issing argued that having a commitment to price stability and announcing a low inflation target were not enough to anchor inflation expectations. Rather, the central bank needs to disclose its policy procedures to the public and assure the pubic that these procedures are capable of maintaining price stability over the long run. Given lags between monetary policy actions and their effects on the economy, intermediate indicators serve as necessary signals of inflationary pressures. While inflation forecasts can serve as one such indicator, Issing thought they should be supplemented with other indicators, including, most importantly, monetary aggregates. In addition, he said, the use of monetary aggregates as intermediate targets for policy increases monetary policy transparency and helps define the responsibilities of the central bank as distinct from institutions responsible for fiscal or wage policy.[7]

Kohn took a slightly different tack, suggesting that inflation targets could limit a central bank's flexibility in responding to shocks. For example, inflation targets that tie monetary policy to a timetable for achieving a specific inflation outcome might prevent a central bank, which is otherwise committed to maintaining price stability, from responding to unexpected developments. For example, inflation targets could be inconsistent with a Taylor-type rule in which the central bank's commitment to price stability is explicit, but the time frame over which price stability is maintained depends on economic circumstances. In the United States, considerable flexibility has been retained in determining the time frame for achieving price stability. As Kohn stated, "Long-run discipline on monetary policy has been provided not by numerical targets but the firm focus of an independent central bank on reducing inflation over the long run, so as to eventually reach price stability—as specified in the Federal Reserve Act."

Conclusions

The symposium concluded with comments from three overview panelists. Andrew Crockett questioned when and whether central banks would take the final step to move from moderate inflation to price stability. He noted that most central banks are not fully satisfied with current inflation yet appear unprepared to pay the price, in terms of lost output, of moving deliberately toward price stability.

Martin Feldstein made a strong case for central banks achieving not merely low inflation but no inflation. He recommended the goal should be to equate the measured rate of inflation to the bias in the consumer price index and suggested the United States achieve the goal in the next four years. He discussed the economic gains from pursuing such a policy and explained why he felt policies that accepted higher inflation were ill-advised.

Finally, in looking to the future of monetary policy in Europe, Jean-Claude Trichet compared the prospective role of the European Central Bank (ECB) in pursuing price stability with the current policy of the Bank of France. Like the Bank of France, the ECB will operate independently under a legal mandate to ensure price stability. Also like the Bank of France, the ECB will likely adopt monetary aggregates as intermediate targets of policy. Echoing the comments of many symposium participants, Trichet emphasized that sound and credible medium-term and long-term objectives are crucial for achieving and maintaining price stability. And, he noted, coping with a changing economy—and coping with changing perceptions about the economy—are essential in the analysis and conduct of central banking.

Endnotes

[1]Fischer did not identify a specific index of inflation to be used as the target of policy.

[2]Summers was not convinced this quality bias needed to be built into the concept of price stability, at least to the extent the concept was used as a long-tun target for monetary policy. He believed the "sticker price" was what people cared about, not quality-adjusted changes in cost.

[3]Fischer cited a recent study by George Akerlof, William Dickens, and George Perry, "The Macroeconomics of Low Inflation," published in the *Brookings Papers on Economic Activity*, no. 1, pp. 1-59.

[4]McCallum made the point that, even if the public's learning process was fully understood, the output effects of a transition period to lower inflation would depend critically on what was assumed about aggregate supply—that is, the economy's "wage-price-output dynamics."

[5]McCallum distinguished between the use of the term "opportunistic policy" to refer to regime design and to the process of transition between regimes. With respect to regime design, McCallum viewed opportunistic policy as "very unattractive." With respect to transition between regimes, he said opportunistic policy "might make some sense, at least on political grounds."

[6]Svensson advocated a slightly different rule. While Taylor specified a formula for adjusting a policy instrument—the federal funds rate—Svensson specified a "target" rule. Specifically, he argued that the central bank should use a *forecast* of inflation as its intermediate target and set its instruments to equate the forecast of inflation to the long-run target for inflation. Svensson suggested such a target rule was superior to Taylor's instrument rule.

[7]Jean-Claude Trichet also advocated the use of monetary aggregates as intermediate targets.

George A. Kahn is an assistant vice president and economist at the Federal Reserve Bank of Kansas City.

Opening Remarks

Alan Greenspan

I am pleased to join in welcoming you all to a conference that will address some of the core issues confronting central banks around the world today.

The more than academic interest being accorded to a conference entitled "Achieving Price Stability" is a testament to the effectiveness of the conduct of monetary policy around the world in bringing inflation to heel over the past fifteen years or so. At the start of the 1980s, it was obvious that the high rates of inflation around the world were corrosive, and that the Federal Reserve and other central banks had to bring inflation down. Under the leadership of Paul Volcker as well as others also present here, that initial objective was accomplished. And now, for the first time in at least a generation, the goal of price stability is within the reach of all the major industrial countries as well as a substantial number of others.

But how will we central bankers know when we have achieved it? Certainly we would deem our policies successful if we removed unproductive price-expectation-driven actions from economic activity, for that is a necessary condition for economic stability and maximum efficiencies. This suggests, from a central banker's point of reference, an operating definition of price stability: Price stability obtains when economic agents no longer take account of the prospective change in the general price level in their economic decisionmaking.

Since we cannot observe expectations directly, we look for proxies. If we believe that expectations are grounded in reality, then the relevant proxy is an index of the actual general price level. But what is the appropriate index?

When prices were rising rapidly by almost any measure in the 1970s, it was perfectly apparent that inflation was distorting economic decisionmaking in a very serious way. There was no need for policymakers to worry about defining the ultimate inflation objective more precisely or choosing a specific price index proxy because it was obvious that the next step on inflation had to be in a downward direction.

But today, with inflation in the United States running in the neighborhood of 3 percent according to the Consumer Price Index (CPI), and considerably lower than that according to some of the chain-weighted indexes from the national income accounts, the issue of what is actually happening to the general price level becomes much more important for monetary policymakers.

Similar measurement problems exist in other major countries. How will we know when price expectations have indeed ceased to be a factor in economic decisionmaking? Indexed bonds may not be as helpful as one might suppose. Indexed to what? Is there a specific aggregate price level index for both evaluation and possible indexing on which we can rely?

Unfortunately, we might as well recognize that we aren't going to get much assistance in this endeavor from conventional textbook models or run-of-the-mill academic discussions. Much of the professional literature on the topic of monetary policy simply assumes that the economy produces goods and services, whose units are well defined and, hence, the task of constructing an aggregate price level is straightforward.

Through the first half of this century, the U.S. economy probably could be thought of, as least to a first approximation, in these terms. After all, it was not particularly difficult to measure the units of most types of agricultural or mining output, and even much of the output of the manufacturing sector could be measured reasonably well in terms of physical units such as tons of carbon steel or board feet of lumber. Even here, of course, prices differed by types of carbon steel and lumber.

However, as we move into the twenty-first century, the concept of a unit of output is becoming increasingly difficult to craft. Today, an ever-growing fraction of overall value added reflects intellectual insight as distinct from physical effort. For a rapidly expanding part of our GDP, the notion of a discrete and well-defined unit of output is becoming progressively illusive.

Obviously, such a development is raising exceptionally difficult issues for price measurement. How, for example, should we decompose the enormous increase in nominal expenditure on medical care in recent years into its "price" and "quantity" components? Consider the case of cataract surgery. Forty years ago, the typical cataract patient had to endure a hospital stay of seven days, and required extensive post-operative vision correction because the eye's natural lenses had been removed. Today, the typical patient is treated on an outpatient basis. Furthermore, in many cases the patient does not require any vision correction after the operation because artificial lenses have been employed. In light of these enormous quality improvements, we obviously cannot treat the unadjusted fee for a single operation as "the price of cataract surgery." Instead, we must attempt to quantify the value of these improvements, and adjust our price indexes accordingly. Advances in arthroscopic surgery pose similar problems.

Examples pertaining to other goods and services abound. What is the appropriate unit of software output? How should we value the convenience of ATMs, or the flexibility that will become available with the advent of personal computer banking? In many cases, the measurement challenge is compounded by the fact that the item in question simply did not exist twenty, or ten, or even two years ago. Clearly, if you cannot define the unit of output, you cannot define price. And even if you succeed in an adequate proxy for unit of output, unless it is substantially unchanged over a period of time, price *change* is not defined.

But daunting though these problems may be, it is worth also recognizing how far we have come in recent years. For example, until 1986, the price of computers was treated as constant in the U.S. national income accounts. To be sure, the computer price series embedded in the national income accounts today may not represent the last word on the matter, but surely they represent a very considerable improvement over the prior state of affairs.

Accordingly, on the one hand, the economy seems irreversibly evolving toward producing more of the impalpable forms of output, and, hence, making it ever harder to define price. On the other hand, economic knowledge is marching—however slowly—toward a more thorough understanding of the issues related to the pricing of such forms of output.

Fortunately, although measurement problems obscure our vision, we know that a general price level must exist in principle. This would be the case even were we unable to measure definitively *any* of the individual prices which make up a general average level. For so long as contracts are being made that involve the exchange of future claims on goods and services denominated in nominal units, the parties to those contracts will have made some implicit or explicit judgment about the forward purchasing power of those nominal units. And those judgments will be embodied in the prices placed on the transaction. On financial markets, for example, as lenders and borrowers exchange current for future claims on goods and services, expectations of future changes in the purchasing power of the currency become embedded in the term structure of interest rates. While backing them out, of course, is no easy task, in part because it requires assumptions about real interest rates as well as term and inflation risk premiums, the presumption that there is a general price level is not in question. Such a presumption is also evident in contracts that specify future financial payments such as forward labor agreements and numerous forms of insurance contracts.

To summarize then, a general price level exists wholly apart from measurement problems; expectations about it can distort economic decisionmaking; and as a consequence, central banks need to be able to judge whether they are achieving their long-run objective of price stability.

As the conference proceeds, I hope we can keep in mind the operational difficulty of knowing exactly to what we are all referring when we speak of "price stability." Finally, I certainly would welcome any discussion as to how central banks can infer information about the price level, and the effects of their policies on it, in the face of imprecise statistical proxies for it.

Why Are Central Banks Pursuing Long-Run Price Stability?

Stanley Fischer

The question posed by the title of this paper has at least two interesting interpretations. The first is why long-run price stability is desirable. The second is what political economy arguments have led to the view that price stability should be the main or only policy goal for the central bank, even though there is a short-run tradeoff between output and inflation.

I shall take up these questions in turn, and also discuss what is and should be understood by (long-run) price stability. One thing central banks do not mean by price stability is stability of the average level of prices. Rather they mean reasonably low inflation, typically 1 to 3 percent per year.

This paper focuses on key issues that arise in considering the adoption of long-run price stability as *the* or *a* goal of monetary policy. The first section sets the background by discussing the allocative costs of inflation. The second and third sections consider the Phillips curve and the growth-inflation tradeoffs, respectively. The fourth section asks why governments nonetheless inflate. In the fifth section, I discuss the optimal rate of inflation, suggesting that, for an industrialized country that has already attained single-digit inflation, it is best to target a rate in the range of 1 to 3 percent. I then turn to political economy issues. The sixth section presents evidence on the public's views of inflation. The paper concludes in the seventh section, which examines the question of why price level stability is increasingly taking precedence as the main stated policy target for the central bank, despite the existence of a short-run Phillips tradeoff.

The costs of inflation

The fundamental reason to pursue long-run price stability is that—as has long been argued by central bankers and is increasingly accepted by academic economists—inflation is economically and socially costly. A comprehensive listing of the economic costs of inflation is presented in Fischer and Modigliani (1978), Fischer (1981), and Fischer (1994), where it is emphasized that the costs of any given rate of inflation depend on the extent to which the institutional structure of the economy—particularly the tax system and especially the taxation of capital—has adapted to inflation. I will not go over these costs, some of which result from the greater uncertainty about inflation that is associated with higher rates of inflation, in any detail here, rather referring the reader to my earlier articles.[1]

The social costs have been less comprehensively catalogued and established, but these too contribute importantly to the public's dislike of high inflation.[2] Opinion polls, which will be discussed below, leave no doubt that high inflation is politically unpopular, a view confirmed by the results of presidential elections in Argentina in 1995, Brazil in 1994, Peru in 1995, and Russia in 1996. And history confirms that high rates of inflation are both socially disruptive and *in extremis* associated with political and social disorder.

Most of the traditional calculations of the economic costs of inflation emphasize its allocative costs. Recently, Feldstein (1996) has presented detailed calculations of the economic costs of inflation in the United States implied by the interactions of existing capital income tax rules and inflation, and concluded that the annual welfare cost of an inflation rate of 2 percent rather than zero is a surprisingly large 1 percent of GDP.[3] Most of this cost derives from the distortion of the intertemporal allocation of consumption caused by the inflation-induced reduction in the real rate of return on saving. The result depends on the non-indexation of capital income taxation. It is so recent, and the calculations so complicated, that it will take some time until the significance of the result and its sensitivity to changes in assumptions can be established.[4,5]

Feldstein also makes the point that, even if there is a short-run tradeoff between inflation and output, the appropriate calculation in deciding whether to reduce inflation requires weighing a one-time output loss against a permanent welfare gain, equal to the capitalized value of the annual welfare gain.[6]

The allocative costs of inflation discussed in this section are important. Most should manifest themselves in lower levels of consumption, income, or perhaps growth, at higher rates of inflation.[7] But they could be outweighed by the Phillips curve relationship between inflation and unemployment, or perhaps by a positive relationship between inflation and growth. We examine those possibilities in turn.

The Phillips curve

It is widely, though not universally, accepted that there is no long-run tradeoff between inflation and unemployment.[8] Three points deserve further consideration: the existence of a short-run tradeoff; the possibility and implications of hysteresis; and the nature of the tradeoff at low inflation rates.

First, there is a short-run tradeoff between inflation and unemployment, equivalently between inflation and output. Two types of evidence are decisive: econometric studies in the United States and elsewhere establish the existence of the tradeoff;[9] and every major central bank assumes the existence of the tradeoff in its policy decisions. Low unemployment and high capacity utilization lead to monetary policy tightening to prevent inflation; and monetary policy is eased during recessions to spur output, once inflation is thought unlikely to increase.[10,11]

Second, there is the important question posed by the work of Blanchard and Summers (1986), of whether there is hysteresis in the behavior of unemployment, namely that the behavior of the unemployment rate is affected by the history of unemployment. Blanchard and Summers suggested that the unemployment rate in Europe followed a random walk, a result they attributed to the role of insiders in wage determination. More generally, the natural rate of unemployment might change, though not necessarily one-for-one, with the actual unemployment rate. In the United States, it certainly appears to be the case that economists' estimates of the natural rate are affected by the recent history of the actual rate. The following rule of thumb roughly describes economists' estimates of the non-accelerating inflation rate of unemployment (NAIRU):

$$u^*_t = 5.0 + 0.3\,(u_{t-1} - 5.0), \tag{1}$$

where u^*_t is the estimate of the NAIRU at time t, and u is the actual rate of unemployment. A similar rule could hold in Europe, where estimates of the structural rate of unemployment have kept rising along with the actual rate.

Equation 1 could describe the behavior of the actual NAIRU over time; alternatively, it is consistent with the true NAIRU being 5 percent. In this latter case, the equation might result from the natural caution of the economic adviser, unwilling to state at times of high unemployment that the margin of unused capacity is very large. Suppose that policymakers were willing to run expansionary policies as long as the actual rate was above the natural rate. Then, if the true NAIRU is 5 percent, equation 1 could mislead policymakers into excess caution at times of high unemployment, and excess optimism at times of low unemployment.[12]

Third, the nature of the Phillips curve at very low inflation rates is central to the discussion of the target inflation rate. It has long been argued that a little inflation greases the wheels of the labor market,[13] and more generally, that a little inflation eases needed adjustments of relative prices. The argument assumes that wage or price cuts are less likely than increases, equivalently that there is downward stickiness of nominal wages or prices.

The result is a long-run Phillips curve that is vertical at high rates of inflation but that displays a tradeoff at lower rates of inflation, as the constraint on reductions in nominal wages increasingly bites.[14] The empirical evidence is so far inconclusive. On the fact of downward wage inflexibility, survey evidence suggests that reductions in nominal wages in the United States are quite common.[15] However, Akerlof, Dickens, and Perry (1996) argue that much of the reported evidence on wage reductions results from response errors to survey questions. Chapple (1996) finds a concentration of wage changes at zero in New Zealand during the low inflation period 1988-1993.[16] Less formal evidence provides some support for the notion of downward wage inflexibility: any academic economist old enough to have been chairperson of the department knows that giving a small nominal increase is disproportionately easier than no change or a wage cut.

At the aggregate level, the data do not speak clearly enough to establish the shape of the Phillips curve at low inflation rates.[17] It must be, though, that downward wage or price inflexibility is a matter of convention, rather than a structural feature of the economy. Money illusion is after all an illusion, one that is likely to yield eventually to the weight of the facts. Most likely, wages that are now inflexible downward would eventually become more flexible if the economy lived through a period of sustained low inflation and/or high unemployment. The logic of the vertical Phillips curve would eventually come to dominate. In the meantime there would be a short-run tradeoff, albeit one that could last a long time.

The evidence on how long it could take the economy to adjust to very low rates of inflation, to reset wage and price setting to an expected rate of inflation close to zero, is mixed. Recent U.S. experience has seen inflation at its lowest level in thirty years with an unemployment rate at the estimated NAIRU and below, hardly evidence of downward price or wage stickiness at recent inflation rates. The aggregate price level declined during the Great Depression

Chart 1
Industrial Countries: Comparison of Average Unemployment Rates During Years with Higher Than Average Versus Lower than Average Inflation Rates, 1975-94

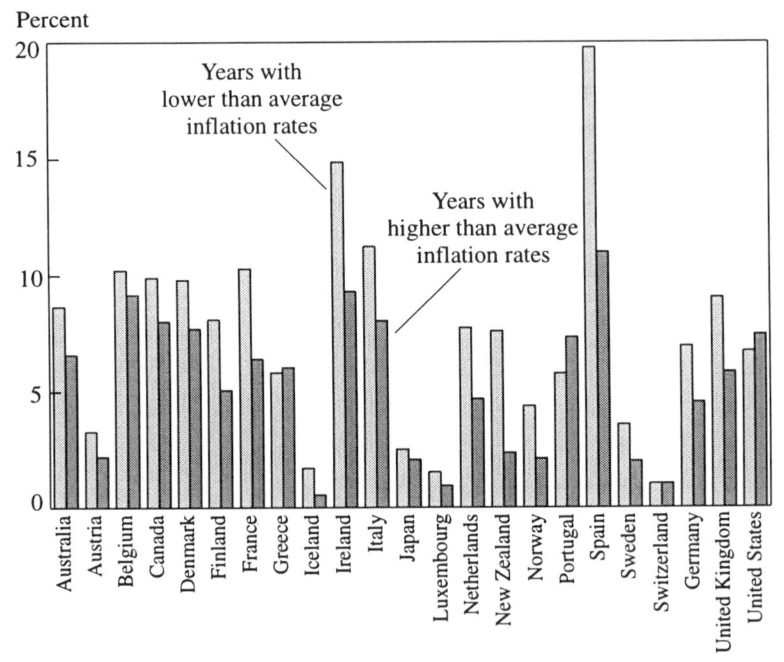

Sources: IMF, International Financial Statistics and OECD, Analytical Database.

of the late nineteenth century, creating political discontent but not protracted unemployment or low growth. The experience of the Great Depression of the 1930s in the United States likewise suggests a costly transition period: prices and wages did display downward flexibility, but not sufficient to prevent massive unemployment.

Recent European experience raises some *prima facie* concerns that the relevant adjustment period may be quite long. Chart 1 shows average unemployment rates in the industrialized countries corresponding to years of below and above average inflation during the period 1975-94. With the exceptions of Greece, Portugal, and the United States, unemployment has been higher when inflation was lower. One explanation for this association is that the natural rate of

Chart 2
Growth and Inflation[1]
(1965-94 average)

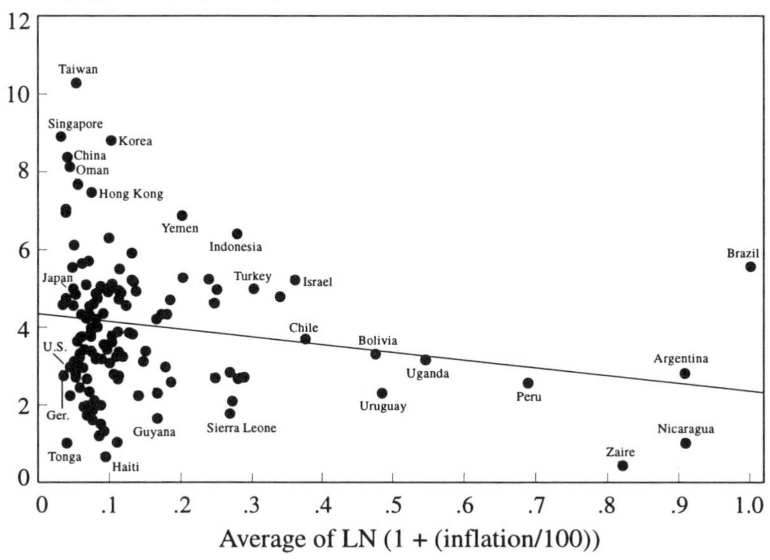

[1]Slope of regression line is -1.905 with a T-statistic of -2.098.
Source: IMF, *World Economic Outlook* Database.

unemployment in most countries has been significantly higher in the low inflation 1990s than in the higher inflation 1970s and 1980s.[18] It is also possible though that the estimated increases in the natural rate of unemployment are consistent with the second interpretation of equation 1, and that in most countries, it will take a long time for asymmetries of price and wage adjustment to be worn down.

Inflation and growth

The simple correlation between growth and (the logarithm of one plus) the inflation rate over the period 1965-94 is negative (Chart 2) and statistically significant.[19] However, the relationship is not very strong and its significance is sensitive to the inflation range considered. For the entire sample period, the correlation between inflation and growth is negative but insignificant for the sample of countries for which inflation averages less than 40 percent; for the sample for which inflation averages less than 10 percent, the correlation is negative and significant.[20] The relationship is also negative and significant for the entire sample for time periods 1975-94 and 1985-94 respectively, and negative but not significant for the lower inflation rate samples during those subperiods.

The inflation-growth relationship has also been studied in cross-sectional growth regressions that include other variables.[21] Despite their widespread use, some problems remain in the interpretation of such regressions. First, they rarely have a clear structural interpretation; rather, they are searches for suggestive correlations. Second, Levine and Renelt (1992) showed that very few of the results established in such regressions are robust, and this holds true also for the inflation-growth relationship.

The inflation-growth relationship is stronger in regressions that control for other variables, including in some (Sarel, 1996) the initial level of income,[22] and in others (Judson and Orphanides, 1996) the rate of investment. The negative inflation-growth relationship is also stronger in panel regressions, such as those in Fischer (1993) and Judson and Orphanides (1996), which take account—appropriately I believe—of both time-series variation within each country as well as cross-country variations.[23] This implies that the time series inflation-growth relationship for individual countries is predominantly negative.[24]

There is, however, controversy about the nature of the relationship at low rates of inflation. Similar theoretical arguments to those that imply the long-run Phillips curve may not be vertical at low inflation rates could also imply that the growth-inflation relationship is positive at very low inflation rates—because asymmetric price adjustments hamper the reallocations of resources necessary to produce growth. Thus, *a priori* considerations suggest that a negative relationship could apply at high inflation rates and a positive or neutral relationship at very low rates. Several attempts have been made to examine this possibility, and to estimate a switching point if one exists.

The most striking results are reported by Bruno and Easterly (1996), who show that 40 percent annual inflation is a threshold above which a country is likely to go into a high-inflation, low-growth crisis. They show also that per capita growth is on average lower than the world average during the crisis period (defined as starting in the year in which the inflation rate first exceeds 40 percent), and then higher than the world average after stabilization to below 40 percent inflation. Results at a lower threshold are either insignificant, or very sensitive to the inclusion of particular observations. These results unambiguously establish that high inflation is bad for growth, and that stabilization to below 40 percent inflation is good for growth. They do not establish the nature of the partial (*ceteris paribus*) growth-inflation relationship at lower inflation rates, although the authors seem to suggest that there is no significant relationship.

There are several regression-based attempts to locate potential nonlinearities in the inflation-growth relationship. Sarel (1996) finds a breakpoint in the relationship at about 8 percent inflation.[25] His estimates imply that the growth-inflation relationship is zero (or slightly positive) at lower inflation rates, and negative at higher rates. By allowing for the possible nonlinearity, Sarel also obtains an increase in the estimated negative effect of (the logarithm of one plus) inflation on growth for high inflation rates.[26] Judson and Orphanides, the main goal of whose paper is to distinguish between the effects on growth of uncertainty about inflation versus the (logarithm of the) rate of inflation, include two breakpoints, at 10 percent and at 40 percent. They find an insignificant but positive relationship at rates below 10 percent, and significant negative relationships at higher rates.[27]

These results leave little doubt that double-digit inflation is bad for growth. However, they leave the nature of the relationship at lower inflation rates uncertain. The simple correlations for inflation rates below 10 percent are all negative in the large sample used in Chart 2, but the coefficient on inflation in multiple regressions is sometimes positive at low inflation rates; the simple correlation is significant but the partial relationship insignificant. In Chart 3, for the period 1975-94, growth rates during very low inflation periods

Chart 3
Industrial Countries: Comparison of Average Growth During Episodes of Low Inflation Versus the 1975-94 Average

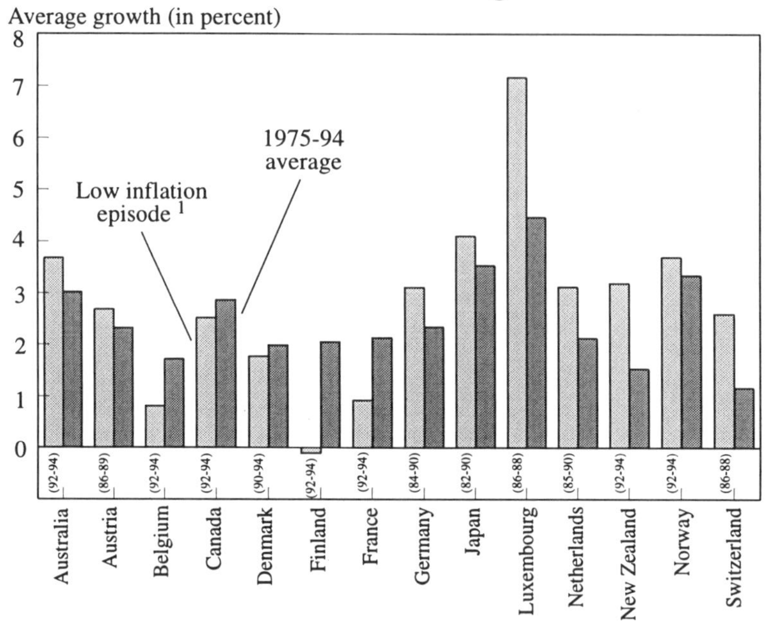

[1] An episode of low inflation for a given country is defined as the longest period of three or more consecutive years of low inflation (less than 3 percent) from 1975 to 1994. (Dates for low inflation episodes are shown in parenthesis).
Source: IMF, *World Economic Outlook* Database.

(less than 3 percent) are compared with growth rates during the entire period, for those industrialized countries that experienced a period of at least three years of inflation below 3 percent. Growth rates are higher during the low inflation periods for nine countries, and lower in five. Chart 3 points, but weakly, to a negative growth-inflation relationship at very low inflation rates, but these results could also be a result of the cyclical timing of inflation and recovery.

Some work has been done for the industrialized countries seeking to identify potential effects of inflation on productivity growth.[28] Higher inflation is associated with lower productivity growth, though cyclical timing relationships or the presence of supply shocks may also play a role.

The overall conclusion must be that it is not possible at this stage to draw any firm conclusion on the relationship between inflation and growth at the very low inflation rates current in the G-7, though there is little evidence for a significant positive association between inflation and growth even at very low inflation rates. The data leave open the possibility that there is a negative relationship between growth and inflation at rates of inflation as low as 1 to 3 percent. Or, there may be no significant relationship when inflation is as low as 1 to 3 percent. Even less is known about the relationship between inflation and growth at negative inflation rates.

Why do governments inflate?

The classic analysis of the costs and benefits of inflation focuses on seigniorage, the revenue obtained by the government from the creation of money.[29] The revenue motive should be understood as applying not only to the direct creation of high-powered money, but also more broadly to the entire process of credit creation. Governments often seek to circumvent budget constraints by using both public and private financial institutions for quasi-fiscal purposes. In addition, some of the financial benefits of high inflation accrue to the private banking and financial system, which typically flourishes in an inflationary environment—and has painfully to contract when stabilization eventually comes.

The rate of inflation that can be justified by seigniorage depends on the efficiency of other methods of raising revenue. A government with a pressing need for revenue, for instance a newly established government in a transition economy, or a wartime government, may well be justified in producing double-digit inflation. Seigniorage is relatively unimportant in most industrialized countries, about 0.5 percent or less of GDP, and would not justify an appreciable rate of inflation.

Although the traditional analysis emphasizes the domestic demand for high-powered money, globalization means that central banks now have to take foreign competition into account in calculating the revenue likely to accrue from seigniorage. In recent years, the Federal Reserve System has earned over $10 billion a year by exporting dollar bills, an amount that would be lower if the Fed had been less successful at controlling inflation (Judson and Porter, 1996).

In addition to the revenue motive, governments inflate because the short- and long-run tradeoffs between inflation and output differ in ways that make inflation costly to stop and almost always tempting to start. An essential element in this tension is captured by the dynamic inconsistency model of inflation developed by Barro and Gordon (1983). These models provide the basis for modern theories of credibility and central bank independence that allow economists to analyze modern central banking in terms used by central bankers themselves.[30]

The essential insight in these models is that, given a low inflation rate and the short-run tradeoff between inflation and output, a government that would prefer output to be above the natural rate is tempted to exploit the tradeoff by running an expansionary monetary policy. Policy is thus subject to an inflationary bias. In equilibrium, private agents will understand the temptation that faces the government, and will adjust their expectations of inflation upward: inflation rises to a level at which its marginal cost, given that it is expected, is high enough to prevent the government from attempting to increase output by seeking an even higher rate of inflation. As a result, the country ends up with no gain in output but with an inflation rate that is higher than socially optimal—unless it can find some institutional device, such as an independent central bank, that enables it to avoid self-defeating temptation.

The optimal rate of inflation

The discussion so far points to the desirability of targeting single-digit inflation, but leaves open the question of where in that range to aim. In this section I discuss the optimal long-run rate of inflation for an industrialized country that has already attained single-digit inflation.[31]

The analytic arguments reviewed in the first section suggest that inflation is costly, and that the optimal rate of inflation is very low, or perhaps even negative.[32] The Phillips curve evidence of the second section of this paper shows no signs of a long-run tradeoff except at very low inflation rates and is thus fully consistent with targeting very low inflation—although the slowness with which wage and price stickiness adjusts to lower inflation could make it optimal to approach the target slowly. The growth-inflation evidence of the third section shows essentially no relationship between growth and inflation in the higher single-digit range, and thus is also consistent with targeting low inflation.

The question then is how low to aim, and particularly why not to aim for the best, zero inflation—or even better, price stability, or perhaps better yet, deflation? Several factors argue for a target measured inflation rate above zero. The first is the revenue motive. However, this is unlikely to justify significant rates of inflation. For instance, in the United States, where the monetary base is 6 percent of GDP, an extra 1 percent of inflation would generate less than 0.05 percent of GDP in revenue. (Admittedly, this sounds more impressive in absolute terms, more than $3 billion.) The second is the possibility discussed above, that the long-run Phillips curve is not vertical at low inflation rates. While the evidence is not decisive, the experiment of pushing to very low rates hardly seems worth trying,[33] particularly since in an economy averaging zero inflation, the inflation rate would have to be negative for a significant amount of the time.

The third and most important factor is the difficulty for monetary policy posed by the lower bound of zero on the nominal interest rate that arises because cash carries a zero nominal interest rate (Summers, 1991). If the expected inflation rate is zero, then it is very difficult for monetary policy to engineer a negative short-run real interest rate.[34] Such a rate may be needed during recessions—and the need would likely be compounded by the inflation rate's being below zero at such a time, thus increasing the lower bound on the real interest rate. The argument here is that inflation greases the wheels of monetary policy. The serious constraints placed on monetary policy in a zero inflation or deflationary environment have recently been evident in Japan. They constitute an important reason to target a low positive rate of inflation rather than zero.

The fourth reason to target a low positive rate of inflation is that the true rate of inflation is below the measured rate. Estimates of the bias in the United States range from below 1 percent per year to close to 2 percent; estimates for Canada and the United Kingdom are around 0.5 percent per year.[35] Germany has recently corrected its measure of inflation to reduce the bias. The impact of this bias on the optimal target rate of inflation is not self-evident if money illusion matters for real resource allocation. It is clear though that if the bias is understood in the capital markets, then the need to keep open the possibility of negative real interest rates would argue for a higher target measured rate of inflation.

These arguments point to a target inflation rate in the 1 to 3 percent range; more specifically, they suggest that inflation should be targeted at about 2 percent, to stay within a range of 1 to 3 percent per year. This is in practice what most central banks mean by price stability; it is also a target that most G-7 central banks have already attained.

It is necessary to specify a range because the inflation rate is not totally controllable.[36] The width of the target band would vary across economies depending on their structure, especially the variance of the exogenous shocks that hit the economy. The lower bound would be taken as seriously as the upper bound.

Two other issues need to be considered in this section: price level versus inflation targeting; and the potential use of indexation to mitigate the costs of inflation. The literal meaning of price stability is stability of the average price level, not low inflation. There is a clear rhetorical benefit to the goal of absolute price stability, the view that central banks should aim to maintain the average level of prices constant over long periods, as in nineteenth-century Britain, where the price level in 1914 was at the level it had been ninety years earlier. The rhetoric typically continues by pointing to the desirability

Figure 1
Inflation Versus Price Level Targeting

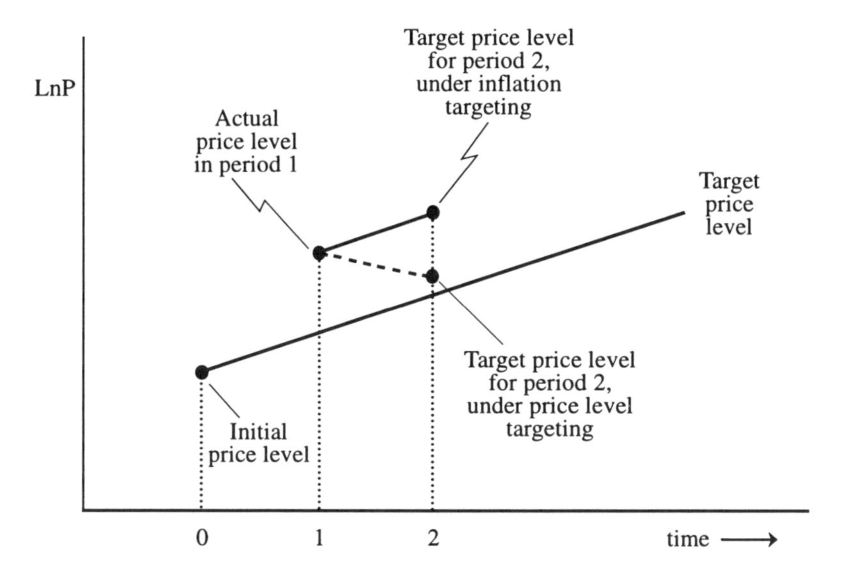

of fostering long-term nominal contracts, for instance, the issue of 100-year nominal bonds. There have recently been some issues of such bonds, but it is not clear what special benefits result. Most of their value in any case derives from the earlier parts of their existence. To the extent that the intention is to ensure that individuals have a safe asset in which to save over the long term, the same effect can be obtained by issuing indexed bonds, as several governments are now doing or planning to do.

More generally, it could be desirable to target a *price level path* rather than the inflation rate. Figure 1 shows the difference. With a price level target, the central bank is always aiming to return to the original path, so that above average inflation would, on average, be followed by below average inflation. With inflation targeting, past failures to hit the inflation target are treated as bygones, and the price level is likely to deviate increasingly from the path it was initially expected to take. (This is known in another context as base drift.) Price level targeting provides greater certainty about the level of prices in the distant future, and thus encourages long-term nominal targeting. However, it puts greater strains on monetary policy, requiring variations in the inflation rate to reverse the effects of previous shocks. Theoretically, the choice must depend on the optimal sharing of the burden of shocks among those differentially affected by inflation.

A particular difficulty arises with price level targeting if the goal is for price level constancy or a very gently rising price path. In these cases, the *expected* rate of inflation would often have to be negative. This would exacerbate the difficulties of monetary policy, if a low or negative real interest rate were needed to deal with recessions.

Pending a fuller analytic answer, it is advisable not to be too ambitious, and therefore, to target a low inflation rate rather than a path for the price level.[37]

We turn finally in this section to indexation. Many of the most clearly identified economic costs of inflation would disappear if the tax system were properly indexed. Why not then comprehensively index the economy, and live with moderate inflation? The answers are clear. In the first instance, comprehensive indexation is difficult and extremely cumbersome:[38] understanding of the convenience of nominal calculations is reinforced by the observation that in high and hyperinflations, countries tend to use a foreign currency as numeraire and increasingly as medium of exchange, rather than to index. Second, inflations do not happen out of a clear blue sky. Whatever the reasons for the inflation, the introduction of indexation would be likely to raise the equilibrium inflation rate. The new higher inflation indexed equilibrium could be worse than the unindexed equilibrium (Fischer and Summers, 1989). If indexation were introduced gradually, the result could be a process of rising inflation.[39] These conclusive objections to comprehensive indexation do not, however, necessarily mean that all indexation is bad; in particular, there remains a good case for the government to issue indexed bonds.

Public opinion and inflation

Alan Greenspan has defined price stability as a situation in which economic agents do not take account of inflation in making their decisions. Periodic alarums in the capital markets when the economy expands too fast reveal that we are not yet there. But sustained low inflation has had a remarkable impact on people's concerns about inflation.

The Gallup Organization has, since the end of World War II, conducted polls that ask Americans what is the most important problem facing the nation. (There was also one poll with this question in 1939.) Chart 4 shows the percentage of respondents answering inflation and unemployment respectively, with actual values of the inflation and unemployment rates plotted on the chart. The answers are, of course, affected by the other national problems on respondents' minds.

For over a decade, from 1972 to 1982,[40] between 30 percent and 80 percent of the respondents regarded inflation as the most serious problem facing the country, this despite the ongoing Vietnam War at the beginning of that period, and the Cold War during the entire period. During that period, the extent to which people regarded inflation as the most serious problem was highly correlated with the actual inflation rate. However, the concern about inflation disappeared rapidly once the inflation rate dropped below 5 percent; inflation has not been a serious issue in the polls since 1986. The lower panel shows that concern about unemployment tracks the actual unemployment rate closely, but that unemployment has never passed the 50 percent mark in the poll.[41]

Chart 5 shows some results from an international poll, taken in March/April 1995, that asked a similar question. Unfortunately, people were asked to name two to three problems rather than one; in addition, the inflation question refers to "inflation and high

Chart 4
United States: Inflation, Unemployment as Nation's Most Important Problem
Comparison with Actual, 1939 to January 1996

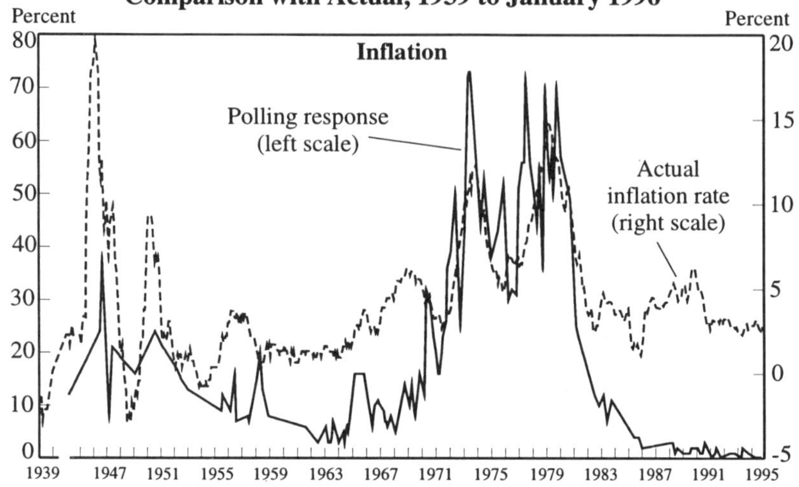

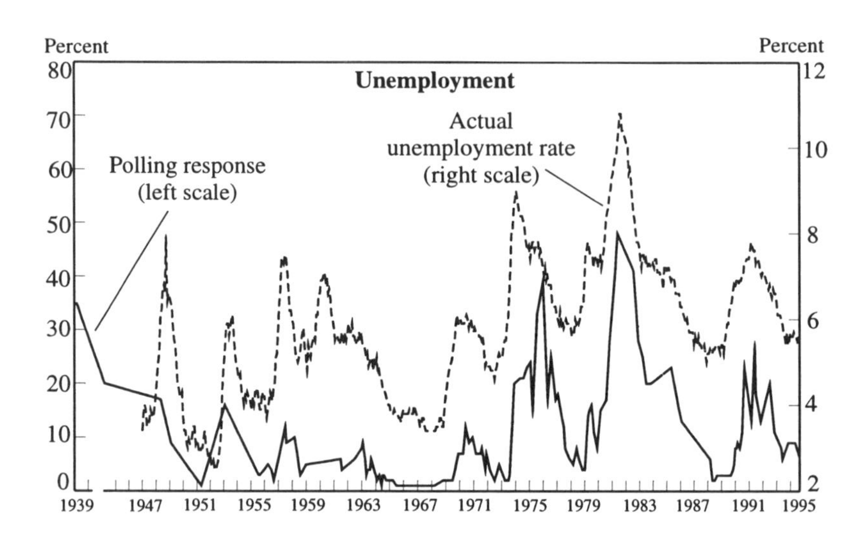

Sources: Gallup Organization; University of Connecticut, Roper Center POLL database, and the WEFA Group INTLINE database.

Chart 5
Inflation/High Prices as One of People's Top Concerns Comparison with Actual Inflation[1]

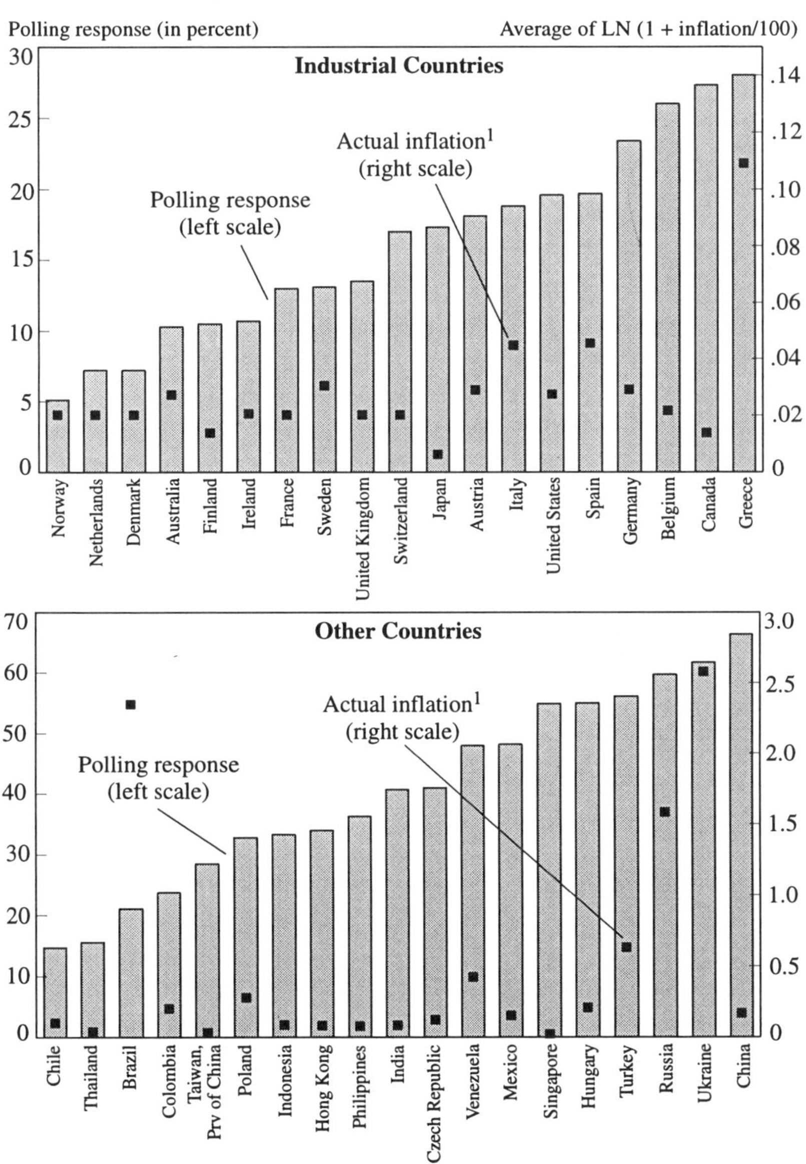

[1] 1993-95 average for LN(1+inflation/100).

Sources: Roper Starch World Wide, Inc. INRA 50th Anniversary Global Survey, March/April, 1995; and IMF, International Financial Statistics.

prices" as the problem. Inflation was not a matter of great concern in any of the industrialized countries, though it is clear that concern about inflation is high, relative to the actual inflation rate, in Japan, Germany, Belgium, and Canada. The concern about inflation and high prices was, for obvious reasons, much higher in some of the nonindustrialized countries (lower panel), including Russia and Ukraine. China and Singapore both stand out for very high concerns over inflation, despite their relatively low inflation rates.

Chart 6 shows that unemployment and recession generally worried respondents in industrialized countries to a much greater extent than inflation, with the anxieties of the Swiss and Japanese standing out relative to their actual experience of unemployment. Unemployment data for nonindustrialized countries are sparse, but it is interesting that there was less relative concern about unemployment than inflation in the five transition economies for which data are shown in the lower panel—no doubt reflecting the very high inflation of the time, and the still relatively low levels of unemployment despite the deep recessions in several of those countries.

Should long-run price stability be the only goal of monetary policy?

There are many good reasons for a country to prefer a low inflation rate, and no great damage is done to the language by describing low inflation as price stability. Central banks should, therefore, be targeting price stability as a major goal of monetary policy.

There is a great deal of confusion though about whether price stability should be the main or the only goal of monetary policy. Central bankers have a tendency to say that price stability should be the only goal of monetary policy, and to shrink from the point that monetary policy also affects output in the short run. That is not hard to understand, for explicit recognition of the powers of countercyclical monetary policy encourages political pressures to use that policy, with the attendant risk that inflation will rise.[42] But it is also problematic and destructive of credibility to deny the obvious, as well as to undertake countercyclical policies while denying doing so.

Chart 6
Unemployment/Recession as One of People's Top Concerns Comparison with Actual Unemployment Rate[1]

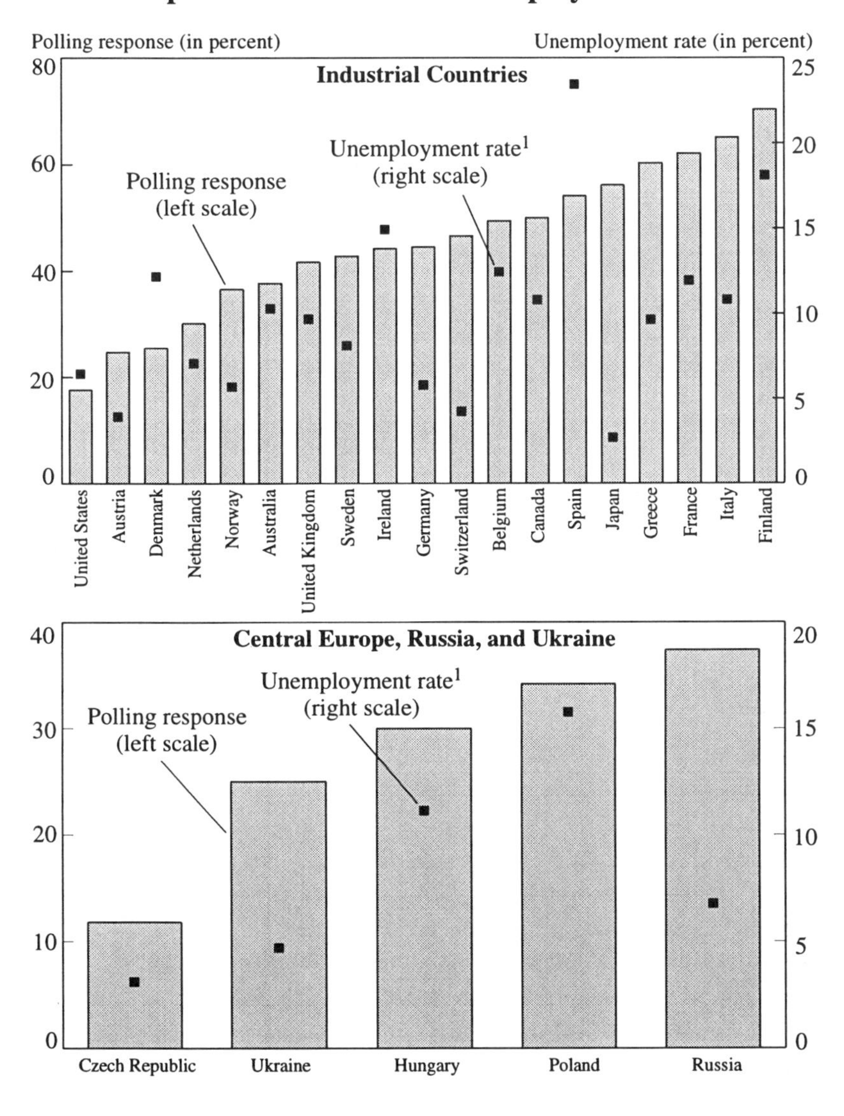

[1] 1993-94 average for industrial countries; 1993-95 average for Central Europe, Russia, and Ukraine.
Sources: Roper World Wide, Inc. INRA 50th Anniversary Global Survey, March/April, 1995; OECD Analytical Database; and IMF staff estimates.

The statement that *long-run* price stability is the sole goal of monetary policy is probably best understood as an attempt to deal with some of the logical and political difficulties raised by the existence of the short-run tradeoff. Policymakers do two things by emphasizing the long-run: they allow themselves a little leeway for short-term countercyclical policy; and they remind proponents of short-term expansionary policies that the short- and long-run consequences of monetary expansion differ.

The current situation, in which central bankers emphasize their long-term responsibilities and downplay or deny the possibilities for countercyclical policies while undertaking them, is untidy but preferable to a situation in which actions would match words as they fail to pursue countercyclical policies. But there should be a way to do better.

Inflation targeting is that way.[43] Once there is an explicit numerical inflation target for monetary policy, and a transparent framework for making policy and holding policymakers accountable for their actions, it is not possible to overlook the potential inflationary consequences of monetary expansion undertaken for short-term countercylical purposes. Nor, if the inflation target is taken seriously, is it possible to miss the beginnings of a process in which inflation creeps up from cycle to cycle, as it did in many of the industrialized countries from the 1950s through the 1980s.

Targeting inflation does not have to mean targeting only inflation. Countercyclical monetary policy should be allowed to work. For the most part—in dealing with demand shocks—the monetary policies implied by inflation targeting are consistent with countercylical policies. It is necessary in the case of supply shocks to find a mechanism that will permit a temporary deviation of inflation from target. Such mechanisms can be and have been designed in countries that have adopted inflation targets, for instance by targeting an underlying inflation rate, or by making allowances for changes in the terms of trade.

As to whether price stability should be the primary target of monetary policy, language very close to that used in the statutes of the new European Central Bank captures the right nuances: long-run price stability should be the primary goal of the central bank, with the promotion of full employment and growth being permitted to the extent that they do not conflict with the primary goal.

Author's Note: The views expressed are those of the author, and not necessarily of the International Monetary Fund. I am grateful to Claire Adams for outstanding research assistance, to Michael Bruno, William Easterly, Martin Feldstein, Jacob Frenkel, John Green, Massimo Russo, Michael Sarel, and Lawrence Summers for their comments, and to Ruth Judson, David Lebow, and David Wilcox for helpful discussions.

Endnotes

[1]Fischer (1981), which provides partial equilibrium estimates of several components of the costs of inflation, includes estimates of the economic costs that arise from the greater uncertainty about inflation associated with higher inflation.

[2]For recent cross-sectional evidence that inflation is associated with increased income inequality, see Bulir and Gulde (1995).

[3]Feldstein assumes that the stated inflation rate exceeds the true rate by about 2 percent, so that the reduction in terms of the measured rate is from 4 percent to 2 percent.

[4]One reason for surprise at the magnitude of the cost is that the triangle rule of distortions suggests that an increase from zero to 2 percent inflation is unlikely to have a large cost. In the case of capital income taxation, an increase in inflation from zero to 2 percent worsens pre-existing distortions, and thus the intuition of the triangle rule is inappropriate; rather, as Feldstein points out, the costs are trapezoids.

[5]There has been an upward trend in general equilibrium estimates of the costs of inflation. A useful review of earlier results is found in Dotsey and Ireland (1996). Their own calculations, which do not include inflation-induced tax distortions, are that the costs of a steady 4 percent inflation amount to about 0.4 percent of GDP. For an earlier general equilibrium estimate, see Cooley and Hansen (1991); see also the comment on this paper by Benabou (1991).

[6]The effective discount rate he uses to capitalize the welfare gain is a little above 3 percent per year.

[7]English (1996) has shown that the share of resources devoted to financial transactions increases with the rate of inflation, which means that inflation tends to reduce output available for consumption or investment.

[8] Fair (1996), working with data from thirty countries, finds that functional forms for price and wage equations that imply the possibility of a long-run Phillips curve tradeoff on the whole perform better than those implying no tradeoff, though he is cautious in drawing conclusions. Bullard and Keating (1995) find no long-run output-inflation tradeoff in a sample of fifty-eight

countries, except for some low inflation countries in their sample, namely Austria, Germany, Finland, and the United Kingdom.

[9]See, for instance, the work of Robert Gordon, as summarized in his 1990 paper. See also Romer (1996).

[10]See Romer and Romer (1994).

[11]As will be argued below, the easing of monetary policy during a recession will be consistent with inflation targeting provided the economy is being disturbed by demand shocks.

[12]The caution in the exercise of countercyclical policy implied by formulation (1) would be warranted if there are not only level but also rate of change effects of unemployment on inflation in the short run, which were not otherwise taken into account.

[13]This is the title of the recent paper by Card and Hyslop (1996).

[14]This argument was presented by James Tobin (1972) in his presidential address to the American Economic Association, and has recently been developed further by Akerlof, Dickens, and Perry (1996). See also Dreze (1992).

[15]See, for instance, Lebow, Stockton, and Wascher (1995), and references therein.

[16]I am grateful to Michael Sarel for this reference.

[17]The work by Bullard and Keating (1995) and Fair (1996) referred to in footnote 8 contains hints of nonlinearities, particularly in the finding by Bullard and Keating of a long-run tradeoff for Germany and Japan. But the possible nonlinearity is not their central focus.

[18]The result could also be due in part to the timing of the responses of unemployment and inflation to changes in monetary policy.

[19]Chart 2 includes data for 138 countries, from the *World Economic Outlook* database of the IMF. Aside from the exclusion of the transition countries and Afghanistan, the sample is the largest possible from among the different databases that were available.

[20]In each case the cutoff point is based on the average of the log of (1+(inflation/100)).

[21]Recent work on this issue is presented in Barro (1995), Bruno and Easterly (1996), Fischer (1993), Judson and Orphanides (1996), and Sarel (1996).

[22]This is probably because the high inflation countries had lower initial incomes, and would on that account have tended to grow more rapidly.

[23]Fry, Goodhart, and Almeida (1996, Chapter 2) report similar results with data from their 45-country Bank of England group.

[24]A negative relationship would obtain if supply shocks predominated (leaving aside questions on the timing of responses of prices and output to a supply shock); this is consistent with the fact that the negative inflation-growth relationship is statistically stronger after 1974 than before. However, that cannot be the whole story, because the relationship is also negative, though not significant, in the earlier period. The weaker relationship in the earlier period may also reflect

the smaller range of variation of the inflation rate, and the fact that data limitations mean there are fewer observations for that period.

[25]Sarel searches for a breakpoint by maximizing the goodness of fit of his regression.

[26]The use of the logarithm of inflation is essentially equivalent to using the continuously compounded rate of inflation. This makes a large difference at high inflation rates. When the continuously compounded rate rises from 0.5 percent per day to 1 percent per day, the annual rate rises from 517 percent to 3680 percent. Cagan's definition of hyperinflation as 50 percent per month corresponds to a daily rate of 1.3 percent, and an annual rate of 11,740 percent.

[27]Negative but insignificant coefficients were found for all three inflation ranges in Fischer (1993).

[28]Fischer (1993) shows that inflation reduces growth through two channels, lower investment, and lower productivity growth. Rudebusch and Wilcox (1994) examined the inflation-productivity growth relationship for the United States and several other industrialized countries.

[29]Fischer (1994) contains a more comprehensive discussion of the reasons for inflation.

[30]See Persson and Tabellini (1994) for a collection of articles that develop this approach.

[31]Several readers have raised the question of the optimal strategy that should be followed in reducing inflation to the single-digit range by a government that has stabilized from high inflation but is currently stuck in a moderate double-digit inflation (Dornbusch and Fischer, 1993). This is not the place for discussing that issue, beyond noting my conviction that in light of the allocative and growth costs of inflation, it is a mistake under these circumstances to try to live with inflation, and that it is necessary to direct policies purposefully at lowering inflation.

[32]In a theoretical article, Friedman (1969) showed that it is optimal under certain circumstances to drive the nominal interest rate to zero, to satiate individuals with cash balances. In the Friedman approach, this means that the inflation rate should be equal to minus the real return on capital. The optimality of the Friedman rule shows surprising theoretical resiliency even though it holds little attraction as a practical policy prescription. See Chari, Christiano, and Kehoe (1996).

[33]This evaluation could change if prices began to show more downward flexibility after a prolonged period of very low inflation.

[34]For simplicity, we do not take into account the possibility that the inconvenience of carrying large sums of cash could allow the nominal interest rate on large denomination instruments to be slightly negative.

[35]Cunningham (1996) develops estimates of the size of the bias in the United Kingdom, and compares his results with those for Canada and the United States.

[36]This issue has been explored for Australia by Debelle and Stevens (1995).

[37]Svensson (1996) claims that price level targeting may also produce a more stable inflation rate. In his comments at the conference, Lars Svensson indicated that the result holds under for certain specifications of the Phillips curve. See also Kiley (1996).

[38]As argued by Martin Feldstein at the conference, indexing capital income taxation to ensure neutrality to inflation becomes even more complicated as the sophistication of financial instruments increases.

[39]My views on the role of indexation are heavily influenced by the experiences of Brazil and Israel, countries which were held out in the 1970s as examples of the benefits of indexation and living with inflation. Inflation in each rose over time, until a growth and/or balance of payments crisis occurred, and a successful stabilization was eventually carried out.

[40]Fischer and Huizinga (1982) examined the determinants of responses to the opinion polls, on both a time series and cross-sectional basis. Shiller (1996) has undertaken polls in the United States, Germany, and Brazil seeking to clarify how people think about inflation.

[41]Former President Ford is supposed to have said that inflation is a more important problem than unemployment because it affects everyone.

[42]This could be interpreted as a shift from a low inflation equilibrium to the bad Barro-Gordon equilibrium.

[43]Green (1996) discusses some of the difficulties and advantages of the inflation targeting framework, which requires the exercise of judgment by the central bank.

References

Akerlof, George, William Dickens, and George Perry. "The Macroeconomics of Low Inflation," *Brookings Papers on Economic Activity,* 1 (July 1996), pp. 1-59.

Barro, Robert J. "Economic Growth in a Cross-Section of Countries," *Quarterly Journal of Economics*, 106, 2 (May 1991), pp. 407-43.

__________. "Inflation and Economic Growth," *Bank of England Quarterly Bulletin,* 35, 2 (May 1995), pp. 166-76.

__________, and David Gordon. "A Positive Theory of Monetary Policy in a Natural Rate Model," *Journal of Political Economy*, 91, 4 (August 1983), pp. 589-610.

Benabou, Roland. "Comment," *Journal of Money, Credit and Banking,* 23, 3 (Part 2), (August 1991), pp. 504-13.

Blanchard, Olivier J., and Lawrence Summers. "Hysteresis and the European Unemployment Problem." *NBER Macroeconomics Annual,* 1, (1986) pp. 15-77.

Bruno, Michael, and William Easterly. "Inflation Crises and Long-Run Growth," World Bank, (June 1996) mimeo.

Bulir, Ales, and Anne-Marie Gulde. "Inflation and Income Distribution: Further Evidence on Empirical Links," International Monetary Fund, *Working Paper* 95/86 (August 1995).

Bullard, James, and John W. Keating. "The Long-Run Relationship Between Inflation and Output in Postwar Economies," *Journal of Monetary Economics*, 36, 3 (December 1995), pp. 477-96.

Card, David, and Dean Hyslop. "Does Inflation 'Grease the Wheels of the Labor Market'?" *NBER Working Paper 5538* (April 1996).

Chapple, Simon. "Sticky Money Wages," New Zealand Institute of Economic Research, *Working paper 96/13* (July 1996).

Chari, V.V., Lawrence Christiano, and Patrick Kehoe. "Optimality of the Friedman Rule in Economies with Distorting Taxes," *Journal of Monetary Economics*, 37, 2 (April 1996), pp. 203-24.

Cooley, Thomas F., and Gary D. Hansen. "The Welfare Costs of Moderate Inflations," *Journal of Money, Credit and Banking*, 23, 3 (Part 2), (August 1991), pp. 483-503.

Cunningham, Alastair. "Measurement Bias in Price Indices: An Application to the U.K.'s RPI," *Bank of England Working Paper Series No. 47* (March 1996).

Debelle, Guy, and Glenn Stevens. "Monetary Policy Goals for Inflation in Australia," Reserve Bank of Australia, Research Discussion Paper 9503, 1995.

Dornbusch, Rudiger, and Stanley Fischer. "Moderate Inflation," *World Bank Economic Review*, 7, 1 (January 1993), pp. 1-44.

Dotsey, Michael, and Peter Ireland. "The Welfare Cost of Inflation in General Equilibrium," *Journal of Monetary Economics*, 37, 1 (February 1996), pp. 29-47.

Dreze, Jacques. *Money and Uncertainty: Inflation, Interest, Indexation.* Banca d'Italia, Roma: Paoli Baffi Lectures on Money and Finance, 1992.

English, William. "Inflation and Financial Sector Size," Federal Reserve Board, Finance and Economics Discussion Series, 96-16 (April 1996).

Fair, Ray. "Testing the Standard View of the Long-Run Unemployment-Inflation Relationship," Cowles Foundation Discussion Paper 1121, Yale University (April 1996).

Feldstein, Martin. "The Costs and Benefits of Going from Low Inflation to Price Stability," National Bureau of Economic Research, 1996.

Fischer, Stanley. "Towards an Understanding of the Costs of Inflation: II," in Karl Brunner and Allan H. Meltzer, eds., *The Costs and Consequences of Inflation*, Carnegie-Rochester Conference Series on Public Policy, Vol. 15, 1981. North-Holland, pp. 5-42.

__________. "The Role of Macroeconomic Factors in Growth," *Journal of Monetary Economics*, 32, 3 (December 1993), pp. 485-512.

__________. "Modern Central Banking," in Forrest Capie and others, eds., *The Future of Central Banking*. Cambridge: Cambridge University Press, 1994.

__________, and John Huizinga. "Inflation, Unemployment, and Public Opinion Polls," *Journal of Money, Credit and Banking*, 14, 1 (February 1982), pp. 1-19.

__________, and Franco Modigliani. "Towards an Understanding of the Real Effects and Costs of Inflation," *Weltwirtschaftliches Archiv*, 114, 1978, pp. 810-32.

Friedman, Milton. "The Optimal Quantity of Money," in M. Friedman, *The Optimal Quantity of Money and Other Essays*. Chicago: Aldine Publishing Company, 1969.

Fry, Maxwell, Charles Goodhart, and Alvaro Almeida. *Central Banking in Developing Countries*. London: Routledge, 1996.

Gordon, Robert J. "What Is New-Keynesian Economics?" *Journal of Economic Literature*, 27, 3 (September 1990), pp. 1115-71.

Green, John H. "Inflation Targeting: Theory and Policy Implications," *IMF Working Paper*, WP/96/65 (June 1996).

Judson, Ruth, and Athanasios Orphanides. "Inflation, Volatility and Growth," Federal Reserve Board, Finance and Economics Discussion Series, 96-19 (May 1996).

__________, and Richard Porter. "The Location of U.S. Currency: How Much is Abroad?" forthcoming, *Federal Reserve Bulletin* (October 1996).

Kiley, Michael T. "Price Level Targeting, Inflation Targeting, and Variability: Does Price Stickiness Matter?" Federal Reserve Board (August 1996) mimeo.

Lebow, David, David Stockton, and William Wascher. "Inflation, Nominal Wage Rigidity, and the Efficiency of Labor Markets," Federal Reserve Board, Finance and Economics Discussion Series, 94-45 (October 1995).

Levine, Ross, and David Renelt. "A Sensitivity Analysis of Cross-Country Growth Regressions," *American Economic Review*, 82, 4 (September 1992), pp. 942-63.

Persson, Torsten, and Guido Tabellini. *Monetary and Fiscal Policy*. Cambridge, Mass.: MIT Press, 1994.

Romer, Christina D. "Inflation and the Growth Rate of Output," *NBER Working Paper* 5575 (May 1996).

__________, and David Romer. "What Ends Recessions?" *NBER Macroeconomics Annual*, 9, 1994, pp. 13-57.

Rudebusch, Glenn, and David Wilcox. "Productivity and Inflation: Evidence and Interpretations." Federal Reserve Board (April 1994) mimeo.

Sarel, Michael. "Nonlinear Effects of Inflation on Economic Growth," *IMF Staff Papers*, 43, 1 (March 1996), pp. 199-215.

Shiller, Robert. "Why Do People Dislike Inflation?" NBER (March 1996).

Summers, Lawrence. "How Should Long-Term Monetary Policy Be Determined?" *Journal of Money, Credit and Banking*, 23, 3 (August 1991) Part 2, pp. 625-31.

Svensson, Lars. "Price Level Targeting vs. Inflation Targeting," Institute for International Economic Studies, Stockholm University, 1996.

Tobin, James. "Inflation and Unemployment," *American Economic Review*, 62, 1 (March 1972), pp. 1-18.

Commentary: Why Are Central Banks Pursuing Long-Run Price Stability?

Lawrence Summers

It is good to be back in Jackson Hole. Let me begin my remarks with a predictable caution. Nothing in what I say is intended as or would properly be interpreted as a comment, either descriptive or prescriptive, on the current or future behavior of the U.S. Federal Reserve, about whose actions the Clinton administration does not comment. Instead, the focus of my remarks will be the broader questions raised in Stan Fischer's paper as well as those of the other authors at this conference about the right framework for monetary policy.

Before saying anything else, I think it is worth highlighting the extent to which economic thinking does change and the impact that the changes have. The core macroeconomic message that I absorbed as a not-very-conscientious MIT undergraduate economics major between 1971 and 1975 was that governments should be more willing to run budget deficits so there would be more demand and more jobs in the economy, and that they were held back by various financial sector troglodytes supported intellectually by people from Chicago. My wife, who was a much better and more conscientious student, came away from her Yale education between 1974 and 1978 with the same set of views along with the additional insight that the Phillips curve was there to be exploited to generate more output since any costs of inflation could be mitigated by indexation.

While there will be differences of opinion here at this conference—it is worth highlighting a central conclusion which is almost universally shared by those concerned with monetary policy. From the starting conditions currently prevailing in almost all economies, there is no continuing benefit in either output, growth, or employment that can be gained by continuously more expansionary monetary policy. Bad monetary policy can have costs—certainly in the form of chronic and costly inflation, and probably in terms of excessively protracted recessions and excessively volatile output, but there are no monetary policy free lunches.

In my comments, I shall address three issues—the choice of an inflation target, the conduct of policy with an inflation target, and the question of multiple objectives for monetary policy.

Choosing an inflation target

I think it is clear enough that high rates of inflation, by which I mean rates that exceed 4 or 5 percent, have obvious costs that outweigh any possible benefits. In addition to the costs usually listed, I would add the cost of efforts to win the zero sum game of getting float. As nominal interest rates rise, it becomes more profitable to delay paying debts one owes, and to collect money owed more quickly. Business success comes to depend more on financial sharpness and less on engineering and marketing. Financial intermediation expands at the expense of real economic activity to an extent not fully reflected by the area under the money demand curve.

The harder questions involve just what low inflation rate is right to shoot for. The universal acclaim accorded to Alan Greenspan's definition of price stability as the level where inflation is not a factor in economic calculations is a tribute to its wisdom and also to its central bankerly ambiguity. Stan Fischer comes down in favor of a range of 1 to 3 percent for target inflation which looks about right to me though it will seem high to some. However, I have some problems with his as well as the standard analysis.

Stan makes two arguments pointing toward a low inflation target that I do not think are quite right. The first points toward growing internationalization and suggests that this reduces optimal inflation on seigniorage grounds. Unless the interest elasticity of foreign demand for U.S. currency is greater than one, which is inconsistent with much of the available evidence on money demand, seigniorage revenues would be maximized and so would the efficiency of U.S. revenue collection by an increase in the inflation rate. Second, he cites Feldstein's calculations of the welfare consequences of inflation-induced increases in capital taxation. Since a country can choose its capital income tax regime knowing its inflation target, I am not sure these costs should really be included. Furthermore, I am suspicious of any analysis which, like Feldstein's, implies that significant deflation would be optimal.

On the other hand, I do not find the argument that one should add to the target rate of inflation to adjust for the consumer price index (CPI)'s failure to take full account of quality change very persuasive. When I think about my future, I think about what it will cost in the future to buy a house or a tennis racket or a college education for my kids, and it's the sticker price, not the quality-adjusted change in cost, that I care about.

I think the central issue in deciding how little inflation is too little is the risk that at excessively low inflation, cyclical downturns will last unnecessarily long. One possible reason is nominal wage rigidity. With low inflation, you can't get real wage reductions without nominal wage cuts, making it harder to get the needed labor market adjustments during downturns. Another reason that I have stressed in earlier work is the zero interest floor on nominal interest rates which translates into a floor on real interest rates; the lower the inflation rate, the higher the floor on real rates. Historically, negative real interest rates have played an important role in facilitating recoveries, particularly in situations of financial strain, and ruling out this degree of freedom for the central bank by achieving zero inflation seems to me to have real risks.

There is another conceptual issue here that I don't think has been adequately aired. As central bankers are fond of stressing, credibility is of the utmost importance. It seems to me that, over some range, a higher inflation objective may actually increase credibility. Because not just the total but also the marginal costs of inflation rise with the inflation rate, it will be easier to convince the public that the central bank will stick with a modest positive inflation rate than that it will stick with a lower rate. The implication of this observation is that expectational errors where the public anticipates more expansionary policy than is delivered are minimized at some non-zero inflation rate. To put this in simpler language—the central banks represented in this room would have a harder time convincing their publics that they would not tolerate any inflation than that they would not tolerate more than 1 percent inflation.

As Stan Fischer's discussion of the available evidence suggests, we do not really have a sound basis for judging the consequences of very low rates of inflation for the behavior of output. There is one empirical fact coming out of the historical experience of the G-10 countries that impresses me. Over the past thirty-five years, countries with less than 3 percent nominal GDP growth in a particular year did not perform well; on average, real GDP growth was negative whenever nominal GDP growth was so low. While this finding may have a number of interpretations, I think there is an important point here: Any central bank that is forecasting nominal GDP growth of less than 3 or 4 percent ought to think carefully about its policy stance regardless of its inflation forecast.

Operating with a commitment to price stability

Many of the papers here discuss the important question of the appropriate pace of disinflation. This question essentially involves weighing the credibility benefits of rapid disinflation against the extra transitional costs involved. This distinction seems right to me. I suspect that standard treatments may overemphasize the costs associated with nominally rigid wages and prices and underemphasize costs associated with long-term fixed nominal financial contracts. An important and appropriate brake on the pace of disinflation is the need to avoid excessive damage to the financial system.

I want to focus on what I think is an important innovation that will support monetary policy in the United States in the years ahead—the Treasury's decision to issue indexed bonds. Indexed bonds are important in two respects. First, their issuance reduces the government's incentive to inflate because indexed debt cannot be inflated away, and because of the direct link they create between increased inflation and higher interest payments in the government deficit. Just as those who sell fire insurance work to prevent arson, and those who sell life insurance worry about the health of their customers, governments that sell inflation insurance will tend to avoid inflating. It is noteworthy in this regard that the industrialized countries that have issued indexed bonds in recent years have all seen significant subsequent improvements in their inflation performance. (See Chart 1.)

Second, and perhaps more important, indexed bonds provide a market-based measure of inflation expectations. Of course, the interpretation needs some care because of tax considerations, risk premia (which may affect the spread between indexed and non-indexed debt), and possible clientele effects. However, these factors change slowly and are unlikely to prevent yield spreads from giving an indication of rising inflation expectations. My own judgment is that markets will over time in the United States prove to be good assimilators of information bearing on future inflation. Note, however, that for the purposes of monetary policy and its credibility, it is not just the rational expectation of future inflation that is relevant but also the actual expectation that is important, and here the indexed bond market will be very hard to beat. If one considers the tremendous stakes that we as a nation have in avoiding increases in inflation or needless sacrifices of output in response to false inflationary indications, it is hard to escape the conclusion that even a small increase in the accuracy of monetary policy would have great value.

There is, of course, the alternative view that indexed bonds erode the natural constituency against inflation and thereby will over time tend to promote inflation. While I think this argument may have merit when applied to certain kinds of inflation indexation, I find it hard to believe that any effects of this kind would be serious as long

Chart 1
Inflation and Indexed Bonds
Year Over Year Percent Change in Inflation Indexes

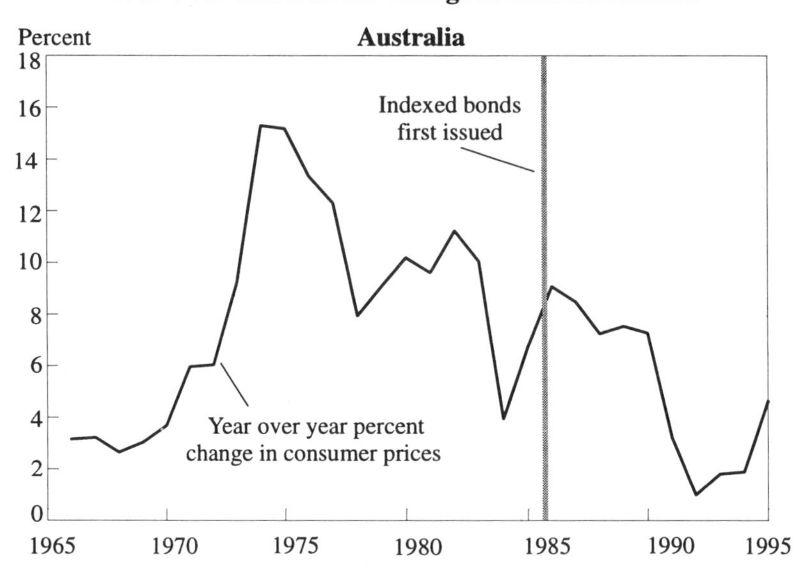

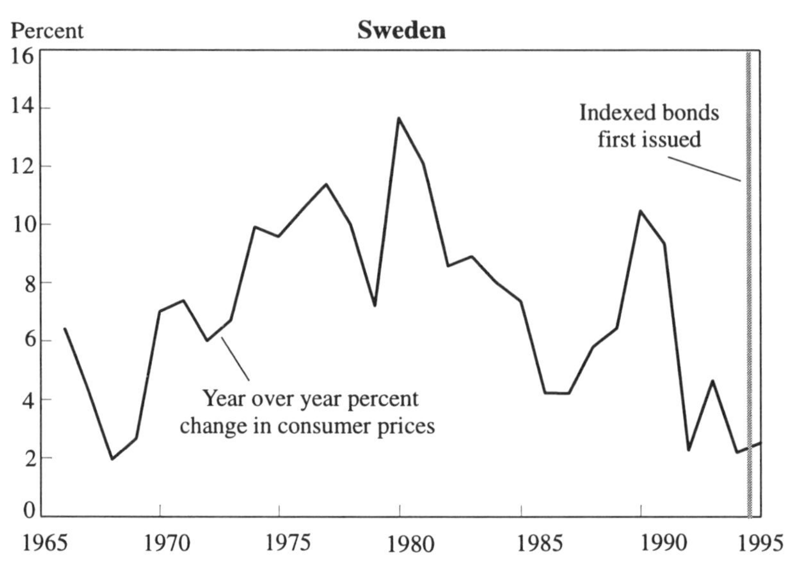

Chart 1 (continued)
Inflation and Indexed Bonds
Year Over Year Percent Change in Inflation Indexes

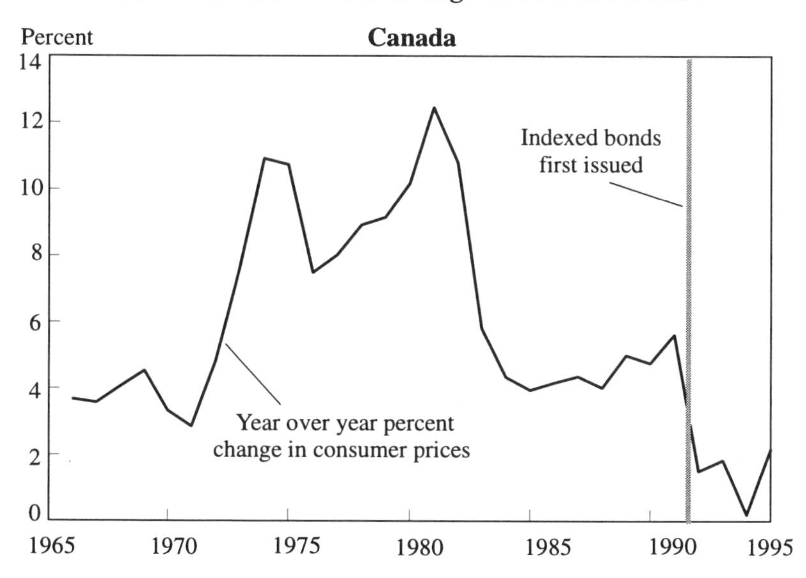

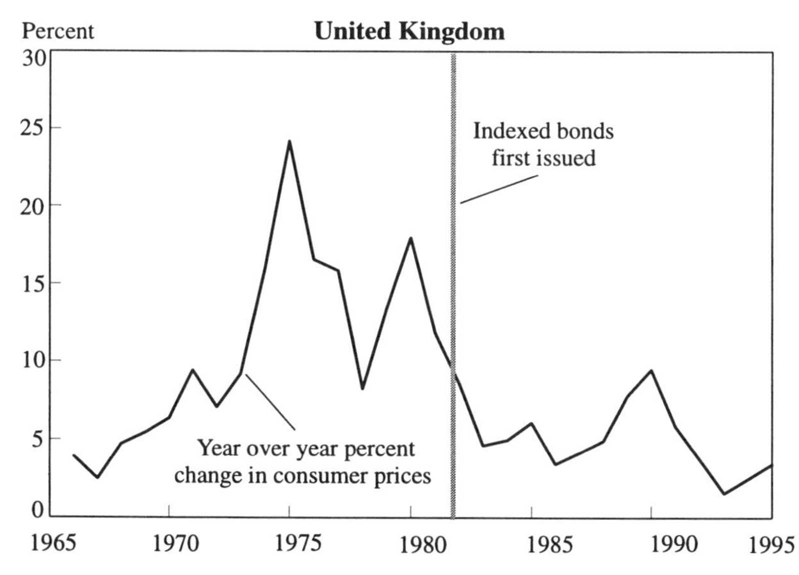

Source: U.S. Treasury: Federal Finance Policy Analysis

as the vast majority of a government's debt is unindexed. In any event, the experience of industrial countries that have introduced indexed bonds is encouraging.

Should only inflation be targeted?

The core of the argument for inflation targeting seems to be this: The overriding goal of a central bank should be price stability somehow defined. An inflation-targeting regime allows for responses to cyclical fluctuations because of the short-run Phillips curve mechanism. Inflation targeting therefore places the appropriate emphasis on price stability, provides for appropriate accountability, and, at the same time, avoids a straitjacket that could cause too much output volatility.

I think this is a reasonable argument as far as it goes. Given the dynamic consistency problem, there is certainly a case for asymmetry in central banks' treatment of output and inflation fluctuations. But I am troubled by the apparent rigidity of some inflation-targeting approaches.

Take an episode like the stock market crash of 1987 or the banking problems encountered in many countries over the last decade. I doubt very much that it would be wise for central banks to consider them only through the prism of their impact on the inflation rate. There must be at least some circumstances where it is appropriate to drive down short-term interest rates to protect financial stability. Indeed, as the world moves away from treating institutions as too large to fail, I suspect the potential role of monetary policy in responding to strains may be increased.

Exchange rates provide a different kind of example illustrating the dangers of rigid targeting. While it is generally felt in countries like the United States that operate with a flexible exchange rate, that monetary policy is best used to pursue domestic objectives rather than to target exchange rates, I think it is reasonable to assert that, in at least some circumstances, monetary policy may need to respond to exchange rate fluctuations. At a minimum, a clear commitment that it would not respond could be quite destabilizing.

A third type of example where overly rigid approaches run risks is situations where fiscal policy is changing rapidly. The virtue of independent central banks as an antidote to the dynamic consistency problem is clear enough. Their disadvantage is that they make coordination of fiscal and monetary policy more difficult. An inflation-targeting approach, mechanically applied, would treat surges of government demand and of export demand in almost the same way. This may not be appropriate, especially if the central bank wants to encourage deficit reduction.

There are many more examples such as these. I think the crucial point is that even if price stability is the overriding objective of a central bank, there are considerations bearing on long-run economic performance that may call for policy responses not captured by simple rules. There is, in the end, no substitute for wise discretion.

Conclusion

I began my remarks by highlighting the magnitude of the changes in macroeconomic thinking over the last twenty years. Similar changes would have been observable over the 1956-1976 period as the importance of money came to be recognized, or over the 1936-1956 period as the Keynesian perspective percolated. It would be a misreading of history to think that we have now identified final truth or that some of the views expressed here will not look archaic twenty years from now. Conditions and analysis will both keep changing and provide grist for the Jackson Hole mill.

General Discussion:
Why Are Central Banks Pursuing Long-Run Price Stability?

Chairman: Gordon Thiessen

Mr. Thiessen: Thank you Larry. My reaction to some of the comments is that I hope we don't take too rigid a view of wage rigidity after a period of some twenty years of high inflation and only four to five years of low inflation. During a period of high inflation, not surprisingly, there is a lot of resistance to nominal wage reduction.

Mr. Sinai: When you look at the question asked by Stanley's paper, "Why are Central Banks Pursuing Long-Run Price Stability?" I still don't understand the answer. And I perhaps ask to have a little discussion of that. Because if you look around the world today outside of the United States, on average, there have been very low inflation rates by the standards of the last twenty some odd years. Unemployment rates are very, very high and I know the answer about hysteresis and the rest of that. But really, what are we waiting for in terms of the optimal results in the world economy and the sacrifices made in the short-run tradeoff? How long is that? And really, why are we pursuing this goal which we have gotten so much closer to in terms of such low inflation rates?

Mr. Fischer: We are pursuing it because there is not much evidence and very little belief that if you ran at a higher inflation rate of 4 or 5 percent, you'd be getting significantly lower unemployment. That's the fundamental reason. There are also the allocative costs of inflation. I believe your basic view is there is a significant tradeoff that lasts a very, very long time, and what we are seeing now is that tradeoff. The bulk of the evidence is not in favor of the existence of such a tradeoff at rates of inflation of 1 to 3 percent. The question you may be asking is what if interest rates were pushed down much lower in Europe in particular. And what would then happen to unemployment? I don't doubt that lower interest rates in Europe now would reduce unemployment somewhat without raising inflation. So I think that's fine. That particular policy prescription which you might have in a variety of countries where inflation is very low and unemployment is very high is one I would agree with. But if inflation in those countries started rising above the 1 to 3 percent range, would you want to keep going? No.

Mr. Sinai: My question isn't about running much higher inflation rates from where we are, but rather, what would be the benefits, and how long in coming would they be, of targeting at a 1 to 3 percent range? And, it is not just a question for you, it is also a question for central bankers, because there is a somewhat implicit but unexplained, I think, set of notions as to what the ultimate benefits would be and how long we would have to wait for them.

Mr. Greenspan: Allen, as you know better than anyone, we are testing some very new views as to the way economies are evolving. Extending on my remarks earlier, what we are looking at is a significantly changing economic structure, especially in the United States and in the industrial countries, in which so-called impalpable, or service-related, outputs have become crucially important. The issue at stake here, is the question of tradeoffs, which Stan and Larry raised, and which was also the issue of the Akerlof, Dickens, and Perry paper. These tradeoffs arise as you approach what we are calling price stability, even though we cannot define it explicitly—largely because of data problems. But I think it is evident from the overwhelming anecdotal data that, as inflation falls, there appears increasingly an endeavor at the firm level to reduce unit costs, largely because expanding profit margins amid overall low inflation becomes increasingly difficult. On a consolidated basis, one must infer that if everyone brings unit costs down, we see significant reductions in hours per unit of output. And, therefore, if the data were to confirm this, we would conclude that as inflation fell, productivity growth would accelerate. The trouble, as you know, is that the data which we are using—whether it is cross-country or temporal—shows that issue only very vaguely. We do get some inherent correlation significance in our measured productivity growth adjusted for the business cycle, and the rate of inflation in the United States. It shows up in Canada, as I recall. But there are serious statistical questions as to just how robust these numbers are. And indeed, if you examine them closely, they stand as rather fuzzy. If the problem is data, there is some evidence that that might be moving toward a resolution. The new set of gross product originating data, which have just been released by the Department of Commerce, I suspect is going to show some very peculiar implied productivity trends in the two and three-digit SIC classifications. For example, you cannot have industries where productivity has been falling for years when it is terribly obvious that profit margins are holding up or rising. It makes no sense. So, you have the first important question as to whether we have a significant measurement problem. And, I think the unambiguous answer is that we do. What is unclear is how we are going to resolve it. The question that Larry and Stan raised on whether it is desirable to have negative real interest rates on occasion clearly is something we have to be aware of. So the tradeoff here, to a large extent, is the improvement implied in real productivity and standards of living from lower inflation against increased monetary policy flexibility. On top of that, we have the very interesting Akerlof, Dickens, and Perry article, which raises a number of provocative issues. One of them that needs to be resolved is whether incidences of a decline in earnings are very rare when you look at job *slots*—and remember it is the jobs not the people which determine unit labor costs. In their model they do endeavor to come to grips with this question. They argue, however, that the firm will be more successful in reducing average wage structures the greater the number of years of losses. And, I would raise the question, which is implicit in what Stan said, namely, as the inflation rate truly falls, does the adjustment process increasingly become more of a factor? In short, do you find the firm's ability to move its wage structure to the left, so that it has a part-negative tail, increases as the inflation rate falls? And clearly, if, indeed, we are getting rising productivity as the inflation rate falls, the nominal distribution of earnings will move to the right and, hence, even the issue of negative nominal changes in wages becomes less significant. These, I think, are the critical questions that we are all endeavoring to answer. I suspect that it may well be that the Jackson Hole symposium in the year 2006 will have the answers to all of these questions. It is correct to seriously question the desirability of bringing down the inflation rate. But I think that, merely observing the obvious hysteresis problem or other issues involved in Europe—which as you may recall we discussed here two years ago—it is an open question whether the problem has to do with inflation or labor market structure. I certainly agree with Stan. What evidence we have clearly suggests that the shift in the views of the economics profession either leading or following central bankers is probably right. But if you are asking for definitive proof without qualification, I don't think our data system at this stage can handle that.

Mr. Thiessen: Thanks, Alan. Yoshio Suzuki.

Mr. Suzuki: As an economist from Japan where the inflation rate is zero in terms of consumer price index and negative in terms of the wholesale price index, I am very much interested in Stanley's argument that tradeoffs may exist at the very low range of the inflation rate. In the Japanese experiences of the past five years, yes indeed, when the inflation rate was declining to zero, the growth rate was also declining and tradeoffs existed. But for the past three years, while the inflation rate has remained at or near zero, the growth rate has been recovering. So, my interpretation is that when the inflation rate was sharply declining, the expected rate of inflation lagged behind the actual one—in other words, the expected rate was higher than the actual one. But when the expected rate converged with the actual one, which was at or near zero, then a tradeoff disappeared. So, my conclusion is that the vertical Phillips curve works in the long run, even in the range of very low inflation. So, Stanley, this is an evidence which is different from yours. What is your response to this? Thank you.

Mr. Thiessen: Okay, I think I had Jacob Frenkel's hand. Then, I will get somebody from the back.

Mr. Frenkel: A couple of comments. The first on Stan's remarks indicating that basically all central banks behave as if they believe in one form or another of a short-term Phillips curve. Witness the fact that when unemployment is low, the rate of monetary expansion is typically faster; and when it is high, then there is monetary tightening. Here, an alternative interpretation would be that those central banks that expand more rapidly when they see low rates of unemployment do so because they believe that the environment of unemployment enables them to expand more rapidly to obtain their inflation target. In other words, they do so not because they want to affect unemployment, but rather because they want to achieve the target and realize they can do it with different rates of monetary expansion depending on the real environment. One remark about Larry Summers' point on coordination. Larry indicated that monetary targeting, or rigid monetary targeting, may cause difficulties in coordinating monetary policy with fiscal policy, especially when the fiscal policy aims at deficit reduction. I am a little bit concerned about even this attempt at coordination, not because it is not nice to talk to governments, but because the time frame and mechanism by which government decisions are implemented are so different. It is very easy to alter monetary policy from one day to the next. It is very difficult to alter fiscal policy once you decide to implement it. So, what is the coordination with? Is it the implementation of monetary policy with the "decision" of fiscal policy? With the "implementation" of fiscal policy, and so forth? And, a final remark about specific words. Larry ended his remarks by saying there is no alternative to "wise discretion." I assume everyone will agree that is better than "foolish discretion," but the real question is, are we likely to gravitate toward wise discretion, or is it better to take the chances in sticking to the target, assuming that otherwise wise discretions will not always arise? Thank you.

Mr. Thiessen: Let me just take one more question/statement, and then I'll let the panelists respond. Steve Grenville, Reserve Bank of Australia.

Mr. Grenville: Thanks. I wanted to make two comments about inflation targets, because they were seen by Stan Fischer as being the key. The first is that a case could be made that the true nirvana of central banks is not meeting an inflation target, but not needing an inflation target. If your reputation is good enough so that you don't need a target, then that is a better position to be in still. And perhaps countries of Europe and Japan, and perhaps even America, are in a better position to make that case than I am. But it does seem to me that if you are not forced to protest your virtue too vigorously and too specifically, then there is a better chance of your virtue remaining unscathed when you are hit by the usual problems that life hands out. The second issue is also on inflation targeting, and I'm afraid it is a bit more parochial. It is close to the issue of how, as a central bank, you manage to put inflation in a prominent position in your rhetoric—I emphasize the word "rhetoric"—and yet retain some discretion to have issues of income in your consideration. In Australia we have found that a key element in doing that is when you set an inflation target, you put a time dimension in it. In our case, we say we will go to this 2 to 3 percent target over the course of the cycle. And, the virtue of having that critical time element is that I think it lets you resolve the two issues of retaining the medium-term and longer-run joys of price stability—while at the same time retaining enough flexibility to do something—perhaps not a lot but something—about the course of real income over the course of the cycle. And, it is that time element in inflation targeting that is important to us. When we set our target, we had the advantage of being able to see what other people had done first in trying to search for better elements to add. It was the time element that was very important to us in fixing our target. Thank you.

Mr. Thiessen: Basically, we have run out of time here, so I ask Stan and Larry to respond briefly to that. Stan, you first.

Mr. Fischer: Thanks. Very briefly. On Japan, I don't doubt that Japanese monetary authorities would have liked to have cut the real interest rate, if they could have, and that the zero constraint on the nominal rate really did have an impact on the speed or lack of speed with which they are coming out of the recession. So that even while

I accept what Yoshio said about the way expectations have adjusted, it is still true that at the zero inflation level there have been constraints on policy. Two other comments. One on Jacob's: I agree that, by and large, if you are dealing with demand shocks, inflation targeting allows you to do both things right—both the countercyclical policy and the inflation targeting go together, as long as you're dealing with demand shocks. It is when you have supply shocks that you need to take some specific account of a tradeoff. On "wise discretion" or true nirvana not requiring an inflation target, that is true; but in the German case, say, there is still a feeling that they need some framework or some indicator. And there is still a reliance on a framework. In that connection, I quote Paul Samuelson, who says, "Given the choice between Bob Solow and an econometric model to make forecasts, I'd choose Bob Solow; but I'd rather have Bob Solow with an econometric model, than Bob Solow without one." Well, I would rather have a very good central banker without a good monetary policy framework than a lousy central banker in a good framework; but I would rather have a good central banker in a good framework. And it is the framework we are talking about.

Mr. Thiessen: Larry.

Mr. Summers: Let me just make two observations. First, I agree with what Stanley said about the Japanese situation. My judgment is that if the underlying inflation rate had been slightly higher, it would have been easier for monetary policy to have been constructive, and that the situation in Japan would not have lasted as long and would have been less serious. There is, I think, a parallel in some ways between the view that people do not accept a wage increasing less than one percent and the aversion that exists to the thought of having a nominal interest rate below 1 percent. Someone could argue, but I think it would be a silly argument, "Look, it is not really a constraint; the interest rate could be brought down from 0.5 percent to .25 percent, so who is to say there is any constraint there?" I don't think that is the way the process works in practice. I would be more comfortable with the view that we should have zero inflation as the target, or 1 percent as the strong target, if somebody were able to present me more happy examples of countries whose economies grew robustly and strongly for periods of a decade with inflation rates in that range. And, it may well be that it could work and would work if it were established for long enough, but I think the evidence is not there and not strong. The second point I would make is, in regard to this question of expectations adjusting, there is no question that, ultimately in the long run, expectations will adjust to almost anything. There is no question in my mind that if you operated in a deflationary environment for long enough, any special taboo about zero on any nominal wage increase would go away. But, I think there is the question of how long it would take. Fundamentally, the output shortfalls happen at times when the amount of inflation is less than the amount that was anticipated. And I think it will be much easier, as I said before, to build credibility in support of a proposition that inflation will not be allowed to rise above a level where the vast, vast majority of relevant opinion thinks it should not be allowed to rise, than it would be to build credibility in support of levels of inflation where there is a large body of intelligent, sensible opinion that thinks it should be allowed to rise. And, that would just counsel caution. This is really just another version of the observation that I think many countries have found that it is like drilling for oil: The lower you get, the harder it becomes to just go a little farther down. And it is really the same phenomenon.

Mr. Thiessen: Thank you, Larry. Let me thank Alan Greenspan, Stan Fischer, Larry Summers. And let us move on to the next topic: "How Should Central Banks Reduce Inflation?—Conceptual Issues."

How Should Central Banks Reduce Inflation?—Conceptual Issues

Mervyn King

It is tempting to give a very short answer to the title of the session—raise interest rates and reduce monetary growth. But when and by how much? That raises two questions which are central to the design of monetary policy. First, starting from an inflationary episode, how quickly should inflation be reduced to its desired level? Second, should monetary policy react to shocks to output as well as to inflation? The two questions are closely related, and are the subject of this paper.

Both questions were faced by the United Kingdom following departure from the exchange rate mechanism (ERM) in September 1992. At that time, the latest published inflation rate (retail price inflation excluding mortgage interest payments) was 4.2 percent, but that was following a recession during which output fell, relative to trend, by almost 10 percent, and the sterling effective exchange rate had just depreciated by 13 percent. The policy challenge was to prevent the depreciation having second-round effects on wages and prices, and to keep inflation falling during a recovery in output that had already started.

The exchange rate link was replaced by a domestic monetary framework defined in terms of an inflation target. The objective was to achieve "price stability" in the long run, defined by the then Chancellor, as a measured inflation rate of zero to 2 percent a year.

But the aim was not to bring inflation down to below 2 percent by the next month, or even the next year. It was to approach price stability gradually. In October 1992 a wide band of 1 to 4 percent for the target range of inflation was announced, with the additional objective of reaching a level below 2.5 percent by the end of the Parliament, a date then some four to five years ahead. The implicit assumption was that it would take approximately five years to make the transition to price stability. In the event, inflation fell below 2.5 percent in March 1994, remained below that level for ten months, but then rose again to just over 3 percent. In August 1996 inflation was 2.8 percent.

In 1995 the target was modified. Monetary policy would aim consistently to achieve an inflation rate of 2.5 percent or less some two years ahead. Shocks would mean that inflation would sometimes be above and sometimes below that figure. But in the long run, if policy were successful in achieving the target, inflation would average 2.5 percent or less. The stated objective of monetary policy was permanently low inflation. There was no mention of output as an explicit consideration in setting monetary policy.

Other countries have shown an equal reluctance to move quickly to price stability. Table 1 shows those countries which have in recent years adopted an explicit inflation target. Except for Australia, in all cases target inflation was below the existing rate of inflation. And in most cases, there was planned to be a gradual transition to price stability. A good example is that of Canada, which planned to bring inflation down from over 6 percent to a range of 1 to 3 percent over four years. New Zealand is a contrast in which the aim was to move quickly from an inflation rate of 7 percent to a range of zero to 2 percent.

Table 2 shows average inflation rates in each decade since 1950 for the G-3 countries and the seven industrialized countries which adopted inflation targets. From a peak in the 1970s and 1980s, inflation declined steadily. But only in Germany, Japan, and New Zealand was there anything other than a slow adjustment to low inflation. Chart 1 compares the path of the inflation rate since 1950

Table 1
Countries With Inflation Targets

Country	Price Index	Date of Introduction	Inflation Rate at Date of Introduction	Inflation Target
			%	
Australia	CPI	1993	1.8	Average of 2%-3%
Canada	CPI	February 1991	6.2	1%-3% from 1995
Finland	CPI	Early 1993	2.6	2% from 1995
Israel	CPI	December 1991	18.0	8%-11% for 1995
New Zealand	CPI	March 1990	7.0	0%-2%
Spain	CPI	November 1995	4.4	Below 3% by 1997
Sweden	CPI	Early 1993	4.8	2% ± 1% from 1995
United Kingdom	RPIX	October 1992	4.2	2.5% or less

for the G-3 countries and the inflation target countries as a group. Not surprisingly, on average the countries which subsequently adopted an inflation target experienced higher inflation than the G-3 over most of the period. It is interesting that following an inflation shock there were rather different speeds of adjustment. Japan, in particular, appears to have brought inflation down more quickly than either the United States or the inflation target countries over the past twenty years.

Is it possible to explain the different responses of the two sets of countries? It is important to distinguish between two speeds of adjustment. The first is the speed at which the inflation target implicit in monetary policy converges to price stability—the optimal speed of disinflation. The second is the speed at which policy offsets a temporary shock to inflation—the flexibility of monetary

Table 2
Inflation by Decade in Selected Countries

Country	Average of:				
	1950s	1960s	1970s	1980s	1990-95
Countries with inflation targets:					
Australia	6.5%	2.4%	9.8%	8.4%	3.3%
Canada	2.4%	2.5%	7.4%	6.5%	2.7%
Finland	6.2%	5.1%	10.4%	7.3%	2.7%
New Zealand	5.1%	3.3%	11.5%	11.9%	2.7%
Spain	6.2%	5.8%	14.4%	10.3%	5.3%
Sweden	4.5%	3.8%	8.6%	7.9%	5.0%
United Kingdom	4.3%	3.5%	12.7%	6.9%	4.6%
G3 countries:					
Germany	1.1%	2.4%	4.9%	2.9%	3.2%
Japan	2.9%	5.3%	8.9%	2.5%	1.6%
United States	2.1%	2.3%	7.1%	5.5%	3.5%

Note: Inflation is measured in terms of the Consumer Price Index, except in the United Kingdom, where RPIX is used, which excludes mortgage interest payments.

policy. In countries with a credible commitment to price stability (or to a stable low inflation rate, as in the G-3) only the second speed of adjustment is relevant. But in countries attempting to change from a regime of moderate or high inflation to one of price stability, there is an additional issue of the optimal speed of disinflation. That depends on how rapidly private sector expectations of inflation adapt to the change in regime.

It has been argued that "the United States is only one recession away from price stability." In contrast, it has been suggested that the United Kingdom is only one expansion away from diverging from price stability. Too slow a convergence on price stability, and too great an accommodation of inflation shocks, have their dangers. The ultimate target becomes less credible. So what determines the opti-

Chart 1
CPI Inflation in the G3 and Inflation Target Countries, 1950-1995

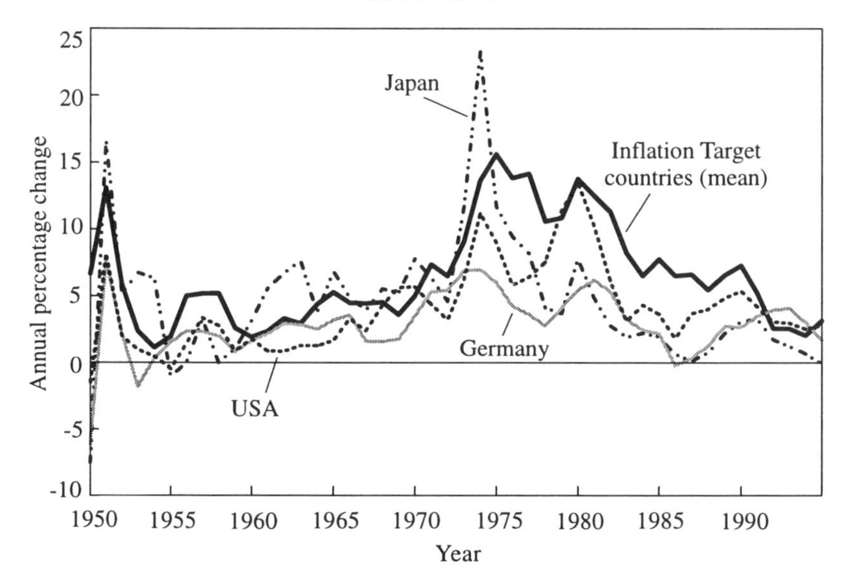

Note: Inflation target countries are those shown in Table 1.

mal speed of disinflation and how flexible should monetary policy be in the face of shocks? Those questions are analyzed in the second and third sections, respectively. I shall assume that the long-term objective of monetary policy is price stability.[1]

The optimal speed of disinflation

In this section I examine the speed of disinflation that would be chosen by a central bank in a world in which monetary policy affects real output and employment in the short run but not in the long run. I shall make two points. First, irrespective of the instruments used to implement it, monetary policy is a combination of an ex ante inflation target chosen each period and a discretionary response to certain shocks. Those shocks are ones to which the central banks can respond before the private sector is able to adjust nominal contracts. Second, in general, it is not optimal to move immediately to a regime of price stability unless that regime can be made fully credible by institutional or other changes.

Following a prolonged period of inflation, why should a central bank not move immediately to price stability? The answer is that there are costs of disinflation, and, moreover, those costs increase more than proportionally with the rate of disinflation. Such costs result from a change in the monetary policy regime—the target inflation rate—because private sector agents cannot easily tell whether the regime has changed or not. Learning takes time. And the longer the period during which inflation was high, the longer it is likely to be before the private sector is persuaded that policy has changed. An unanticipated disinflation will depress output because wages and prices take time to adjust to the new lower price level (relative to expectations). Disinflations in both the United States and the United Kingdom in the early 1980s proved costly in terms of lost output and employment.

The speed at which expectations adjust during that transition will influence the magnitude of the output loss. A central bank can lower those costs by reducing the gap between private sector inflation expectations and the inflation target implied by its own monetary policy. A target is credible when the gap is zero. Indeed, "rational expectations" are defined as those where expected inflation is equal to the inflation target. But the mere announcement of a commitment to price stability as the basis for monetary policy is unlikely to generate full credibility quickly. Indeed, in a deeper sense, expectations are likely to be influenced by the commitment to price stability among the public at large. Institutional changes such as central bank independence, may improve credibility; but when they do so, it is largely because they reflect a commitment among the public to the objective of price stability.

The optimal speed of disinflation depends, therefore, on the real output costs of changing expectations held by the private sector about the intentions of the central bank to reduce inflation. Those costs reflect the existence of a short-term tradeoff between inflation and output. Such a tradeoff reflects nominal stickiness in wages and prices, which results from the cost of processing information in order to determine the prices which it is optimal to charge, as well as incomplete adjustment of expectations to changes in the monetary policy regime. In a survey of 200 firms, Blinder (1994) found that "almost 80 percent of GDP is repriced quarterly or less frequently." Both nominal stickiness and slow adjustment of inflation expectations play a role in the analysis set out below. Nominal stickiness means that the central bank can affect output in the short run because monetary policy is able to respond to at least some of the shocks hitting the economy before wages and prices can be adjusted by private sector agents. I do not assume that the central bank has private information—except about its own preferences for price stability. There can be few decisions where the relevant information is more widely available to, and analyzed by, the public than monetary policy. But the central bank may be able to respond to a shock before all wages and prices have adjusted, and it is that speed of response which enables monetary policy to influence the extent to which shocks impact on output or inflation. Of course, there will be some shocks to which even the central bank will find it difficult to respond in time, and such shocks introduce a random element into the behavior of inflation despite the best efforts of central banks to control the price level.

The speed at which expectations adjust to changes in inflation was a key element in the expectations-augmented Phillips curve of Friedman and Phelps. In their model, expectations adjusted slowly to changes in actual inflation, and the central bank could raise output for a time by raising the inflation rate. At a constant inflation rate, expectations would be consistent with actual inflation, and unemployment would be at its natural rate. It was the assumption of rational expectations that enabled Lucas (1973) to undermine the theoretical plausibility of even a short-run tradeoff. Monetary policy could not affect output because expectations adjusted immediately. Only when the private sector had incomplete information about monetary policy could changes in money affect output. That is because, in the Lucas model, agents are uncertain about how to interpret changes in nominal prices. Do they reflect changes in the aggregate money stock or are they changes in relative prices?

Confusion can exist for awhile because neither the money supply nor the aggregate price level is perfectly observable. Such an assumption is not plausible empirically. The world is not short of statistics on money and inflation. But nominal stickiness—nominal contracts which last for several periods—mean that future inflation matters. And agents, although able to observe current money supply, may be uncertain about how the central bank will conduct monetary policy in the future. So differences between actual and anticipated monetary policy will affect output.

A change in the way monetary policy is conducted will alter private sector expectations. It is not sensible to ignore that aspect of a change in monetary policy, as was done in the more extreme Keynesian models. Equally, however, it is too extreme to suppose expectations adjust immediately to a new regime. Learning takes place in real time. As Brunner and Meltzer put it,

> "Both positions are unacceptable. The Keynesians failed to recognize that people learn and are not locked into their beliefs and behavior. The new classical macroeconomists introduce learning but neglect costs of acquiring information. Neglect of these costs leads them to exaggerate the speeds of learning and response in the marketplace and the knowledge that people have about the future in a changing and uncertain world." (1993, p.132)

Nevertheless, Sargent (1986) has argued that a sharp disinflation may be preferable to gradualism because expectations adjust quickly. There is no doubt that the "rational expectations" approach to understanding changes in monetary regimes has been very important. When governments change behavior, agents learn. But how do they learn and over what time span? Those are the key questions the answers to which determine the optimal speed of disinflation. In Sargent's view, "gradualism invites speculation about future reversals, or U-turns, in policy" (p.150). Excessive gradualism surely does so; but so does excessive radicalism. Sargent's strictures on gradualism relate primarily to paths toward price stability that are accompanied by large and persistent government budget deficits. On that I fully agree. Unless budget deficits are reduced to levels consistent with price stability, no commitment to price stability is credible. In what follows I shall assume that deficits are on a path consistent with price stability in the long run.

I shall examine the role of learning in a simple model of aggregate demand and supply.[2] For those who enjoy equations, a good many are given in the appendix. There are three equations for the three key variables: aggregate supply, aggregate demand, and the money stock. The model is standard—with one exception. In the recent literature on the "inflation bias" of discretionary monetary policy, it has become fashionable (despite the best efforts of McCallum, 1995, 1996) to assume that the central bank aims for a rate of unemployment below the market-generated natural rate of unemployment. Put simply, the central bank uses monetary expansions to create jobs which do not exist in the long run. In contrast, I shall assume that the central bank does not use monetary policy as a substitute for microeconomic structural reforms. Because it is not trying systematically to push unemployment below the natural rate, there is no "time inconsistency" in monetary policy. By relating monetary policy to macroeconomic rather than microeconomic goals, there is no "inflation bias" and hence no obstacle to the achievement of price stability.

The model is simple. First, aggregate supply exceeds the "natural" rate of output when inflation is higher than was expected by agents when nominal contracts were set. Positive price surprises make it profitable for firms temporarily to increase output. Output is also subject to random shocks. These are of two types. The first (type 1 shocks) are shocks which can be observed by the central bank before monetary policy is determined, but which the private sector observes only after wages and prices have been set for that period. Monetary policy can respond to those shocks. The second (type 2 shocks) cannot be observed by the central bank until after policy has been set for that period. They may not be observable until data are published some months after the event. Type 2 shocks will introduce additional randomness into inflation and output, but are not central to the choice of monetary strategy.[3]

Aggregate demand is positively related to real money balances and to expected inflation. That is the reduced form of a system in which the demand for money is a function of nominal expenditure and nominal interest rates, the demand for goods is a function of real money balances and the real interest rate, and the real interest rate is equal to the nominal interest rate less the expected inflation rate.

The final relationship describes the process by which the central bank determines the growth of the money supply. In the technical jargon, monetary policy is a "reaction function" which determines policy as a function of changes in observable economic variables. Each period the money supply (or, equivalently, the short-term interest rate) is set by the central bank in full knowledge of the size of the shock to output, which it has been able to observe. The expectations of the private sector that influence demand and supply are, however, formed before agents can observe the shock. That reflects nominal stickiness in setting wages and prices. It is possible, therefore, to express the monetary policy reaction function as a choice by the central bank of two variables. The first is an inflation target for that period, defined as the value of the inflation rate which the central bank would like to achieve in the absence of any shock to output. The second term is the discretionary response by the central bank to the observed shock that leads it to choose values for interest rates or monetary growth that are an appropriate response to the shock. It is shown in the appendix that it is possible to compress the model into two equations—for inflation and output. These are:

$$\text{inflation} = \text{inflation target} + R_I(\text{type 1 shock}) + \text{type 2 shock}$$

$$\text{output} = \text{natural rate} + b(\text{inflation target-expected inflation}) + R_O(\text{type 1 shock}) + \text{type 2 shock}$$

where R_I and R_O are coefficients which describe the effects of monetary responses to type 1 shocks on inflation and output respectively, and b measures the impact of inflation surprises on output.

There are two points to note. First, *any* monetary policy can be described as a choice of (1) an *ex ante* inflation target and (2) an optimal response to observable shocks. An inflation target is not a particular form of setting monetary policy; rather, it is its generic form. That is why the difference between an inflation target regime for monetary policy and a regime based on a monetary target can easily be exaggerated. Choosing the inflation target, however, does not uniquely define monetary policy. There is the subsidiary question of how policy should respond to shocks. It is important to distinguish these two aspects of policy in order to avoid confusion between changes in trend inflation, which are monetary, and changes in price levels caused by real shocks.

Second, inflation can differ from the long-run desired level which corresponds to price stability, for three reasons. First, the inflation target itself may differ, at least temporarily, from zero. Second, it may be optimal to accommodate a temporary inflation shock. Third, there may be other shocks to inflation about which the central bank can do little in time to prevent their feeding through to the final price level. Since the shocks average to zero over a period, it is clear that a central bank can achieve price stability by setting its inflation target to zero (or whatever measured inflation rate corresponds to price stability).

The two equations determine inflation and output as a function of the choices made by the central bank (the inflation target and the discretionary response to a shock), the expected inflation rate, and the shock to output. For any given model of learning by the private sector about how the central bank will set its inflation target it is possible to solve for the actual paths of inflation and output (see the appendix).

Suppose that inflation has averaged some positive rate for a period, and that both expected inflation and the implicit inflation target are consistent with that rate. If the central bank now announces that it intends to pursue price stability in the future, what will happen to inflation and output? That depends on how quickly expectations adjust to the new monetary strategy. Three cases may be analyzed corresponding to different models of learning. These are rational expectations; exogenous learning, in which expectations adjust along a path that is independent of the inflation out-turn; and endogenous learning, in which the speed of learning depends on the policy choices made by the central bank.

A fully credible change in regime

A change to a regime of price stability that is fully credible means that private sector expectations are consistent with the adoption of a new inflation target corresponding to price stability. When expected inflation equals the actual inflation target chosen by the central bank, there is no systematic deviation of output from its natural rate. Policy can achieve price stability without any expected output loss. The optimal strategy is to move immediately to a zero inflation target. There is, however, one exception, even in the case of full credibility. In an open economy, nominal wage and price stickiness may mean that, after a change to a regime of price stability, the exchange rate rises to a level above its long-run equilibrium corresponding to the new monetary policy, causing a short-term rise in the real exchange rate. Such Dornbusch overshooting of the exchange rate depresses the demand for domestically produced output. In that case the time horizon for a move to price stability is determined by the duration of nominal stickiness.

Exogenous learning

In general, an announcement by the central bank that in future the inflation target will be consistent with price stability does not command immediate credibility. It takes time for the private sector to be convinced that the target will be chosen to be consistent with price stability. The private sector will try to learn about the true preferences of the central bank. Their pronouncements will not necessarily be taken at face value. Modeling learning is difficult. As Sargent argues:

> "The characteristics of the serial correlation of inflation are inherited from the random properties of the deep causes of inflation, such as monetary and fiscal policy variables." (1986, p. 113).

There is no unique way to model rational learning. Nevertheless, it seems implausible to suppose that learning takes place immediately upon a switch to a new monetary regime. By moving rapidly to price stability, a central bank can hope to demonstrate that it is committed to price stability. Indeed, in a world in which there are only two kinds of central banks—"tough" and "weak"—it has been shown that a "tough" central bank will disinflate just fast enough to differentiate itself from a "weak" central bank that might otherwise be tempted to pass itself off as a true inflation-fighter. (Vickers, 1986, Persson and Tabellini, 1990). In practice, there is a spectrum of views on inflation that might be held by a monetary authority, and it becomes much more difficult to learn where on that spectrum a central bank lies. Successful regime shifts usually occur when public opinion is behind the need for a dramatic reform, and hence the sustainability of the reform is more credible. That support is less obvious for a shift from low and moderate inflation rates to price stability than when tackling a hyperinflation. To be credible, the change in regime must be widely understood and thought likely to persist. For that to be the case, it is insufficient for a central bank to make a public announcement; the change must also be thought acceptable to a wider public. Consider the following example of a clear regime shift suggested by Sargent,

> "It is arguable that pegging to a foreign currency is a policy that is relatively easier to support and make credible by concrete actions, since it is possible to hook the domestic country's price expectations virtually instantaneously onto the presumably exogenous price expectations process in the foreign country." (1986, p.121).

When Britain joined the ERM in 1990, inflation expectations did not jump to those in Germany or other "inner" core members of the ERM. Inflation expectations did fall modestly, and they rose again when Britain left the ERM in September 1992. But the process of learning about the government's commitment, both to the ERM and to price stability, did not stop upon entry to the ERM. That shows that a regime shift may be easier to identify in theory than in practice.

Much of the process of learning about central bank preferences is independent of the actual evolution of inflation itself. Central bank behavior reflects the degree of external support for its objectives. And since the ultimate basis for a central bank commitment to price stability is a wider public support for that objective, it is not easy to forecast how quickly a central bank will be able or willing to move toward price stability. In practice, learning is continuous. The idea that private agents are trying to learn about a fixed point—the long-run inflation target—misses some important aspects of behavior. Central banks are not static institutions. There is turnover among members of the governing board, and new ideas about monetary policy are continually injected into the policy debate. Since central banks' views change, private agents need to learn continuously about those views.[4] The significant reduction in inflation in the industrial countries over the past twenty years surely derives at least as much from the gradual acceptance that there is no long-run tradeoff between inflation and unemployment as from changes in preferences about inflation itself. It is worth examining, therefore, the consequences of a learning process that is exogenous to the short-run path of inflation.

If expected inflation exceeds the inflation target, then there are systematic output losses during the transition to price stability. It would be costly to pursue price stability from the outset. It is possible to calculate the optimal transition path given the objective of minimizing deviations of inflation from the desired level of zero and of output from its natural rate. There is a tradeoff between the two. Too slow a reduction in the inflation target implies inflation remains high for a long period; too rapid an approach to the long-run target means large output losses.

It is shown in the appendix that when expected inflation converges on price stability at an exogenous rate, then it is optimal to set the inflation target at a constant proportion of the exogenous expected inflation rate. That proportion depends upon (a) the weight attached to the importance of keeping inflation close to price stability relative to keeping output close to its natural rate, and (b) the impact of inflation surprises on output. The inflation target converges gradually to price stability, but is always below expected inflation. Inflation itself also falls gradually.

The "gradualist" path to price stability is, in general, preferable to either a "cold turkey" strategy, in which the inflation target is set to zero from the outset, or an "accommodation" strategy in which the inflation target declines in line with expected inflation. The former involves greater output losses during the transition and the latter involves larger deviations of inflation from price stability.

Figure 1a shows an example in which expectations decline steadily, and linearly, over a fixed period of length T. Both output and inflation adjust to their long-run values gradually over time. If the relative importance which the central bank attaches to minimizing deviations of inflation from price stability relative to deviations of output from its natural rate is denoted by a, and b measures the impact on output of price surprises, then the cumulative output loss during the transition to price stability is $[ab/(a+b^2)]\ \pi_0\ (T/2)$, where π_0 is the initial inflation rate.[5] Plausible values are $a = 0.25$ and $b = 0.5$ for quarterly data. Hence the cumulative output loss along the optimal transition path from an initial inflation rate of 10 percent a year to price stability when learning is complete only after ten years is 12 percent of the initial level of annual output. That can be contrasted with the cumulative output loss under the "cold turkey" strategy of over 24 percent.

Random shocks to the economy make the path less smooth than that shown in Figure 1a. It is possible to simulate the shocks, and Figure 1b shows a path both during and after the transition to price stability for parameters of the random process generating shocks fitted to U.K. data. Figure 1b plots output each quarter and inflation over the previous twelve months since they are the usual definitions of published statistics. Not surprisingly, the twelve-month inflation rate changes more smoothly over time than does quarterly output. The path to price stability contains periods in which inflation rises before converging to zero.

Figure 1a
Inflation and Output With Exogenous Learning

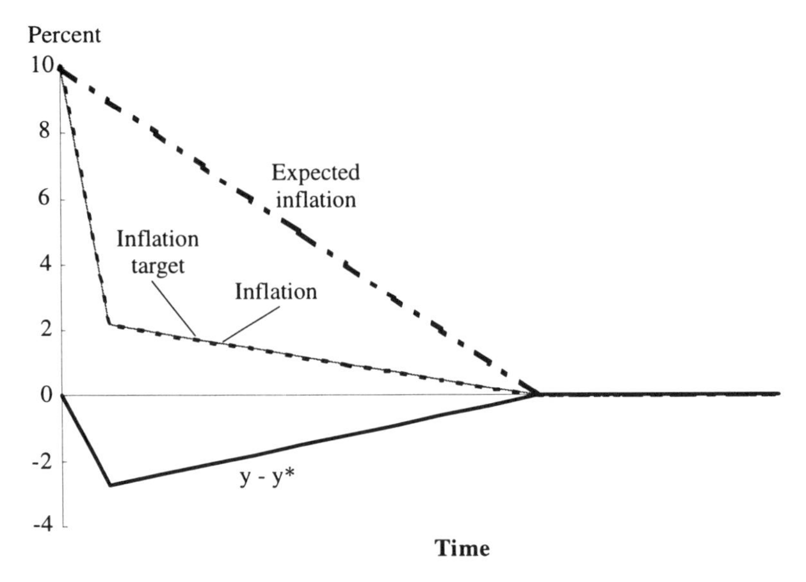

Endogenous learning

In the previous section it was argued that there are good reasons to suppose that, in trying to learn about the future inflation target of the central bank, many of the relevant factors are exogenous to the path of inflation itself. But a central bank may try to convince the private sector of its commitment to price stability by choosing to reduce its inflation target toward zero quickly. One might call this "teaching by doing." The choice of a particular inflation target influences the speed at which expectations adjust to price stability. Each period the private sector can look back and infer from the shocks that occurred in the past the inflation target that was chosen in the previous period. It then updates its belief about the current inflation target according to how fast the actual inflation target itself adjusts to price stability. I call this a case of endogenous learning. The optimal speed at which the inflation target approaches zero is derived in the appendix for the special case of a constant updating parameter. As in the case of exogenous learning, price stability is

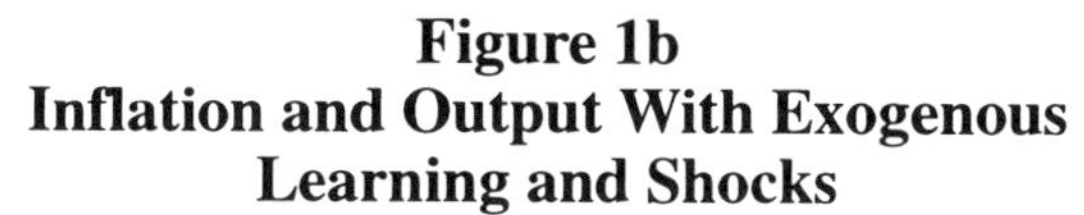

Figure 1b
Inflation and Output With Exogenous Learning and Shocks

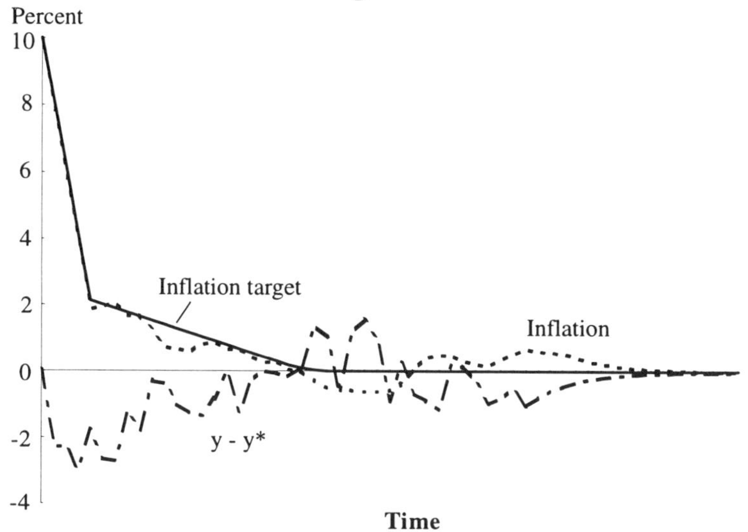

reached gradually, and an example is shown in Figure 2. In general, the weight attached to past observations of the inflation target will depend upon the perceived uncertainty of the commitment to price stability. With a stable institutional arrangement for monetary policy, credibility is likely to grow over time. But any uncertainty over the continuation of the new regime, perhaps because of a lack of public support, slows down the acquisition of credibility.

The rationality attributed here to private agents—in which they can observe past shocks and so infer the previous period's inflation target—means that the optimal degree of flexibility in monetary policy is unaffected by whether learning is endogenous or exogenous. If, however, learning depends on the actual rate of inflation rather than the inferred inflation target, then it may be optimal not to accommodate temporary inflation shocks for fear that doing so might lead to higher inflation expectations in the future. In this case in the early stages of the transition to price stability it is optimal to pursue a much less flexible monetary policy than would be desirable once credibility had been attained.

Figure 2
Inflation and Output With Endogenous Learning

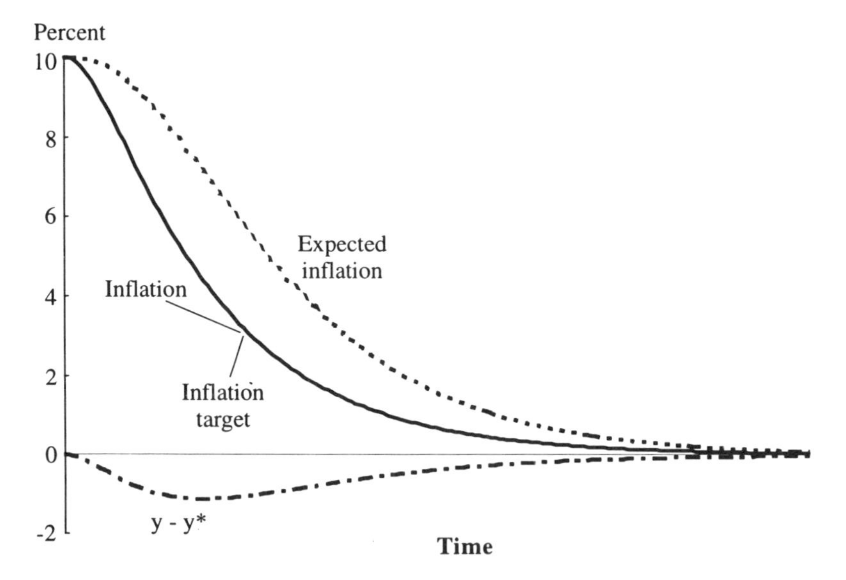

The general prediction of the learning models is that the inflation target—and hence actual inflation—will fall faster in the earlier years of the transition and will always lie below expected inflation. That appears to have been the U.K. experience during the 1980s. Chart 2 shows expected inflation derived from a comparison between the yields on nominal and index-linked government bonds and the actual inflation rate. The predicted pattern holds with the exception of the period toward the end of the decade when the pursuit of price stability was temporarily suspended. The data are not ideal for the purpose of making comparisons with the model. Estimates of expected inflation are available only from 1982, some three years after the initial change in regime, and they refer to inflation expected some ten years ahead because of difficulties in estimating accurately the short end of the yield curve. But the general pattern is clear, and seems to have been repeated in the renewed attempt to reach price stability in the 1990s. It is evident

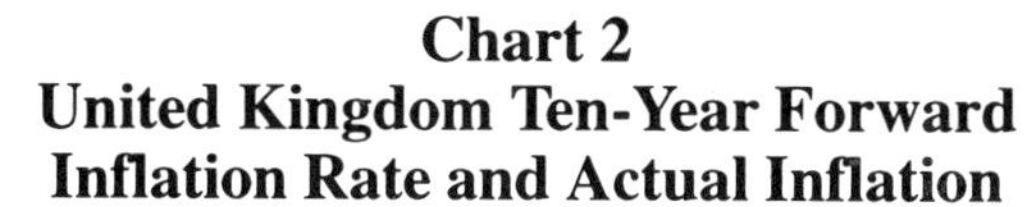

Chart 2
United Kingdom Ten-Year Forward Inflation Rate and Actual Inflation

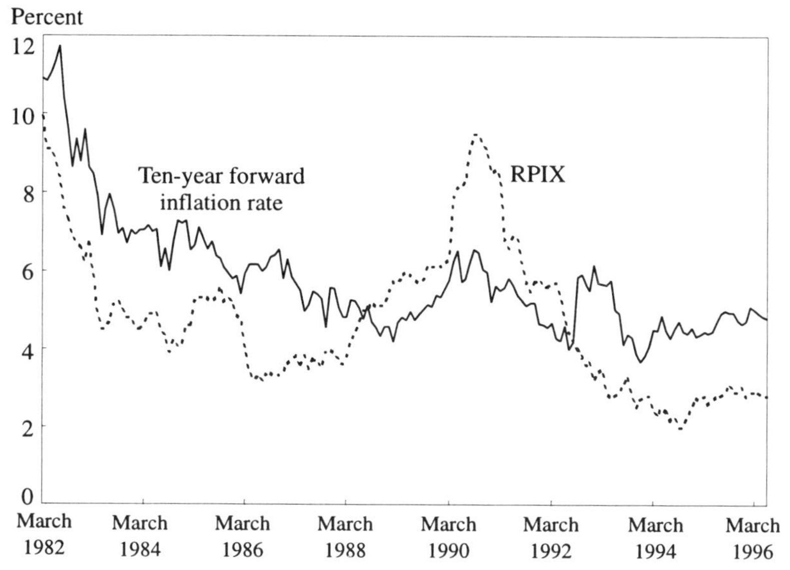

that the United Kingdom has not achieved credibility in its stated inflation target. The data in Chart 2 can be used to estimate the learning model given by equation 22 in the appendix. From 171 observations, the estimated value of the updating parameter ρ is 0.921 with a standard error of 0.023. For the case considered above where $a = 0.25$ and $b = 0.5$, this estimate implies that it takes just over six years before the inflation target falls from 10 percent to 5 percent a year.

Table 3 and Chart 3 provide information on the two speeds of adjustment of inflation discussed above. The upper panel of Table 3 shows the change in inflation from a cyclical peak to the next trough in a number of industrialized countries. The speed at which inflation was brought down is shown together with the average inflation rate over the period 1965 to 1995. The data refer to completed cycles over that period. The average speed is a mixture of the speed of disinflation and the rate at which temporary shocks to inflation are

Table 3
Inflation Changes Over the Cycle

Country	Change from peak to next trough (pp) (1) (b) (c)	Number of quarters (2)	Change in inflation per quarter (1)/(2)	Ranking (a)	*Average inflation 1965-1995*
Germany	-3.8	11	-0.6	6	*3.6*
U.K.	-8.6	6	-1.5	13	*8.1*
U.S.	-5.2	10	-0.5	5	*5.3*
Italy	-6.8	9	-1.1	11	*9.2*
Japan	-4.7	7	-0.9	9	*5.0*
France	-3.9	12	-0.3	1	*6.4*
Canada	-3.2	8	-0.4	2	*5.6*
Belgium	-5.2	9	-0.5	4	*5.0*
Netherlands	-4.1	7	-0.7	7	*4.5*
Sweden	-6.2	8	-0.9	10	*7.0*
Switzerland	-4.7	9	-0.5	3	*3.9*
Australia	-6.5	9	-0.7	8	*7.0*
New Zealand	-8.9	11	-1.2	12	*8.7*

Country	Change from trough to next peak (pp) (1)	Number of quarters (2)	Change in inflation per quarter (1)/(2)	Ranking (a)
Germany	4.0	11	0.5	1
U.K.	8.6	8	1.1	11 =
U.S.	5.3	9	0.6	5
Italy	7.2	7	1.1	13
Japan	4.3	7	0.7	9
France	3.8	8	0.5	2
Canada	3.1	5	0.6	4
Belgium	4.4	9	0.5	3
Netherlands	3.7	8	0.7	7
Sweden	6.3	9	1.1	11 =
Switzerland	4.6	8	0.7	8
Australia	6.3	11	0.6	6
New Zealand	7.8	10	0.9	10

(a) Ranking is from lowest to highest rate of change of inflation.

(b) For peak-to-trough or trough-to-peak half cycles started and completed between March 1965 and 1992

(c) Inflation as measured by the three month moving average of the annual rate of change of the CPI

Source: IFS

allowed to die away. Countries with a credible commitment to stable low inflation have inflation slopes—defined as the reduction in inflation per quarter—of around 0.5. Countries with worse inflation records, such as the United Kingdom, Italy, Sweden, and over much of the period New Zealand, show much steeper slopes with an absolute value around unity. There does seem to be evidence that the two speeds of adjustment are different. In the lower panel of Table 3, similar calculations are presented for the change in inflation from a cyclical trough to the next peak. A similar pattern emerges, reflecting the speed with which the lower credibility countries allowed inflation to rise in the 1960s and 1970s. Chart 3 plots the profile of inflation for selected G-10 countries over the period 1965 to 1995. The difference in the inflation slopes is evident.

There is one additional cost of a disinflation in which actual inflation falls faster than expected inflation. With government debt fixed in nominal terms, the burden of the debt rises when there is unanticipated disinflation. At last year's Jackson Hole conference I called this "unpleasant fiscal arithmetic" (King, 1995). Too rapid a disinflation can, therefore, add to the fiscal burden. But there is a ready solution at hand—the use of index-linked debt.

The optimal flexibility of monetary policy

The previous section discussed the optimal speed of adjustment from some initial inflation rate to price stability. Although the overriding objective of monetary policy is price stability, that does not uniquely define monetary policy. Inflation can differ from the target level because of either type 1 or type 2 shocks. Price stability is better defined as a situation in which the inflation target is equal to the expected rate of inflation and both in turn equal zero. That corresponds better with Alan Greenspan's definition of price stability in which inflation does not affect significantly decisions by economic agents, and leaves open the choice of the optimal response to type 1 shocks. In general, it is optimal to accommodate part of any such shock. The fraction that is accommodated depends upon the relative weight attached to deviations of inflation from price stability, on the one hand, and to deviations of output from its natural

Chart 3
Inflation in Selected G10 Countries

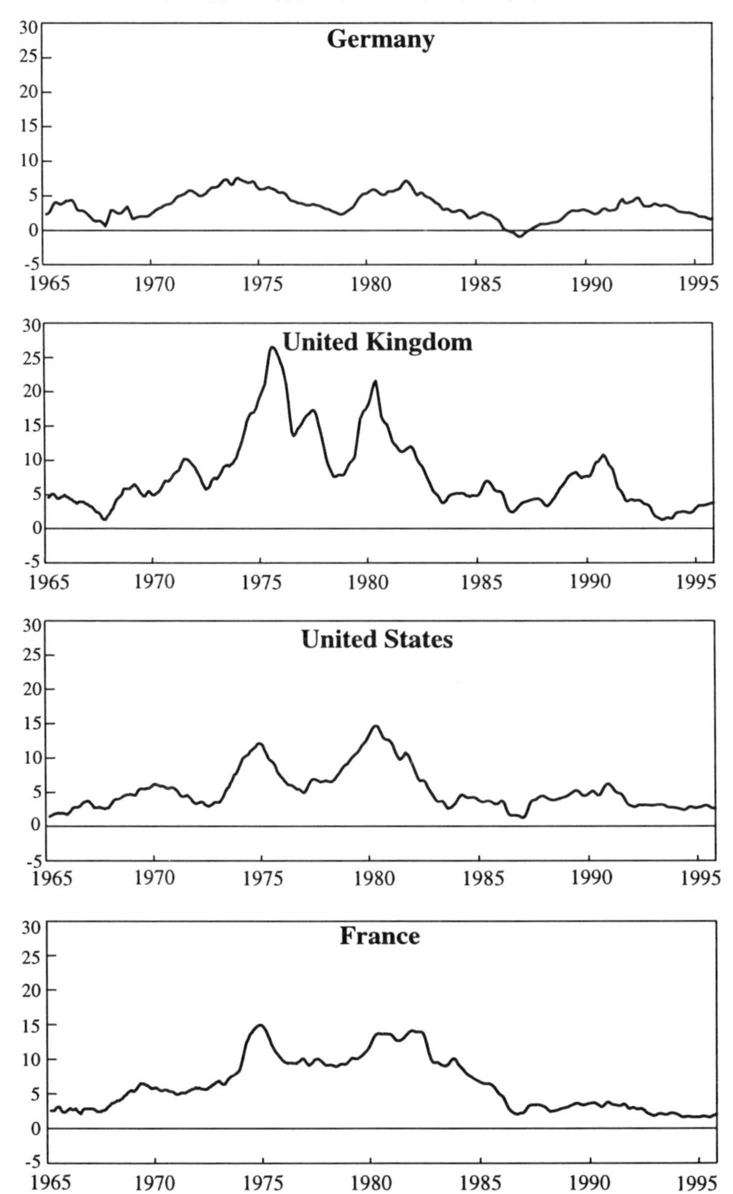

Chart 3 - continued
Inflation in Selected G10 Countries

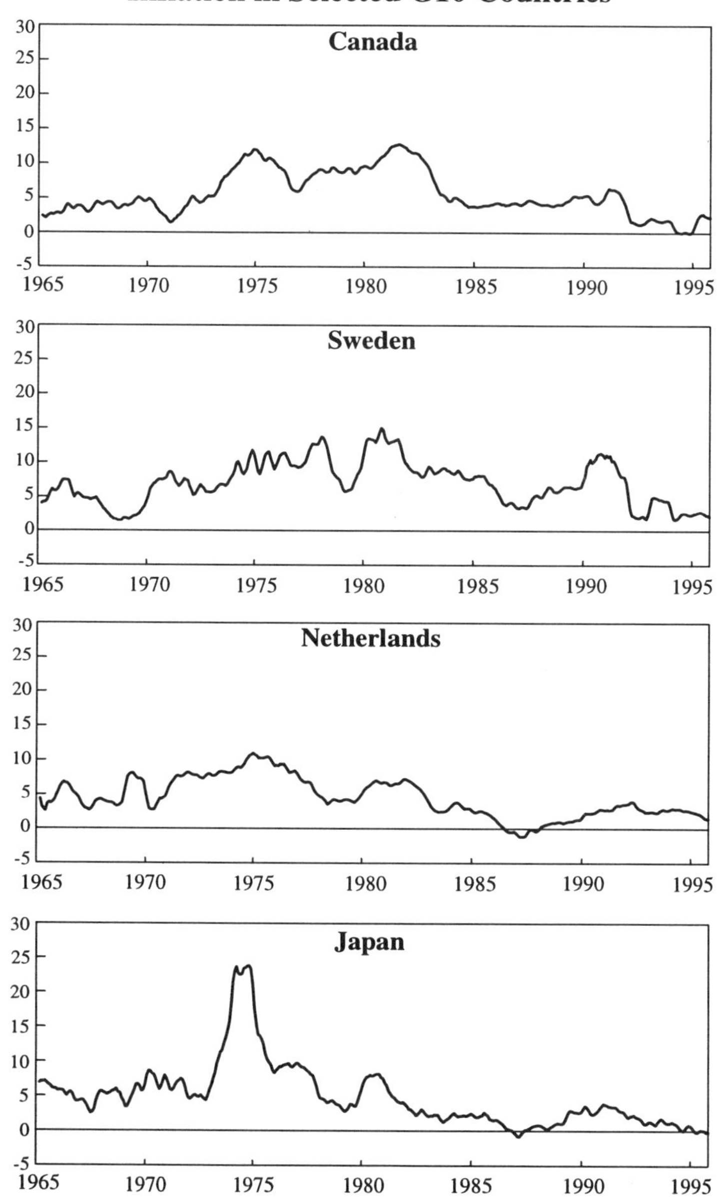

Source: ONS for United Kingdom, IFS for other G10 countries.
United Kingdom inflation rate is for retail prices excluding mortgage interest payments (RPIX), headline CPI for all other countries.

rate, on the other.[6] As John Crow has argued, a mandate of price stability does not absolve a central bank from taking countercyclical actions, but its purpose is "to ensure that such actions when taken do not build in an inflationary bias, not that they not be taken at all."[7]

In most cases the optimal degree of accommodation of temporary shocks is quite separate from the optimal speed of disinflation. But when learning depends on past inflation, matters are more complicated. Any accommodation of an upward shock to inflation, albeit temporary, affects future expectations of inflation. That in turn increases the output costs of any given inflation target. Hence, especially in the early stages of the transition to price stability, it pays not to accommodate as much of the inflation shock as would be optimal once expectations have adjusted to price stability. A central bank that is embarking on the road to price stability cannot afford to engage in as much flexibility in monetary policy as can a central bank which has established a track record for a commitment to price stability. There is a tradeoff between credibility and flexibility. But that tradeoff exists only during the transition to price stability. That may explain why there is little empirical evidence of a tradeoff between credibility and flexibility in cross-section data.

There is a further reason for caution in a transition to price stability. It is clear from the literature on time inconsistency of monetary policy that a central bank which tries to stabilize output around a level in excess of the natural rate can create an inflationary bias. During the transition, it is important for the central bank to convince the market that it is not trying to use monetary policy to achieve a level of output in excess of the natural rate as a substitute for structural reforms. In the absence of a track record of price stability, it is quite possible that the market may be suspicious that a central bank is trying to do just that. This is quite distinct from the issue of the speed of learning. And it suggests why central banks are extremely cautious in their use of language to describe how output affects monetary policy. It is easy for economists to make a clear, logical distinction between two different models. But it is vital for a central bank to ensure that markets do not suspect it of behaving according to one model rather than the other. And that is not straightforward when the key variables—the natural rate of unemployment and the output gap—are not observable. Hence, even though it may be perfectly rational to accommodate temporary shocks to inflation, the need to ensure that markets do not suspect other motives implies the importance of caution in the language used by central banks about output stabilization. Words matter. Indeed, actions may be safer than words.

Another aspect of the link between the two elements of monetary policy—the inflation target and the response to shocks—has surfaced in the recent proposal for an "opportunistic" approach to disinflation, an idea associated with Alan Blinder.[8] An analysis of the opportunistic model has been provided by Orphanides and Wilcox (1996). The opportunistic approach implies that when inflation is either too high or too low the approach to price stability is as analyzed above. But when inflation is in an intermediate range, the inflation target is not reduced any further unless there is a negative inflation shock. When such a shock occurs no attempt is made to benefit from a temporary excess of output over trend—the shock is fully accommodated. The inflation target is then ratcheted down. There is an asymmetric approach to positive and negative shocks when inflation is in the intermediate range. Positive shocks are suppressed; negative shocks are accommodated. Why would a central bank behave in this way? Orphanides and Wilcox identify two conditions under which a central bank might pursue such a strategy. First, its attitude to current inflation must depend on the path of inflation in the recent past. To quote the example given by Orphanides and Wilcox,

> "an opportunistic policymaker evaluates a 3 percent rate of inflation today less favorably if inflation yesterday was 2 percent than if inflation yesterday was 4 percent. In the former case, an opportunistic policymaker might well aim to drive output below potential, whereas in the latter case, she would aim simply to hold output at potential."

Second, the central bank pursues output stabilization when inflation is low, and price stability when inflation is high. An opportunistic central bank which starts with low inflation will focus on output stabilization even if inflation drifts upward for a time.

But that strategy may be observationally equivalent to that of a central bank which uses monetary policy to target a level of employment in excess of the natural rate—that is, to create jobs that are not there—and incurs the inflation bias of discretion. Equally, a central bank that waits for negative inflation shocks before reducing inflation may also appear similar to a central bank that is trying to achieve unemployment below the natural rate. The loss of credibility may then create output losses when inflation is reduced.

So far I have examined learning by economic agents. But central banks learn also. An optimal monetary strategy can be expressed in terms of a predetermined rule only if the procedure for updating the policy rule can itself be written as a rule. Since there is no unique optimal learning strategy, that is unlikely. But if discretion is inevitable, then why has it been suggested that several central banks have, in fact, followed rules, in particular the rule suggested by John Taylor?[9] The Taylor rule implies that nominal short-term official interest rates should be set such that the real interest rate differs from the real interest rate that would hold at the natural rate of output by an amount which is proportional to the excess of output over its natural rate and the excess of inflation over its target rate. It is vital to distinguish between two uses of the Taylor rule. The first is as a normative rule for policy. The second is as a positive description of the behavior of central banks in practice. The Taylor rule implies a correlation between real interest rates, output, and inflation. In the normative sense, causation runs from interest rates to output and inflation. But such a correlation exists in any economy that behaves according to the simple model presented in this paper. It is easy to show that, for *any* choice of inflation target and response to temporary shocks, the linear relationship between real rates, output, and inflation is identical to the Taylor rule (see appendix). Any set of observations can be rationalized as a Taylor rule for a suitable choice of inflation target. Hence it is impossible to distinguish between those central banks which are following a Taylor rule and those which are not. Differences show up in the time paths of inflation and output, not in the relationship between real interest rates, inflation, and output.

The main lesson from the discussion of rules is the importance of trying to ensure that private sector expectations are consistent with the monetary strategy pursued by the central bank. It is the predictability of policy rather than the fact that the policy can be expressed in terms of a rule that is crucial. If the exercise of discretion is inevitable, then predictability implies a significant degree of transparency in the setting of monetary policy. Explanations by the central bank of the rationale for policy help to increase predictability and reduce volatility. Monetary policy in both the United Kingdom and the United States in recent years has clearly not followed a simple rule. But it has been somewhat more predictable than at times in the past. One consequence is that quite small changes in official interest rates—or even a decision *not* to change rates—have led to significant movements in short-term market rates and hence to short-term real interest rates. Charts 4 and 5 show the short end of the yield curve in the United Kingdom and the United States, respectively, from January 1994. In both countries modest movements in official rates led to significant changes in expected three-month market interest rates over the following twelve to twenty-four months. Rates moved in anticipation of future policy changes, and the yield curve did a lot of the work in altering the stance of monetary policy.

Conclusions

The main point of this paper is simple. The design of monetary policy in the transition to price stability must take seriously learning by both economic agents and the central bank. No successful transition can be designed that ignores learning by private sector agents about the implicit inflation target of the monetary authority. Equally, pure rational expectations models are not a good basis on which to base policy because they ignore the process of learning. Models of learning under conditions of bounded rationality are few and far between. As Sargent puts it,

Chart 4
United Kingdom Three-Month Interest Rate Expectations[1]

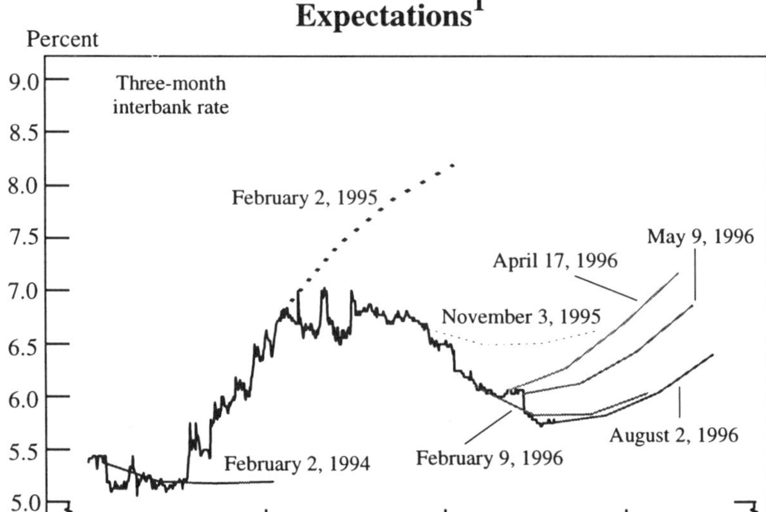

[1] Based on a combination of sterling interest rate futures contracts.
Sources: Bank of England and LIFFE.

> "We might have prejudices and anecdotes to guide our preferences among transition strategies but no empirically confirmed informed theories." (1993, p.1).

The search for a simple policy rule to guide the transition is an illusion. But central banks can try to accelerate the learning process by "teaching by doing;" in other words, making clear their own preferences and explaining their own view of how the economy behaves. Like economic agents, central bankers do not have a fixed stock of knowledge. They learn—especially from conferences at Jackson Hole—and the product of this learning should be communicated to the public at large. That is one reason why transparency is important. A switch in monetary regime from hyperinflation to low and stable inflation is likely to be sufficiently dramatic that the behavior of inflation itself communicates the change to agents.

Chart 5
United States Interest Rate Expectations[1]

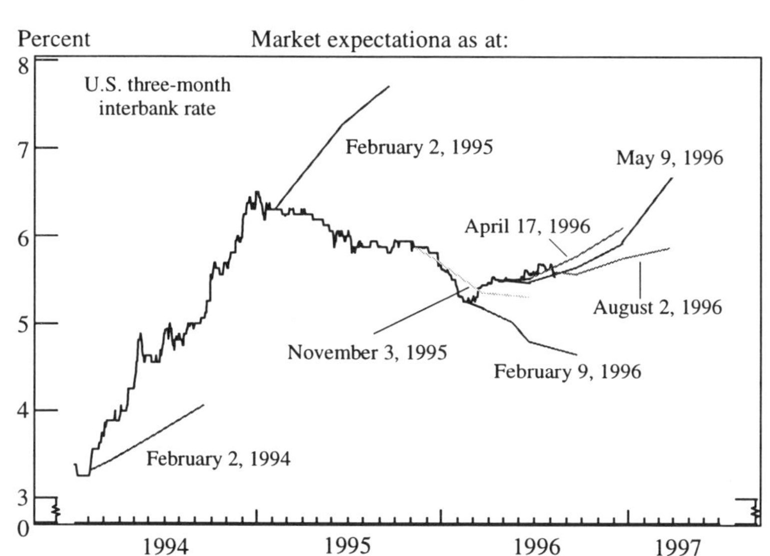

[1]Based on a combination of U.S. Dollar interest rate future contracts.

But the transition from low or moderate inflation to price stability will be more difficult to detect. In those circumstances, transparency can help to speed up learning by both private agents and the central bank.

The overriding objective of monetary policy should be price stability. But two subsidiary questions arise. First, how fast should a central bank disinflate in order to reach price stability? Second, how flexible should policy be in accommodating temporary inflation shocks in order to avoid costly volatility in output? An optimal monetary strategy is a choice of an *ex ante* inflation target and a discretionary response to temporary shocks. In general, the optimal speed of disinflation is a gradual approach to price stability, but one in which the inflation target is always below expected inflation and falling. There should also be some accommodation of temporary shocks. Any response to such shocks should be more cautious in the early stages of a transition in order to speed up learning by the private sector of the central bank's commitment to reducing the inflation target. None of that is surprising. It is merely the best practice of successful central banks that combine a choice of an inflation target with some degree of flexibility in response to shocks. What successful central banks have in common is not a particular intermediate target to guide policy, but rather a common policy reaction function.

Author's Note: I am grateful to the two discussants, Rudi Dornbusch and Bennett McCallum, and to Andrew Haldane and Neal Hatch for helpful comments and suggestions.

Appendix

Optimal disinflation

The propositions about the optimal speed of disinflation discussed in the main part of the paper can be demonstrated rigorously in a simple macroeconomic model which combines nominal wage and price stickiness and slow adjustment of expectations to a new monetary policy regime. The model has three key equations—for aggregate supply, aggregate demand, and money supply. This last equation is the central bank's policy reaction function.

Aggregate supply in period t, y_t, is given by a reduced form supply function (or short-run Phillips curve)

$$y_t = y_t^* + b(\pi_t - \hat{\pi}_t) + \varepsilon_t \tag{1}$$

where y_t^* is the "natural" rate of output, π_t is the inflation rate, $\hat{\pi}_t$ is the private sector's expectation of the central bank's target inflation rate in period t, and ε_t is an aggregate disturbance which is assumed to be white noise. All variables other than inflation and interest rates are measured in natural logarithms.

Aggregate demand is a function of real money balances and expected inflation.[10]

$$y_t = c(m_t - p_t) + d\hat{\pi}_t \tag{2}$$

$$\pi_t = p_t - p_{t-l} \tag{3}$$

where m_t is the money stock.

Each period the money supply (or, equivalently, the short-term interest rate) is set by the central bank in full knowledge of the size of the shock to output (the realization of ε). The expectations of the private sector which influence demand and supply are, however, formed before ε is observed. That assumption reflects nominal rigidities in setting wages and prices, and other nominal contracts.

Given the linear structure of the model, and the serially uncorrelated nature of the supply shock, the most general form of a monetary policy reaction function is

(4) $$m_t = \lambda_{1t} + \lambda_{2t}\,\varepsilon_t$$

Note that the money supply process is allowed to vary on the transition path to price stability.

For any given policy reaction function, the model can be solved to give paths for output and inflation in each period as a function of private sector expectations, the aggregate shock, and the parameters of the model. Substituting equation 4 into equations 1 to 3 yields

(5) $$y_t = y_t^* + b\alpha_t + \left(\frac{b(d-c)}{b+c}\right)\hat{\pi}_t + \beta_t\,\varepsilon_t$$

(6) $$\pi_t = \alpha_t + \left(\frac{b+d}{b+c}\right)\hat{\pi}_t + \left(\frac{\beta_t - 1}{b}\right)\varepsilon_t$$

where

(7) $$\alpha_t = \frac{c\,(\lambda_{1t} - p_{t-1}) - y_t^*}{b+c}$$

$$\beta_t = 1 + \frac{b(c\lambda_{2t} - 1)}{b+c}.$$

I shall assume that the central bank has rational expectations in the sense that it understands that output and inflation are generated by equations 5 and 6. It is possible to rewrite the monetary policy reaction function in terms of the central bank's choice of an inflation target each period. The inflation target is defined as the rational expected value of inflation before ε is realized which is given by

(8) $$\pi_t^* = E\pi_t = \alpha_t + \frac{b+d}{b+c}\hat{\pi}_t\,.$$

Substituting into equations 5 and 6 yields

(9)
$$y_t = y_t^* + b(\pi_t^* - \hat{\pi}_t) + \beta_t \varepsilon_t$$
$$\pi_t = \pi_t^* + \left(\frac{\beta_t - 1}{b}\right) \varepsilon_t .$$

Monetary policy is a choice of an *ex ante* inflation target, π_t^*, and a response to stochastic shocks described by the choice of β_t.

Consider a switch from a monetary policy regime in which inflation has averaged π_0 to a regime of price stability in which average inflation is zero. What is the optimal transition path? That will depend upon how quickly private sector expectations adjust to the new regime. It is useful to consider three cases: (1) a completely credible regime switch: private sector expectations adjust immediately to the new policy reaction function—this is the case of rational or model-consistent expectations; (2) exogenous learning: expectations adjust slowly along a path exogenous to the actual policy choices made in the new regime; (3) endogenous learning: the speed of learning depends on the policy decisions made in the new regime.

Case 1: Fully credible regime switch

With a completely credible regime change, private sector expectations are consistent with the new inflation target:

(10)
$$\hat{\pi}_t = \pi_t^*$$

Hence

(11)
$$y_t = y_t^* + \beta_t \varepsilon_t$$
$$\pi_t = \pi_t^* + \left(\frac{\beta_t - 1}{b}\right) \varepsilon_t .$$

Since the level of output is independent of the inflation target, policy can aim at price stability without any expected output loss. The optimal policy is to move immediately to a zero inflation target.

Case 2: Exogenous learning

The central bank announces that it intends to move to a regime of price stability, defined as a regime in which the unconditional expectation of inflation each period is zero. But the private sector adjusts its beliefs about the inflation target only slowly, and at a rate that is exogenous to the monetary policy decisions taken in the transition. From equation 9, it follows that if expected inflation exceeds the inflation target then there are systematic output losses during the transition to full credibility. It may be costly to pursue price stability from the outset of the new regime. How should the central bank choose the inflation target during the transition? From case 1 it is clear that once credibility has been established, it is optimal to set the inflation target to zero. During the transition, optimal monetary policy is a sequence for the pair $\{\pi_t^*, \beta_t\}$. Let the loss function of the central bank be defined over the expected value of the squared deviations of inflation from its desired level of zero and of output around the natural rate.[11]

$$L_t = aE\pi_t^2 + E(y_t - y_t^*)^2. \tag{12}$$

Denote the length of the transition to full credibility under exogenous learning by T. Assuming no discount factor, the loss during the transition is

$$L = a\sum_{t=1}^{T} \left\{\pi_t^{*2} + \left(\frac{\beta_t - 1}{b}\right)^2 \sigma_{\varepsilon t}^2\right\} + \sum_{t=1}^{T}\left\{b^2(\pi_t^* - \hat{\pi}_t)^2 + \beta_t^2\sigma_{\varepsilon t}^2\right\}. \tag{13}$$

Differentiating w.r.t. π_t^* and β_1 gives the optimal monetary policy as

(14)
$$\pi_t^* = \frac{b^2}{a+b^2}\hat{\pi}_t$$
$$\beta_1 = \frac{a}{a+b^2}.$$

Provided that learning is exogenous, the optimal transition to price stability is to allow inflation to fall gradually. The inflation target should start out at a fraction of the initial inflation rate, and then decline as a constant proportion of the exogenous expected inflation rate. The expected cumulative output loss in the optimal transition is

(15)
$$CYL \equiv \sum_{t=1}^{T} E(y_t - y_t^*) = b\sum_{t=1}^{T} (\pi_t^* - \hat{\pi}_t)$$
$$= -\frac{ab}{a+b^2}\sum_{t=1}^{T} \hat{\pi}_t .$$

The optimal path may be contrasted with the two extremes of pursuing price stability from the outset—a "cold turkey" strategy—and setting the inflation target to accommodate inflation expectations—an accommodation strategy. The "cold turkey" strategy is defined by

(16)
$$\pi_t^* = 0 \quad \forall t.$$

On average, price stability is achieved even during the transition period, but only at the cost of an expected cumulative output loss of

(17)
$$CYL_{CT} = -b\sum_{t=1}^{T} \hat{\pi}_t .$$

A strategy of full accommodation is defined by

(18)
$$\pi_t^* = \hat{\pi}_t.$$

It is clear from equation 9 that such a strategy eliminates any output loss, but at the cost of inflation falling only at the exogenous rate of decline of private sector inflation expectations.

In all of these cases it can be seen from equation 14 that the choice of β_t, the flexibility of monetary policy in the face of shocks, can be separated from the choice of the optimal inflation target during the transition.

A convenient representation of exogenous learning is that expectations adjust linearly over a fixed horizon of T years:

(19)
$$\hat{\pi}_t = \left(\frac{T-t}{T}\right)\pi_0 \qquad 0 < t \leq T.$$
$$= 0 \qquad\qquad t > T$$

With that specification, the cumulative output loss under the "cold turkey" strategy is

(20)
$$CYL_{CT} = -b\left(\frac{T-1}{2}\right)\pi_0 .$$

Along the optimal path the output loss is

(21)
$$CYL_{OPT} = -\left(\frac{ab}{a+b^2}\right)\left(\frac{T-1}{2}\right)\pi_0 .$$

Case 3: Endogenous learning

The speed at which expectations adjust depends on actual inflation experience, and hence on policy choices made during the transition. A convenient representation of this learning process is

(22)
$$\hat{\pi}_t = \rho\hat{\pi}_{t-1} + (1-\rho)\,\pi^*_{t-1}.$$

The smaller is ρ, the faster is the learning process. For a positive value of ρ, expected inflation converges asymptotically to the inflation target. Equation 22 is, however, problematic. For a well-defined change of regime it is likely that ρ will decline over time under rational learning as more weight is placed on the lagged inflation target in the optimal updating rule. But with, for example, Markov switching between regimes, ρ may not decline. Even with rational learning, it is unlikely that expected inflation will jump to the new inflation target.

The model of learning in equation 22 assumes that agents can infer last period's inflation target by adjusting *ex post* for the effect of the previous period's shock on monetary policy. That is more rational than assuming that agents look only at past inflation. But if learning does depend on the actual rate of inflation, as would be the case if agents could not observe the shock *ex post*, then the optimal flexibility of monetary policy interacts with the optimal speed of disinflation. Rewriting equation 22 using the lag operator L

(23)
$$\hat{\pi}_t = \frac{(1-\rho)L}{(1-\rho L)}\,\pi_t^*.$$

Since learning occurs over an infinite horizon, the loss function may be defined as

(24)
$$L \equiv \sum_{t=1}^{\infty} (1+\theta)^{-t} \left\{ aE\pi_t^2 + E(y_t - y_t^*)^2 \right\}$$

where θ is the time discount rate.

Substituting equations 9 and 23 into the loss function and differentiating w.r.t. π_t^* yields the following second order difference equation for the optimal inflation target

(25)
$$\pi_t^* = \pi_{t-1}^* \left\{ \frac{2(a\rho+b^2)}{(a+b^2)} \right\} - \pi_{t-2}^* \left\{ \frac{a\rho^2+b^2}{a+b^2} \right\}.$$

The optimal degree of flexibility in monetary policy, measured by β, is the same as in the case of exogenous learning.

When learning is defined over the actual rate of inflation accommodating temporary shocks affects expected inflation in the future.

The central bank can invest in credibility by refraining from such stabilization in the early stages of the transition.

Finally, the model generates data that look as though the Taylor rule had been followed. Under the Taylor rule, official nominal interest rates are set so that the short-term real interest rate equals the "natural" rate plus terms related to the deviation of output from trend and inflation from its target rate:

$$r = r^* + \lambda_1(y - y^*) + \lambda_2(\pi - \pi^*). \quad (26)$$

For any monetary policy $\{\pi^*, \beta\}$ it is the case that the model leads to an equation of the form of equation 26 because all three variables (expressed as deviations from their natural or target rates) are proportional to the shock . Hence it is crucial to distinguish between a normative and a positive interpretation of equation 26.

Endnotes

[1]The case for price stability was restated at this conference by Fischer (1996); recent estimates of the cost-benefit analysis of moving from moderate inflation to price stability were given by Feldstein (1996).

[2]An early analysis of the problem can be found in Taylor (1975).

[3]The formal analysis in the appendix ignores type 2 shocks which add only random noise to the paths of output and inflation, and do not alter the optimal speed of disinflation.

[4]The importance of continuous learning was stressed by Balvers and Cosimano (1994).

[5]A formal derivation of this result with discrete time periods is shown in the appendix.

[6]Details are provided in the appendix.

[7]Letter to the *Financial Times*, January 8, 1996.

[8]Alan Blinder's views were set out in an opening statement at his confirmation hearing before the U.S. Senate Committee on Banking, Housing, and Urban Affairs in May 1994.

[9]Taylor (1993), Clarida and Gertler (1996), Stuart (1996).

[10]The aggregate demand function is the reduced form of the three-equation system:
(i) demand for money $m_t = p_t + y_t - \gamma i_t$
where i_t is the nominal interest rate;

(ii) demand for goods $y_t = \delta(m_t - p_t) - \theta r_1$

(iii) definition of the real interest rate $r_t = i_t - \hat{\pi}_t$

Hence in equation 2, $c = (\theta + \gamma\delta) / (\theta + \gamma)$ and $d = \theta\gamma$.

[11]Note that the loss function does not assume that the central bank is using monetary policy to target output in excess of the second-best natural rate as is assumed in those models which generate an inflationary bias of discretionary monetary policy.

References

Balvers, R.J., and T.F. Cosimano. "Inflation Variability and Gradualist Monetary Policy," *Review of Economic Studies,* 61, 1994, pp. 721-38.

Blinder, A. "On Sticky Prices: Academic Theories Meet the Real World," in N.G. Mankiw, ed., *Monetary Policy*, 1994. Chicago: University of Chicago Press.

Brunner, K., and A.H. Meltzer. *Money and the Economy: Issues in Monetary Analysis*, 1993. Cambridge: Cambridge University Press.

Clarida, R., and M. Gertler. "How the Bundesbank Conducts Monetary Policy," National Bureau of Economic Research Working Paper 5581, mimeo.

Feldstein, M.S. "The Costs and Benefits of Going from Low Inflation to Price Stability," paper presented at the NBER Conference on Monetary Policy and Inflation (January 1996), mimeo.

Fischer, S. "Why are Central Banks Pursuing Long-Run Price Stability?" in *Achieving Price Stability*, proceedings of a symposium sponsored by the Federal Reserve Bank of Kansas City in Jackson Hole, Wyo., August 29-31, 1996.

King, M.A. "Monetary Policy Implications of Greater Fiscal Discipline," in *Budget Deficits and Debt: Issues and Options,* proceedings of a symposium sponsored by the Federal Reserve Bank of Kansas City in Jackson Hole, Wyo., August 31-September 2, 1995.

Lucas, R.E. "Some International Evidence on Output-Inflation Tradeoffs," *American Economic Review*, 63, 1973, pp. 326-34.

McCallum, B.T. "Two Fallacies Concerning Central Bank Independence," *American Economic Review Papers and Proceedings*, 85, 1995, pp. 207-11.

______________. "Crucial Issues Concerning Central Bank Independence," NBER Working Paper 5597, 1996, mimeo.

Orphanides, A., and D.W. Wilcox. "The Opportunistic Approach to Disinflation," Federal Reserve Board Discussion Paper 96-24, 1996, mimeo.

Persson, T., and G. Tabellini. *Macroeconomic Policy, Credibility and Politics,* 1990. London: Harwood Academic Publishers.

Sargent, T.J. *Rational Expectations and Inflation*, 1986. New York: Harper and Row.

______________. *Bounded Rationality in Macroeconomics,* 1993. Oxford: Oxford University Press.

Stuart, A. "Simple Monetary Policy Rules," *Bank of England Quarterly Bulletin,* 36, 1996, pp. 281-7.

Taylor, J.B. "Monetary Policy During a Transition to Rational Expectations," *Journal of Political Economy,* 83, 1975, pp. 1009-21.

______________. "Discretion Versus Policy Rules in Practice," *Carnegie-Rochester Conference Series on Public Policy,* 39, 1993, pp. 195-214.

Vickers, J. "Signaling in a Model of Monetary Policy with Incomplete Information," *Oxford Economic Papers,* 38, 1986, pp. 443-55.

Commentary: How Should Central Banks Reduce Inflation?—Conceptual Issues

Rudiger Dornbusch

Inflation is a dramatic problem; all available evidence supports the view that it undermines growth and social stability at the very roots. Containing inflation, therefore, is an utmost priority. But the recognition that inflation is destructive leaves still a host of important questions as to how best to deal with the inflation problem. Importantly, it leaves the question where to draw the line, where to start thinking about tradeoffs.

Work reported in a large number of studies demonstrates that high inflation lowers a country's average growth performance. There is divergence of views on exactly where "high" starts. Work at the World Bank, for example, draws the line at 40 percent—anything more is demonstrably counterproductive, anything less may be a growth problem but that is harder to show. Other studies move much further down in setting the threshold for counterproductive inflation. Thus a recent International Monetary Fund (IMF) study finds support for the view that adverse growth effects emerge at inflation rates of only 8 percent. Even more ambitious work looks for counterproductive effects in the range of 0 to 3 percent and comes out in favor of a zero-inflation target as the only growth-friendly strategy.

There is one common thread to all this discussion: nobody has claimed inflation is good for growth, at any level. That contention, if it ever existed, is just gone. The overwhelming presumption today is that inflation is no help at all, that it is totally undesirable. The remaining issue is to know whether there is a temporary cost in bringing down inflation, how high this cost—if any—might be, and accordingly, what is the range of inflation rates where inflation is the number-one policy issue. Interestingly, the World Bank study referred to above has one answer: above 40 percent inflation, reducing inflation increases growth. At lower rates of inflation, the issue becomes less clear-cut as we will see in a moment. Before getting to that topic, it is helpful to dispose of one easy issue: extreme inflation.

How to get out of extreme inflation

It is no longer controversial to assert that extreme inflation is impossible without sustained, extreme money creation. True, the rise in velocity driven by the extravagant cost of holding money—the flight from money—is part of the inflation process. But extreme inflation does not happen just by chance. The source is always and everywhere, as Firedamp has long claimed, extreme money creation, which, in turn, is linked to the financing of budget deficits. If anything above 40 percent growth (per year) hurts growth, extreme inflation—20, 30, 40 percent per month—certainly takes its toll in full measure. There is no question that stabilization is a sine qua non for growth.

That leaves two important questions. One is *when* to stabilize and the other is *how.* There is a school of thought that claims waiting is a good idea: the longer and more extremely inflation runs its course, the more disorienting the process for the public. In the end, the public will come to endorse whatever is necessary to stop inflation. Starting too early just means failed sterilizations and a loss of credibility.

That view is wrong for two reasons. First, stabilizations almost everywhere are not made of a single, decisive package which overnight abolishes the problem. On the contrary, it is rather a process of a protracted search for the countless things that have to be done in the public sector to reduce the deficit and increase competition and accountability. At the outset none of them is enough. But looking back from a successful stabilization invariably reveals a long history of efforts that ultimately add up to enough. Waiting merely advances destruction of the economy's immune system and its social structure. These are very hard to put back together. That was the case in Germany, Austria, and Hungary in the 1920s; it may yet be the case in Russia or Ukraine today. Sometimes it may be desirable to destroy the existing social structure, but that surely goes far beyond the agenda of inflation control and it is definitely not a technical issue in optimal stabilization.

The next question then is how to stop an extreme inflation process. There is no doubt that *a regime change* must occur. The term is much abused in the literature, but in this context it is appropriate and decisive. The fiscal regime must be changed so that the budget no longer needs to be financed by the central bank. Almost invariably that means balancing the budget; possibly the goal may be less ambitious if there is plausible financing from the capital market. One way or the other, the central bank has to be out of the business of printing money to finance the government. Moreover, this needs to be institutionalized in a way that goes beyond mere promises. They will have been broken already far too often in the past; something better is needed to show what is new. Here is the point where institutional arrangements matter—currency boards, constitutional amendments, and the like.

In a situation of extreme inflation an economy becomes spontaneously dollarized. If dollar deposits are allowed, dollar deposits become the rule. If they are not allowed, dollar holdings in the form of currency and offshore deposits via capital flight will take the role of local currency deposits. That process can be documented for all and any high-inflation country. The implication of this almost complete domestic demonetization and the corresponding dollarization is quite central. If the economy is already near fully dollarized, going there all the way is only a small step. It merely amounts to recognizing that everyone is already on board and it is just the government that is not. Nothing is more definitive in terms of regime change than taking the extra step. That was true in the 1920s with a restoration of the gold standard in the demonetized economies of Germany or Austria and it is true today from Argentina to Russia.

There are three ways to take advantage of the fact that foreign exchange will have become central in a hyperinflation. The smallest and least definitive move is to just peg the local, stabilized currency to the dollar or the next best stable money in the region. That is good for a start, but it won't last as a credible anchor; it throws most of the regime change weight to the money supply process and the budget. Since nothing very institutional has happened, relapse into the old pattern of inflation can happen easily.

A far stronger move is the drift to a currency board system such as Argentina practices. The rules of central banking are changed in a dramatic fashion, and irreversibly. Money creation is tied to foreign exchange inflows and outflows; a hard line is drawn between the central bank and the treasury. True, all that could be reversed, but only by an act of Congress and that means a financial collapse before the debate even gets under way. But there might be a debate about softening the system and latent fears about the implications of overvaluation. This leads to advocacy of an even stronger system—moving outright and fully on the dollar.

Even this system comes in two ways: 100 percent dollarization with absolutely no domestic money creation—monetary teetotaling—or leaving room for a home money (and local heroes on the coins and bills) in small denominations. It is tempting to leave some room for local heroes, but second thought is appropriate: who would want to be the dignitary or hero depicted on a debased currency? Surely history books are better places than schmutz-money.

Two points reinforce the view that *full* dollarization is preferred to a currency board. First, as long as there is some local money, residual uncertainty about reversal or the hard policy and devaluation is always present. This is apparent in Argentina, for example, where after four years of the currency board, there remain interest differentials between peso and dollar deposits of the same maturity at the same financial institutions. The discussion never stops, particularly outside the country where the belief in a "permanent and irreversible" regime change is always taken with a grain of salt. Second, an anecdote from Poland in the 1920s makes the point that poor public finance always finds a way to the printing press. A new central bank had been created (by Edwin Kemmerer, the money doctor of the 1920s) with full gold standard and complete independence. But coinage was left to the treasury. For a brief period, inflationary coinage by the treasury resulted in one more bout of inflation. Of course, it could not go very far since coins are harder to produce and physically cumbersome. This must be one of the weirdest inflation episodes in history.

The basic inference is that countries who have plain and simply failed to control their money, have reached the most complete debauchery of their monetary system, should spend a few decades on the dollar or the deutsche mark. Their history shows that having a national money is a threat to growth and international standing; the lesson for us is to get rid of it. Arguments about seigniorage are misplaced when the attempt to collect 1 percent of GDP costs 2, 3, or more percent in growth.

There is another way to make the story palatable. Why should a country like Hungary or Poland hang around cultivating their own money, running precarious disinflation attempts with overvaluation in the wings? All of Europe, which they are desperately trying to join, is moving ahead to the recognition that a Europewide money gives them more stability and better economic performance. The soft currency countries of Eastern Europe should be in the forefront since they need the extra stability more than anyone else. The IMF should routinely advise, as part of the move from hyperinflation to stability, moving on the dollar, the deutsche mark, or the *Eurodollar.*

The political argument against this strategy, voiced all too often in countries where money has been debased as completely as can be done, speaks for itself: our national currency is like the flag. These people surely would think twice before doing to their flag what they have done to their money!

The currency arrangements are only one part of successful action. At least as important is a shift on the fiscal side. The stabilizing government needs to balance the budget, no less. And that must be accomplished in a lasting and productive fashion. Emergency taxation is a poor way of going about the task; restructuring government spending, privatization, and closing loopholes has to be nine-tenths of the action.

The more waste there is in government, the better the scope for strong fiscal sanitation and hence, support in monetary stability. The government is not bankrupt; it is just mismanaged. The more extreme the willingness to adopt monetary institutions or the dollar, the more firm the ground on which reconstruction takes place.

Destroying a money is not easy. It takes years and years of dedicated work. Not surprisingly, reconstructing monetary stability is not an issue of a year or three. It takes a decade or more. Countries that have gone all the way into destruction and have then rebuilt are rightly hypersensitive about the institutions that guard the new stability and about any compromises that might renew their bad experiences in however minor a way. They are right to be uncompromising.

Moderate inflation

Countries with 15 percent inflation per *month* must stabilize with urgent priority. Nothing is likely to be more important. Countries with 15 percent inflation per *year* certainly should not belittle inflation. They definitely should attempt, on average, to bring inflation down. But they must see this as one of a number of priorities and they should view it as a process of five or even more years. Accepting the right perspective on moderate inflation is important because otherwise, severe recession, super high real interest rates with resulting banking problems, and currency overvaluation with the risk of a collapse might be the result rather than the dramatic success hoped for on the inflation front.

To appreciate the point, it is useful to look at an inflation representation in a formal way: inflation this year is what it was last year (this is the indexation effect) except for the influence of real appreciation, which tends to lower inflation, slow down public sector inflation (at the cost of bigger deficits), or recession.

$$\pi_t = \pi_{t-1} + \alpha(e - \pi_t) + \beta(p - \pi_t) + \varphi y$$

where π is the current rate of inflation, e the rate of depreciation, p the rate of increase of public sector prices, and y the output gap. The equation summarizes the proposition that inflation today is what it was yesterday—via formal or implicit indexation or "inertia" as it is often called—except for the accelerating influence of real depreciation, increasing real public sector prices, or overheating. Disinflation then requires real appreciation of the exchange rate (with resulting trade deficit risks), reduced inflation in the public sector prices (with resulting budget deficit risks), old-fashioned recession, or the always-suspect *incomes policy* which can never be a substitute for financial discipline, but may help coordinate the disinflation. Something has to give. Inflation reduction does not come from ceremonious incantations of the central bank or a spontaneous outbreak of credibility.

Chile, for example, has had an average inflation over the past ten years of 17 percent. At the outset, it was 30 percent; in the early 1990s, it was still double digit, and today, ten years later, it is down to 7 percent. The average growth rate for the 10-year period was 7 percent.

At the outset, a deep recession with near 30 percent unemployment set the tone for sharply lower rates of price increase. From there, productivity growth not outrun by wage increases and careful footwork by the central bank have gradually done their work. Chile's approach has been exemplary, particularly in the past few years where the central bank has refused to overreach and squeeze inflation down to the fashionable 2 percent of the industrialized countries. Chile's policymakers recognize that strong growth, modernization, and integration in the world economy are not held back by 6, 10, or even 15 percent inflation, but could be seriously hampered if overambitious disinflation created a macroeconomic problem.

Mexico's experience in the 1990s is the opposite—exaggerated emphasis put on inflation, exaggerated urgency to get to 2 percent,

Chart 1
Mexico: Exchange Rate and Prices

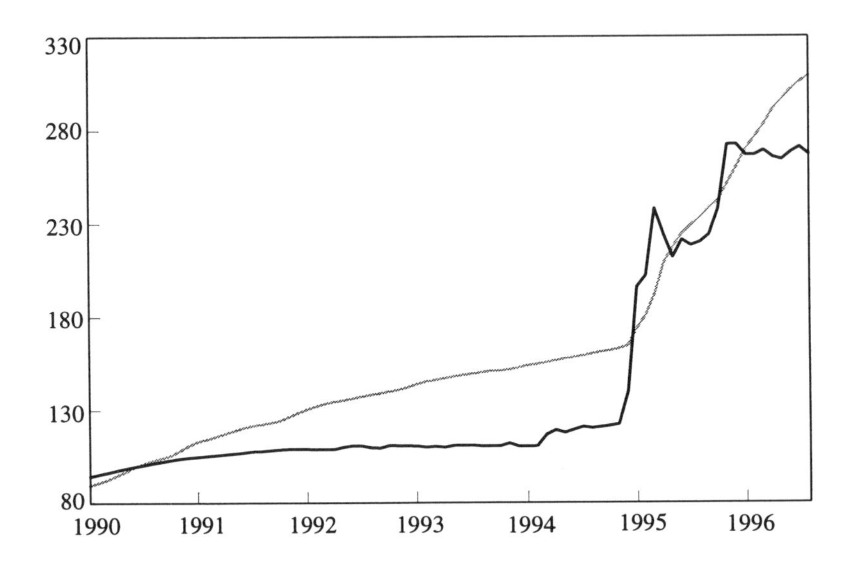

dangerous imperviousness to overvaluation. The intransigent wish to bring down inflation in the context of an incomes policy that allowed significant wage increases led, year after year, to mounting real appreciation. However, in a country where trade had been liberalized and deregulation led to the shedding of labor in many sectors, real *de*preciation was called for. The cumulative real appreciation in the end amounted to more than 40 percent! The Mexican currency crisis was not surprising; in fact, it is what was predicted and had been predicted. The surprise was the extent of meltdown.

One would have thought that the severity of the recent experience might have taught Mexican policymakers a lesson—stay far, far away from an exchange-rate-based stabilization. Yet, precisely that same strategy is being pursued yet again. Of the huge real depreciation of 1995, much less than half is left. Even in the face of more than 20 percent inflation, monetary policy supports a peso that is flat

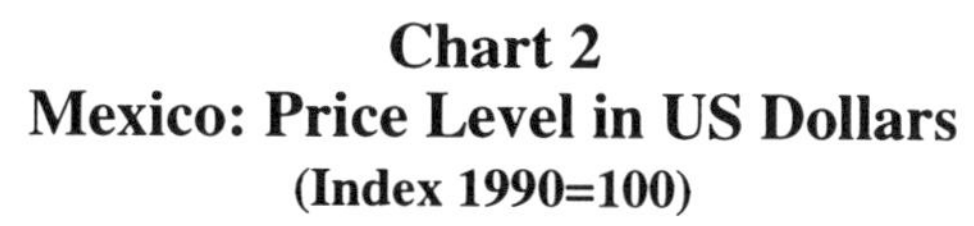

Chart 2
Mexico: Price Level in US Dollars
(Index 1990=100)

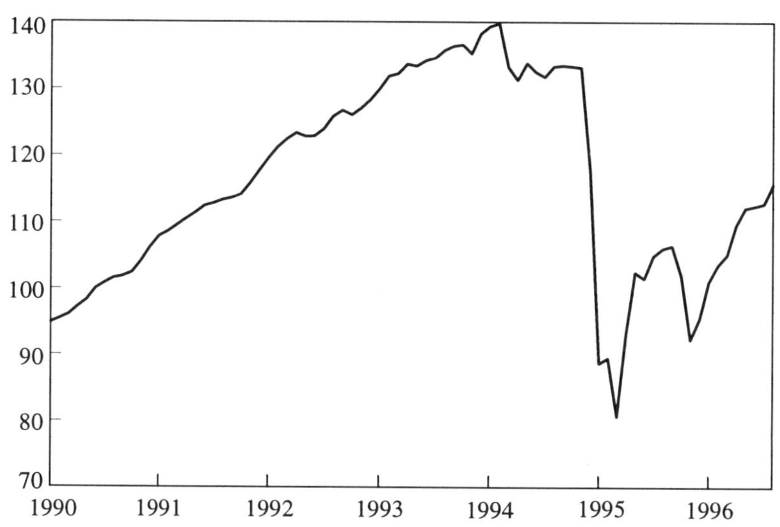

rather than depreciating at the pace of inflation. It is said to be a "flexible" rate, but in between interest rate and aggregates policy, it manages to keep the peso, keep the capital coming, and risk preparing yet another instance of overvaluation. (See Charts 1 and 2.) It is early to express that concern, but this is the appropriate time since correction of the course remains easy. Once a large overvaluation has built up—as in Mexico in 1994 or presently in Brazil—it is difficult to expect that inflation can fall below world trends sufficiently to bring a remedy. A vast empirical review of the experience with real appreciation reported by Goldfajn and Valdes shows clearly that large overvaluations have little chance of a mild end.

The central lesson in stabilizing moderate inflation is that it is very perilous, indeed, to use the exchange rate for anything but a very transitory, initial consolidation effort. The exchange rate cannot carry most or even much of the burden of stabilization. Nor can

Chart 3
Inflation and Growth
(level scale)

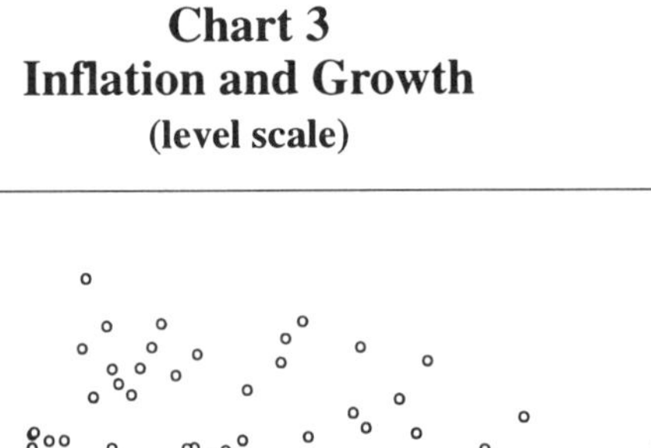

monetary policy do the job all by itself. Fiscal policy and competition must do a very substantial portion of the work.

The concern for inflation is altogether appropriate, but single-mindedness is not. In the face of moderate inflation, growth also must be part of the discussion. It is not correct to argue that there can be no growth in the presence of inflation, nor is it right to state that even moderate inflation is a detriment to growth. Chart 3 shows a cross-section of growth rates for a large group of countries with inflation in the range of 5 to 20 percent. It is hard to see any evidence of a relationship between inflation and growth. In the absence of a cost in terms of growth foregone, that suggests a more gradual disinflation strategy is acceptable.

Of course, it might be argued that the only stable inflation is zero inflation. That is the kind of dogmatic posture which has no empirical foundation. For the past decade or more, countries have been at work reducing inflation or at least containing it. Countries with moderate inflation rates, such as Chile, have perfectly well managed to achieve *gradual* reductions without either compromising the credibility of that strategy or sacrificing growth. On the contrary, the fact that inflation was steadily—over twelve years—falling but growth was strong throughout, made the program a textbook case of successful inflation fighting. Mexico's case, by contrast, is a series of failures and blunders as result from half-baked ideas about credibility, inflation kills, and the like. Chile today is a low inflation country; Mexico is once again back to intolerably high inflation. The right message is that inflation must come down and that there is never room for complacency; that is not the same as inflation reduction first, growth later.

References

Bruno, M. "Does Inflation Really Lower Growth?" *Finance & Development*, (September 1995), pp.35-8.

Dornbusch, R. "Overvaluation and Disinflation." Unpublished manuscript, Massachusetts Institute of Technology, 1996.

__________, and S. Edwards. "Exchange Rate Policy and Trade Strategy," in B. Bosworth and others, eds., *The Chilean Economy,* 1995. Washington, D.C.: The Brookings Institution.

__________, and S. Fischer. "Moderate Inflation," *The World Bank Economic Review* Vol. 7, No. 1, 1993, pp.1-44.

Goldfajn, I., and R. Valdes. "How Does Real Appreciation End?" NBER Working Paper, 1996.

Vegh, C. "Stopping High Inflation," *IMF Staff Papers* Vol. 39, No. 4, 1992, pp. 626-95.

Commentary: How Should Central Banks Reduce Inflation?—Conceptual Issues

Bennett T. McCallum

It was a pleasure to study Mervyn King's wide-ranging and ambitious paper, which raises a number of very interesting issues, some of which I will comment upon in the following paragraphs. In calling Mervyn's paper "ambitious," what I mean is that it tackles two or three distinct conceptual problems, each of which is important enough that a solution would be regarded as a major accomplishment for an academic researcher. I am amazed that Mervyn has the time and energy to do all this work while keeping British monetary policy from going astray. But maybe it is the case that the Chancellor's attitude toward Bank of England independence has the effect of leaving Mervyn with more time for such activities.

Why no inflationary bias?

In any event, there are several points that I will try to address. The first of these concerns Mervyn's position regarding the necessary existence of an inflationary bias in nontransitional monetary policy-making[1] and the related notion of an inevitable tradeoff between flexibility and commitment. His conclusion for nontransitional (that is, within regime) periods is the same as the one that I have promoted in a pair of recent papers (McCallum, 1995a, 1996), namely, that there is no necessary inflation bias or flexibility vs. commitment tradeoff. This conclusion differs, of course, from the one that is prevalent in the dynamic inconsistency literature.[2] It is important to note, however, that our reasons for reaching this conclusion are quite different. In particular, Mervyn assumes that the central bank has no *desire* to have unemployment rates below (or output rates above) their natural-rate values. My argument, by contrast, retains the literature's usual assumption that central banks would like to keep unemployment below the natural rate but suggests that thoughtful central bankers recognize that attempting to do so would be counterproductive on average; consequently they adopt a committed or "rule-like" manner of conducting policy. Naturally I believe that my assumption is the more realistic of these. I believe, that is, that central bankers would in fact like to keep unemployment below the natural rate value[3] *if* they could do so with no fear of inflationary consequences being generated thereby. For example, I suggest that the Fed's policymakers would prefer for U.S. unemployment rates to average around 4.0–4.5 percent rather than 5.5–6.0 percent if this would entail no inflationary pressures. In other words, I contend that it is realistic to specify $k > 0$ in an objective function of the form

$$\omega(\pi_t - \pi^*)^2 + (1 - \omega)\,[y_t - (\bar{y}_t + k)]^2 \tag{1}$$

where π is inflation, y is the (log of) output, $\bar{y}$ denotes the natural-rate value of y, π^* is the target inflation rate, and the weight ω satisfies $0 < \omega \leq 1$. The point is that the first term, not the second, reflects the central bank's concern for inflation, which is distinct from its concern for unemployment.

This issue is really quite important, in the following way. Suppose that in fact $k > 0$ as most of the analytical literature presumes. Then the validity or invalidity of numerous conclusions in this literature hinges on the correctness of my contention that central bankers can, if they choose, behave in a committed fashion. If my contention is correct, for example, striking recent results by Debelle and Fischer (1995) concerning monetary-fiscal interactions and by Svensson (1995, 1996) concerning inflation targeting are fundamentally misleading, because they are based on the presumption that noncommitted behavior prevails.[4] With respect to the evidence, my hypothesis provides—as, admittedly, does King's—an explanation for the absence of empirical findings of a tradeoff between inflation variability and output growth variability, as mentioned by Fischer (1994), among others.

Before going on, I think I should take a minute to explain what I mean by committed or rule-like behavior on the part of a central bank. Of course I agree with John Taylor (1993a) that literally adhering to a specific numerical formula for setting instrument values is not presumed; everyone knows that central banks cannot reasonably be expected to do that. Thus, what I mean by rule-like behavior is that in selecting interest rate (or other instrument) settings month by month, the central bank is systematic in its responses to prevailing conditions and also forward-looking enough to abstain from attempts to exploit existing inflationary expectations. It takes account, that is, of the fact that the private sector's expectations will not be systematically incorrect—although there will be substantial expectational errors occurring at random—which implies that it is fruitless to try to regularly exploit any short-run Phillips relationship. This does not mean, it must be emphasized, that the central bank forgoes short-run stabilization actions in responding to shocks. In terms of the model in Mervyn's appendix, the central bank does respond to shocks like his ε_t but it acts as if $\pi_t - \hat{\pi}_t$ is unaffected by its choice of the period-t instrument setting.

Monetary policy rules

So, with that interpretation, let me go on to the subject of some specific patterns of rule-like behavior and for the sake of brevity refer to them as policy rules. The most prominent such rule today is, of course, the one described by John Taylor in his 1993 Carnegie-Rochester conference paper, whereby the central bank sets its nominal interest rate instrument so as to produce an expected real rate equal to the long-term average real rate plus upward adjustments whenever inflation and/or output are above their target and natural-rate values (or downward adjustments when either is below). With respect to this rule of Taylor's, Mervyn emphasizes that it is essential to distinguish between positive and normative interpretations or uses of the formula. With that proposition I would agree heartily. But Mervyn goes on to suggest that, because inflation and output deviations are in his model proportional to current shocks, any choice of inflation target and response to shocks yields the same interest rates as implied by Taylor's rule.[5] To quote from his paper, "Hence it is impossible to distinguish between those central banks which are following a Taylor rule and those which are not." This statement is evidently supposed to apply to charts like those that we have seen in several publications recently, charts that compare actual and Taylor-rule paths of the federal funds rate or the clearing banks' base rate in the United Kingdom. Well, I do not understand this claim. Of course, actual interest rates rise and fall with expected inflation, as do Taylor-rule rates, so their values will be reasonably close together when actual inflation is reasonably close to the target value. But if you look at the data from the 1970s, before some important central banks decided that inflation was, in fact, dependent upon monetary policy, then the rates called for by Taylor's formula are not at all close to actual rates. From the start of 1974 continuously until late 1980, John's rule always calls for a federal funds rate at least 300 basis points higher than actual, with a discrepancy of over 1,000 basis points for a while in early 1980. And the difference was even greater in the United Kingdom, showing clearly that policy was not anything like that called for by his rule.[6]

All of this is not to suggest that I would favor Taylor's rule over all others. It seems to me a rather good guide to policy behavior, one that would almost certainly have prevented the inflation of the 1970s if it had been followed. But as a policy guide, I continue to be attracted to the nominal income growth rule, with a base money instrument, that I have been promoting for the past decade (see McCallum, 1995b). In this regard, a diagnostic application to the British economy of my rule as well as John's is provided in the recent Bank of England *Quarterly Bulletin* paper cited by Mervyn (Stuart, 1996). I have some complaints about that paper—it states falsely that "both rules require knowledge of the output gap" (which mine does not) and its handling of trend output in my rule appears inappropriate—but nevertheless, the reported exercises show accurately that my rule calls for much tighter monetary policy in the

United Kingdom during the years 1988-1990, whereas Taylor's does not.[7] In retrospect, I think that most observers would agree that U.K. monetary policy was, in fact, too loose during those crucial pre-exchange-rate-mechanism (ERM) years.

There are two more things that I would like to say about my proposed rule before returning to our main topic. First, the fact that I express it in terms of a monetary base instrument does not imply that it could not be implemented with a funds rate instrument. My (1995b) paper for the Bank of Japan's Seventh International Conference includes a study (which Mervyn wrote a comment upon) in which I explore a procedure for adjusting a funds rate instrument from week to week so as to hit quarterly time paths for the monetary base that are specified by my rule. Interest rate variability would be somewhat greater than at present but not very much. Second, the fact that GDP data is only published quarterly, and is then revised, is not a serious problem. What the logic of my rule actually calls for is some measure of nominal aggregate spending. I am confident that an index based on the monthly consumer price index (CPI) and industrial production indexes, for example, would serve quite well in that capacity, and perhaps some such constructed measure would even be preferable in principle.[8]

Transitions between policy regimes

Now let me back up to the earlier portion of Mervyn King's paper that is concerned with transitions following changes in policy regimes—such as a shift to a new, lower inflation target. Here Mervyn argues that there will typically be output losses during disinflationary transitions, basically because it takes time for the private sector to *learn* that the central bank's inflation target has changed, and that a reasonably slow gradualist path will result in less cumulative output loss than a sharp, abrupt movement toward the lower inflation target. These conclusions he justifies by analysis with a simple analytical model in which aggregate supply behavior is represented by a familiar equation that relates output (relative to its natural-rate value) to the surprise component of current inflation. The aggregate demand function is also familiarly obtained by solving the nominal interest rate out from log-linear IS and LM functions.[9] This is a very standard model, but for the purposes of this analysis I would contend that its reliance upon the aggregate supply relation (1) is unsatisfactory. The problem is not that there is anything particularly wrong with this specification,[10] but rather that there are many other models of aggregate supply behavior in the literature and many of them would yield different implications in this context. To emphasize the multiplicity of competing specifications, let me quote from a recent paper of mine on inflation targeting (McCallum, 1996, p. 17):

> It is not just that the economics profession does not have a well-tested quantitative model of the quarter-to-quarter dynamics, the situation is much worse than that: we do not even have any basic agreement about the qualitative nature of the mechanism. This point can be made by mentioning some of the leading theoretical categories, which include: real business cycle models, monetary misperception models, semi-classical price adjustment models, models with overlapping nominal contracts of the Taylor variety or of the Fischer variety, models with nominal contracts set as in the recent work of Fuhrer and Moore, NAIRU models, Lucas supply function models, MPS-style markup pricing models, and so on. Not only do we have all of these basic modeling approaches, but to be made operational, each of them has to be combined with some measure of capacity output—a step that itself involves competing approaches—and with several critical assumptions regarding the nature of different types of unobservable shocks and the time series processes generating them. Thus there are dozens or perhaps hundreds of competing specifications regarding the precise nature of the connection between monetary policy actions and their real short-term consequences. And there is little empirical basis for much narrowing of the range of contenders.

Of course, if all these models had similar implications for Mervyn's disinflation analysis, the multiplicity would not matter. But they definitely do not, a point that I will illustrate by reference to a recent article by Larry Ball (1994), which uses a different model of aggregate supply. In Ball's analytical experiment, a disinflation is announced and is assumed to be perfectly credible by the private sector, which is like Mervyn's case (1). But whereas Mervyn's model implies that there will be no expected output loss regardless of the disinflation path, Ball's implies that output depends sensitively upon the path and, in fact, that a well-chosen rapid disinflation can generate an *increase* in cumulative output.[11] Thus the results of the experiment are drastically different, just because of the different assumptions regarding aggregate supply. The one used by Ball is not an obscure or crazy choice, moreover, but is essentially the same as the overlapping nominal contracts model developed by Taylor (1979, 1993b). I might mention that a version of Ball's result was published much earlier by Taylor (1983).

My purpose here is *not* to suggest that Ball's analysis is superior to Mervyn King's. To the contrary, I find the latter's conclusion more plausible. The point, rather, is that we do not possess adequate knowledge of wage-price-output dynamics to permit any well-founded conclusions to be developed regarding disinflationary transition periods, even if specifics of the public's learning process were agreed upon (which they certainly are not).

This lack of knowledge concerning wage-price-output dynamics plays a very important role, it should be emphasized, in my way of understanding the desirability of an inflation-targeting regime or one that attempts to keep constant the growth rate of nominal income. If we did understand accurately this dynamic process, it is hard to see why more short-run activism would not be justified, as is argued by some critics of these more inflation-focused regimes. That is one reason why it is important not to be seduced by striking results generated in the context of one particular model—*any* particular model.

Opportunistic policymaking

Finally, I would like to conclude with a few remarks on the topic of "opportunistic policymaking," which Mervyn discusses briefly.

To put it bluntly, I think there is a basic inconsistency that is marring much of the current discussion of this subject. What I have in mind is a failure to distinguish between regime design and the process of transition between regimes. Thus the actual analysis in the paper by Orphanides and Wilcox (1996) is entirely concerned with regime design, that is, with the analysis of what type of objective function would rationalize an "opportunistic" regime. That analysis is skillful and, in my opinion, makes an opportunistic regime—policy rule, if I may use the term—look very unattractive. But the title of the Orphanides-Wilcox paper refers to "disinflation," which should be thought of as a transition to a regime with lower inflation than was accepted previously. Now it seems to me that a kind of opportunistic approach to that type of transition might make some sense, at least on political grounds. If a painful disinflationary move to a new regime is to be undertaken, it may be sensible to wait for an "opportune" time to begin. But that is quite a different matter from an opportunistic way of behaving within an established regime. In any event, clear thinking about this subject, among others, requires a clear distinction between regime design and the transition between regimes.

I suspect that actual central bankers may be inclined to object to that distinction, for the reason that these categories are not clear in practice. But I will argue that at the level of conceptual thinking—to use the term in the title of Mervyn's paper—it is necessary to make this distinction. For we have a well-developed theory of expectation formation within an ongoing regime, but virtually no theory at all of expectational behavior during transitions between regimes.

Mervyn's paper does respect this distinction quite nicely; my few objections to his analysis stem from other small matters. All in all, I found his paper very stimulating. I was initially inclined to think that, from the perspective of British monetary policy, it is somewhat worrisome that four years after the end of the U.K.'s ERM regime, Mervyn should still be giving so much thought to transitional issues. But, of course, that thought is inappropriate, since Mervyn's topic was assigned to him and it is one that certainly involves disinflationary transitions.

Endnotes

[1]Here I am referring to a central bank that has considerable independence and is not constrained by any externally imposed rule or target, but is sensitive to public opinion.

[2]See, for example, Fischer (1994) or Persson and Tabellini (1994).

[3]This wording should not be taken to imply that the natural-rate value is constant through time.

[4]Svensson's (1996) paper in this volume suggests that price level targeting dominates inflation targeting, but his reasoning presumes—I believe unrealistically—that discretionary policymaking prevails.

[5]Throughout, my comments pertain to the version of King's paper that was presented at the symposium.

[6]When actual inflation is 10 percent, the term $0.5(\pi_t-2.0)$ itself contributes 400 basis points.

[7]In that regard, see also the useful recent study by Dicks (1996).

[8]A word should be added about the choice between what Svensson (1996) terms "target rules vs. instrument rules," both Taylor's rule and mine being examples of the latter. Svensson argues that "with new information about structual relationships ... a target rule implies automatic revisions of the reaction function." This argument involves, however, a basic misunderstanding of a central part of my thinking, and I'm sure John Taylor's, namely, that our simple instrument rules are intended to be robust to model specification. It would be, I believe, a major mistake to design a rule on the basis of any specific model because the profession does not know what the correct model is. My rule and Taylor's are designed to work *reasonably* well in a wide variety of models, and thus (perhaps) in reality. So no change in rule would be made in response to new information. Furthermore, with regard to language, I would argue that this particular terminology is undesirable since it blurs an important distinction. Thus a target is just that, a target. The word rule should be used only with reference to a formula or guide for setting instrument values.

[9]There is actually a misspecification in the demand function since real and nominal interest rates in period t differ by the expected value of Δp_{t+1}, not Δp_t, but there is no need to dwell upon that here. (Here p_t is the log of the price level in period t.) On the other hand, the specification is richer than the most standard one, because King's IS function includes a real-balance effect.

[10]Although it performs rather poorly in empirical work.

[11]See Ball (1994), pp. 285-6.

References

Ball, Laurence. "Credible Disinflation with Staggered Price-Setting," *American Economic Review* 84 (March 1994), pp. 282-9.

Debelle, Guy, and Stanley Fischer. "How Independent Should a Central Bank Be?" in J.C. Fuhrer, ed., *Goals, Guidelines, and Constraints Facing Monetary Policymakers*. Boston: Federal Reserve Bank of Boston, 1995.

Dicks, Michael. *Rules as Tools: An Investigation into the Usefulness of Policy Rules*. New York: Lehman Brothers Global Economics, 1996.

Fischer, Stanley. "Modern Central Banking," in F. Capie and others, *The Future of Central Banking*. Cambridge: Cambridge University Press, 1994.

King, Mervyn. "How Should Central Banks Reduce Inflation?—Conceptual Issues," in *Achieving Price Stability*, proceedings of a symposium sponsored by the Federal Reserve Bank of Kansas City, Aug. 29-31, 1996.

McCallum, Bennett T. "Two Fallacies Concerning Central Bank Independence," *American Economic Review Papers and Proceedings 85* (May 1995) (a), pp. 207-11.

__________. "Monetary Policy Rules and Financial Stability," in K. Sawamoto, Z. Nakajima, and H. Taguchi, eds., *Financial Stability in a Changing Environment*. London: Macmillan Press, 1995 (b).

__________. "Inflation Targeting in Canada, New Zealand, Sweden, the United Kingdom, and in General," *NBER Working Paper No. 5579*, 1996.

Orphanides, Athanasios, and David W. Wilcox. "The Opportunistic Approach to Disinflation," Finance and Economics Discussion Series 96-24. Washington, D.C.: Board of Governors of the Federal Reserve System, 1996.

Persson, Torsten, and Guido Tabellini. *Monetary and Fiscal Policy-Volume I: Credibility*. Cambridge, Mass: MIT Press, 1994.

Stuart, Alison. "Simple Monetary Policy Rules," Bank of England *Quarterly Bulletin* 36 (August 1996), pp. 281-7.

Svensson, Lars E.O. "Optimal Inflation Targets, 'Conservative Central Banks,' and Linear Inflation Contracts," *NBER Working Paper No. 5251*, 1995.

__________. "Commentary," this volume.

Taylor, John B. "Staggered Wage Setting in a Macro Model," *American Economic Review Papers and Proceedings* 69 (May 1979), pp. 108-13.

__________. "Union Wage Settlements During Disinflation," *American Economic Review* 73 (December 1983), pp. 981-93.

__________. "Discretion Versus Policy Rules in Practice," *Carnegie-Rochester Conference Series on Public Policy* 39 (Autumn 1993) (a), pp. 195-214.

__________. *Macroeconomic Policy in a World Economy: From Econometric Design to Practical Operation*. New York: W.W. Norton, 1993 (b).

General Discussion:
How Should Central Banks Reduce Inflation? —Conceptual Issues

Chairman: Gordon Thiessen

Mr. Thiessen: Thank you, Bennett. As a result of the use of discretion on the part of your chairman, we are running a little late here. So, let's start the discussion right away. Questions? Yes, David Hale.

Mr. Hale: Mervyn, you gave a good paper on the transition toward lower inflation among existing central banks. Could you speculate for a minute how you would apply your paper to the new European Central Bank, which begins operations in two years? If we assume monetary union occurs, what can that new central bank learn from the experiences you outlined in your essay?

Mr. Thiessen: Mervyn, why don't you go ahead?

Mr. King: I'd like to respond to Ben (McCallum) too, after I respond to David (Hale). Well, of course, the European Central Bank—if and when it starts—will inherit its position with inflation rates in the member countries close to something that one would call price stability. So I think the fundamental question I was given to answer in this examination paper, which deals with the transition from moderate or high inflation to price stability, is not one that would immediately apply. Now I think the general lesson of the question of learning is one that is very important for the European

Central Bank. There will not be a track record or behavior of that new governing body, or even of the new head of that central bank, to follow. And that will make things rather tricky. And I think the important questions will be how the markets will form expectations about what the European Central Bank will do, and what sort of pressures it will come under, because there is no doubt that one of the criticisms that has been made of the design of the European Central Bank is its lack of accountability. There will, therefore, undoubtedly be a much greater public debate about the role of that central bank and the way in which it reaches decisions than is the case presently, I think, with central banks in the individual member countries, which have reached a stable situation. It will be something new and the question of learning will be very much in the cards. Now I think Ben made a point that unfortunately as economists we understand very little about how learning takes place and about the transition between regimes. One should not criticize economies for that because there are always issues that have to be researched and explored. But it is certainly an unknown factor that concerns many people looking forward to the European Central Bank, which is why I think, if I may roughly paraphrase some views put forward by Otmar Issing: There is a good deal to be said unto the European Central Bank, if and when it starts, for combining both the monetary targets, which have been used successfully by the Bundesbank, with an inflation target, which clearly states the objectives of policy to everyone in Europe, and which will have the other attractions alluded to this morning by Stan Fischer and others. So that may be a useful way forward.

Mr. Thiessen: Okay, there is a question over here.

Mr. Ford: Mr. Dornbusch, you made a very interesting argument that, perhaps in certain situations, entire economies should just switch to the dollar and get on with stabilization through that route. I am curious. Would you cite some examples of where this has been tried in the real world? Also, suppose that some country did try this and got stabilization—how would they then make the transition, if ever, back to their own currency?

Mr. Dornbusch: I must disappoint you, because very few countries have taken the full medicine. Panama has gone very far in that direction. And it served them well except when they quarreled with the United States and suddenly were short of supplies. But, think of Hungary. Hungary is about to embark on a Latin American experiment—exchange rate-based stabilization. In the central bank, there are three groups—one supports fixing the rate to get inflation down. The second group is reading Chilean books to tell the others—that you actually can do well by going down slowly over ten years. The third group is reading books on Mexico, because they are saying what's happening is already bad. Why don't they go on the deutsche mark and save themselves ten years of monetary experiment, and focus on what really matters—namely, the whole, real economy? And 15 percent inflation is not the end of the world compared to a terrible economy. So I believe there needs to be far more encouragement to go in that direction in countries where there is just no plausible reason to run their own money and no expectation that in ten years they will do it with any success.

Mr. Thiessen: There is a question back there.

Mr. Daianu: If one relates the focus put on learning to the previous discussion, it seems to me that in a way the whole debate on monetary policy and what the central banks should aim at in the long run was like in a vacuum at the end of the day; one needs to embed monetary policy into the overall policy content. It is not clear to me that learning by doing is enough. It may be that learning is quite impossible because of major impediments to a central bank in pursuing price stability, although the central bank sees that as its long-term fundamental objective. It may be the case that the central bank has to educate. This may sound presumptuous, because the central bank has its own cognitive limits, but, frequently, performing well is not necessarily the only way to muster public support and it may even be unrealistic in this respect when its track record, history, is more than insufficient—like the transforming economies. It may be that there is a rationale for trying to educate, convince people—to tell people, "Look, we need cooperation, we need support"—because without that, one cannot expect the central bank to have the required strength and the stamina to pursue the long-term goal. And the second comment I want to make is this: I empathize to a large extent with what Professor Dornbusch said. But nations have icons, and icons are important. A national currency may be badly used, may be debauched by policy, but it does not mean that going in the direction suggested is necessarily the best way from a longer perspective—particularly when political sensitivities are extremely high.

Mr. Thiessen: Rudi wants one sentence before we collect a few more comments here.

Mr. Dornbusch: You said "debauched" yourselves, so I don't have to say it. It is totally, totally an old-fashioned political argument of the Third World to say national money is a great thing, even after hyperinflation when everybody holds dollars. I don't think it is really heroic to stick to the national currency. Look at Argentina. What they are really proud of is to have moved away from a totally managed domestic money—and the emphasis is on "managed."

Mr. Brinner: I wanted to get Mervyn's (King) reaction to the "information content" of inflation-indexed bonds. In the prior panel, we heard Larry Summers say that the markets will be good assimilators of information and particularly good projectors of things like future inflation. I have a different verdict. I think it looks like "amateur hour" out there pretty often. For example, if you look at studies of heating oil futures, you find that the weather in suburban Connecticut (where the traders live) really matters a lot. Or, if you look at the 10-year, I repeat *10-year,* Treasury bond, you see it moves about half as much as the *one-month* industrial production index growth for the United States. Both of these are clearly greatly disproportionate responses. So if we are going to target inflation, I would hate to see us use the changes in the inflation-indexed bonds versus other bonds as reliable indicators of inflation to come. I don't think there is much information content, and I wonder if Mervyn would disagree with that?

Mr. Thiessen: Let me collect another comment. I've got to give the next question to my colleague, Chuck Freedman, because what is the point of having your own colleague here, if you don't give him a chance to ask questions?

Mr. Freedman: Thank you, Governor. I just want to follow up on the last question. In Chart 2, Mervyn treats the difference between the conventional bond and the real return bond as an estimate of the expected rate of inflation, and uses that as evidence in terms of the relationship between the actual rate of inflation and expected rate of inflation. But, my understanding of the Bank of England's own conclusions on these matters is that the conventional bond and real return bond is not really very meaningful in terms of the level of expected inflation, and one would want to focus only on the change in this measure as an estimate of the change in the expected inflation rate. Yet, what Mervyn seems to be doing is drawing a lot of information from the level. I was just wondering, how much weight can you put on the level in this kind of analysis?

Mr. Thiessen: All right. Let's let our panelists respond to that. Mervyn, let's start with you.

Mr. King: Two or three quick points. Let me pick up first the comments on index-linked bonds. I don't think any wise central banker—Larry Summers has encouraged us to be wise—would ever describe markets as amateurs. So I am not going to do that. And, I think we can learn something about inflation expectations from index-linked bonds. There are obviously difficulties in doing it. We have described this at great length in various working papers, and risk premia and so on make it difficult. But, two observations: When Britain joined the exchange rate mechanism, there was a clear jump in the price of index-linked bonds and the expected rate of inflation fell, as we anticipated. We changed the regime for monetary policy. When we left the exchange rate mechanism, what was very clear within forty-eight hours was that the expected inflation rate five or ten years ahead, not the next year or the year after, but five or ten years ahead, was somewhat higher. That was brought down when a new monetary policy regime was introduced. So there is some evidence there that these things move in ways one can think of as being *a priori* sensible. That is a far cry from saying that you can get precise calibrations of inflation expectations. But, I look forward to the introduction of U.S. index-linked bonds, which may avoid some of the technicalities of ours, which make expectations more difficult to extract, perhaps, a more liquid market and one in which it will then be possible to examine this whole question further. But I think it will be unnecessarily pessimistic to suppose that one could not embark at least on a serious research program to see what we can learn from the yields on these bonds. And, I would have thought that was one of the great benefits of their introduction. In the text, Chuck, I was much more cautious about what one could say than in the brief comments I made, so I think you will see in the text that you can still learn something from levels; but rates of change were the key element in the comments in the text on the rate at which inflation and the inflation target declined. A comment about learning: I described it in the text as "teaching by doing." The role of education of central banks is important. And I think for the following reason: There will always be shocks to the economy that affect the inflation rate. And it will always be necessary for central banks, I suppose, to say, "Well, of course, things didn't work out in quite the way that we might have anticipated." And the only way to make that a credible statement is *ex ante* to put forward a clear intellectual framework within which decisions are being made that makes it more likely that *ex post* the people will give you credit for the fact that you could not have anticipated an unpredictable shock, rather than simply wrap yourself in sufficient mystery so that no one can tell *ex post* whether it was a shock or whether in fact your understanding of how the economy works was simply faulty. Now, therefore, there is a question of openness. It is not a question of claiming that we know a great deal. And, I think one of the absolutely crucial elements to any policy of openness and transparency is a suitable degree of modesty in what we understand. Without that, the policy will clearly fail. And that is the challenge and it is not easy with a press that typically wants clear and unambiguous statements. Openness does not mean a lack of ambiguity. We do not understand enough about the world, as Ben (McCallum) explained. And, one very final comment on Ben's point about my comments on the Taylor rule. It is important to distinguish the normative and positive for the following reason: When looking at data on the 1970s, it is possible to say, of course in retrospect, if the Taylor rule had been followed, we would have done better. My point, however, is that if the British government had been following the Taylor rule, but with a very different inflation target than price stability, then you might well have seen exactly the correlation in the data that in fact we see. And the difficulty in trying to claim that governments have been following the Taylor rule is that once you make adjustments for the fact that it is not plausible to suppose that in the 1970s the British government was following price stability, it was not. And the intellectual revolution that has taken place since then, which has let countries be more committed to price stability, and seeing the advantages of that policy, that revolution has been at least as responsible, I think, for the fall in inflation as has the change in the technical way in which monetary policy has been made. The two things probably go together. If you are not committed to price stability, you will not spend a lot of time thinking about the design of monetary policy rules.

Mr. Thiessen: Rudi.

Mr. Dornbusch: I would just like to supplement my earlier answer to the gentleman from Romania. European Monetary Union (EMU) is happening. People are giving up the national icons, even Italy, which cherishes the lira, is hoping to get into EMU. Isn't now the time to modernize and say we are going to do the same kind of thing? So I think there is today a strong, strong argument for doing so. The second, moderate inflation—15 percent—if you just say no higher but from here on we go down, isn't that the slippery slope and the next thing you are at 16 percent and where is the end? I think that a clear capping and a policy announcement of what you in fact are planning to do will help a lot. Take Mexico—and I finish with that. Everybody is revising up the forecasts: No, the peso will not decline during the rest of the year. They have 17 to 18 percent inflation. Put those two problems together and it's no wonder they aren't investing, because they are waiting for the next problem. So monetary policy is not in a vacuum. Inflation-fighting is not in a vacuum. It must not be overburdened by other problems in the economy. And it must be able to go to second place when a lot of success has been accomplished and the rest is ten years.

Mr. McCallum: Well, I had very little to say in my comments about the real subject, I guess, of this session, which is about moving from a high-inflation regime to a low-inflation regime—except to say that I think we don't know how to really plan that movement accurately. So, how should you do it, then? Well, to me the right strategy to follow is to think quite a bit about where it is that you want to go, to really try to decide upon the regime that you want to get to—what targets and what instruments you are going to use—and then just go there, taking about three years to do it. Along the way, make institutional changes that will make your efforts appear serious and certainly make changes that will give the central bank the ability to get you there. In other words, spend some time looking at the New Zealand experience and see what they did. That is my strategy.

Mr. Thiessen: Thank you very much. Well, we will hear more about the New Zealand strategy, I guess, after the coffee break. Thank you, panelists—Mervyn King, Rudi Dornbusch, and Bennett McCallum. And thank you, all.

Reducing Inflation in New Zealand: Some Practical Issues

Donald T. Brash

I have been set a large task today, and will necessarily be rather selective in dealing with the questions posed. In particular, I will concentrate on just a few aspects of the topic assigned to me: first, the importance of an overall macro- and micro-policy framework which is supportive of a price stability goal; second, how our inflation target has been made operational; third, the results to date; and, finally, an assessment of the public response to this brave new world of contracted price stability.

The framework for price stability

My starting point is very simple. A sound monetary policy may be the essential ingredient for achieving price stability but, if it has to act on its own in an otherwise hostile environment, it may fail or only succeed at a very high cost. In particular, it is important for there to be widespread political support for the goal of price stability, not just among those who compose the government of the day, but among those who are thought likely to have a reasonable chance of forming future governments. If that support does not exist, then, however well-intentioned and skilled the central bank may be in implementation of monetary policy, that policy will lack credibility as there will be a widespread expectation that the goal will not endure. If expectations of inflation are not reduced to low levels, then inevitably, the realization of price stability will be costly and difficult to achieve. A framework which makes the objectives of monetary policy transparent to everybody—government, central bank, financial market participants, and members of the public—can be enormously helpful in reducing inflation, and in reducing the transitional costs of getting there.

In an important respect, New Zealand's ability to persist with a rigorous reform program over a period of twelve years sprang from the demonstrable failure of prior policy approaches. I won't dwell on the New Zealand experience prior to 1984, since many of you will have some general familiarity with it. Very broadly, deteriorating economic performance over the period from the 1950s had been met with policy responses that relied heavily on protection, administrative controls, and subsidies. Not surprisingly, the result was slow growth, growing internal and external indebtedness, rising unemployment, and persistent double-digit inflation.

There was popular will for change and a new government was elected in 1984. That government was ready to adopt a fundamentally different view of the role of the public sector, and to embark on a breathtakingly broad program of reforms to put that view to work. Primarily, this involved two strands: the development of a prudent and sustainable set of macroeconomic policies, of which price stability was a key part; and secondly, a comprehensive program of microeconomic or structural reforms, involving removal of barriers to domestic and international competition, the elimination of subsidies and other sectoral incentives, a complete overhaul of the tax system, a reshaping of the public sector to make it operate more efficiently, and a significant reform of functioning of the labor market, aimed at increasing flexibility.

On the macroeconomic policy front stand two "landmark" policy initiatives—the Fiscal Responsibility Act of 1994 and the Reserve Bank of New Zealand Act of 1989. Both adopt a common framework which aims to check the normal incentives of governments to put short-term electoral gains ahead of longer-term public interests. Both rely heavily on mandated transparency and public accountability to achieve that incentive shift. Both require public political commitment to longer-term objectives, and periodic public accounts of progress toward those longer-term objectives. Together they have been successful in facilitating a significant shift with respect to behavior and outcomes in fiscal and monetary policy.

Both of these major pieces of legislation now command substantial public and political support, although I would have to acknowledge that it is monetary policy and the Reserve Bank Act which remain the more controversial and more "challenged" at this point.

The Reserve Bank Act establishes the framework within which monetary policy is to be conducted. It specifies an objective, defines responsibilities and accountabilities, and mandates transparency of the policymaking process at each stage. Very briefly, the act specifies "stability in the general level of prices" as the sole objective of monetary policy, requires the establishment of a contract or Policy Targets Agreement (PTA) between the Governor and the Minister of Finance to give specificity to that objective (currently defined as the achievement of consumer price index [CPI] inflation between 0 and 2 percent over each 12-month period, after adjusting for specified "caveats" to allow for supply shocks), and provides authority for the Governor to formulate and implement monetary policy to achieve that objective without further reference to the government.

In this way, the objective of monetary policy remains firmly in the hands of the public's elected representatives, but constrained by:

—the need for the PTA to be consistent with some reasonable interpretation of the act's requirement for the single monetary policy objective of "stability in the general level of prices;"

—the requirement that the PTA be made public and tabled in Parliament; and

—the need to find a Governor who is prepared to accept the PTA and commit himself to achieving it.

Under this framework, the formulation of day-to-day monetary policy lies squarely in the hands of the Governor. The performance of the Governor is assessed, and his continued tenure in office is determined, with direct reference to the terms of the PTA. I can assure you that the combination of a public contract, and formal accountability for producing outcomes in accordance with that contract, provides very powerful incentives for the Governor to ensure that monetary policy decisions are, indeed, consistent with the PTA.

Perhaps as important, this same structure provides similarly powerful constraints on politicians who might wish for a little more latitude in the conduct of monetary policy on occasion. Within the terms of the act, the Minister of Finance can direct the Governor to take account of other economic objectives in addition to (or even in substitution for) price stability. However, such instructions must be issued formally and publicly, and will lapse after twelve months unless renewed.

To appreciate the force of these provisions, put yourself in the position of a Minister of Finance who thinks that the tough stance being adopted by the central bank is hurting his re-election prospects. You want the central bank to ease up, but they are simply seeking to achieve the objectives laid down in the publicly agreed policy target, and are being seen by the financial market to be doing just that. Your only route to getting the central bank to ease up is to publicly direct that it drop, for twelve months, the statutory price-stability-only objective and replace it with something else. It is very hard to conceive of anything other than a negative market reaction to the news that price stability had been modified or abandoned. And it is very hard to conceive of a net benefit arising to electoral prospects from the ensuing rise in interest rates and fall in the exchange rate.

Transparency of the objective-setting and policy formulation and implementation process is clearly the key to effective accountability, and is also essential to the willingness of politicians and the public to devolve operational independence to the central bank. In our case, the transparency mechanism is provided by the PTA and the requirement to publish at six monthly intervals a *Monetary Policy Statement*, which must review the implementation of monetary policy during the preceding period, specify the means by which the bank intends to achieve the objectives of the PTA in future, and state the reasons for adopting those policies and means.

These statements are required to be referred to Parliament. In addition, they may be reviewed (and generally are) by a Select Committee of Parliament, which may (and usually does) call the Governor to give evidence and further explanation in a public hearing.

The accountability process is given further substance by way of the bank's board of directors. The board has no role in the formulation of policy—as noted earlier, that responsibility rests solely with the Governor. Rather, it is the role of the board to scrutinize the performance of the Governor in terms of the requirements of the PTA. Accordingly, the board formally reviews each *Monetary Policy Statement* with respect to its consistency with the PTA. Moreover, where inflation outcomes depart from those specified in the PTA, the board formally reviews the adequacy of the Governor's performance, and reports publicly on its findings to the Minister of Finance. Again, I can assure you, from uncomfortable recent experience, these processes are taken very seriously by all concerned, and the transparency of the process imposes a very high standard of discipline, rigor, and credibility on all participants.

Translating an inflation target into an operational target

In New Zealand, as in most countries, monetary policy has its effects on inflation through three main channels:

—directly through effects on inflationary expectations;

—directly through the exchange rate and its impact on domestic prices; and

—indirectly through interest rates and the exchange rate,

and the effect which they have on incomes and hence, via demand pressures, on prices.

Most discussion tends to center on the interest rate and exchange rate mechanisms, but we have put a lot of weight on the role of inflationary expectations and, therefore, on policy credibility. We have put a great deal of effort into conditioning public inflationary expectations. It is important that price setters understand and accept that shocks will not result in inflation being allowed to move beyond our target range (or, if it does, that the departure will be temporary). To that end, we try to make our monetary policy "reaction function" as clear as possible.

Policy operates in a forward-looking framework. Each quarter, we make a projection for inflation two to three years ahead, on the basis of some stylized and publicly disclosed assumptions about fiscal policy, interest rates, and the exchange rate. We then spell out what monetary conditions will be required if inflation is to be in the middle of our target range one to two years ahead. We also explore how the reality may depart from our stylized projection, and discuss how monetary policy might respond to such departures. These quarterly inflation forecasts have become by far and away the single most important ingredient in the monetary policy decisionmaking process.

In making our projections, we rely on estimates of the effect that changes in the exchange rate and interest rates have on inflation.

The direct effect from the exchange rate to inflation, via import prices (and those of exportables), tends to be the fastest and most predictable, and in the early years of the disinflation process we tended to give predominant attention to what the exchange rate was doing. Indeed, for some years we gave the impression that adjusting monetary policy to ensure that the trade-weighted measure of the New Zealand dollar moved within our perceived exchange rate "comfort zone" was our only concern.

A change in interest rates also has some early effect on the CPI since, unlike many other countries, New Zealand has new house prices captured directly in its CPI. However, this direct interest rate effect is relatively small.

The indirect effects of both the exchange rate and interest rates work their way through to the CPI in a more diffuse fashion, but are mostly felt within two years.

The New Zealand dollar is freely floating in that, while we certainly do seek to ensure, by adjusting monetary policy, that the exchange rate evolves in a way consistent with our inflation target, we have not intervened in the foreign exchange markets since the New Zealand dollar was floated in March 1985. Nor does the bank "fix" any particular interest rate. Access to the bank's discount window is priced at a margin over short-term market interest rates, and so varies from day to day. We recognize, of course, that we cannot determine the *mix* of monetary conditions at any point; we cannot shift the balance between the exchange rate channel and the interest rate channel. It is, therefore, necessary to accept a degree of "trading off" of interest rate and exchange rate pressures, while looking for outcomes which are consistent with our inflation target.

In our stylized and transparent world, we have sometimes thought it might be helpful and efficient to have a Monetary Conditions Indicator that combined the exchange rate and interest rate effects into one readily communicated measure. However, despite quite extensive work in that area, we have not yet found a single set of coefficients that adequately captures that tradeoff in a manner which is useful for policy communication purposes.

Between our quarterly publication of either a formal *Monetary Policy Statement* or a set of *Economic Projections*, our internal Monetary Policy Committee meets weekly to review market conditions and new data. That committee also sets the longer-term agenda for research, and reviews the products of our research effort. While those weekly deliberations on current monetary conditions may occasionally lead us to a conclusion that current conditions are inconsistent with the longer-term price stability goal, and thus cause us to take some action, we prefer to base any such responses or shifts in policy stance on the more substantial quarterly projections. Either way, the trigger for action is a judgment that a continuation of current monetary conditions would risk inflation outcomes at or near the edges of our targeted inflation range within the policy relevant period.

One useful consequence of this approach to the operation of monetary policy is that we rarely actually *do* anything other than publish inflation projections, and occasionally comment on the evolution of market conditions relative to those assumed in our projections. So long as market participants understand our policy reaction function, believe that we will act consistently with that reaction function, and accept that we have the capacity to inflict some bottom-line pain when taking action, then their incentives are to anticipate the monetary conditions consistent with our inflation target, and trade accordingly. As a consequence, there have been only three events since early 1991 in which we have felt obliged to take explicit monetary policy actions by varying our key policy instrument.

Action, in our case, generally means an adjustment to the aggregate quantity of "settlement cash" provided to our settlement or "clearing" banks. Adjustments to that quantity alter the risk of banks being forced into discounting to clear their daily settlement obligations or, alternatively, finding themselves holding surplus settlement cash (or reserves) at the end of the day earning sub-market returns. Other possible, but less preferred, forms of action for us include adjustments to the margin-over-market rates applied at the discount window, or adjustments to the volume of "discountable" securities provided to the system.

In essence, our monetary policy implementation structure retains the hallmarks of its quantity-based origins. However, over the years we have tended to de-emphasize the significance of the underlying quantities, and focus a little more on the key prices: interest rates and the exchange rate. One point of philosophy has remained constant through this evolution: we have little, if any, informational advantage over the market. Market participants know what our objectives are, and they know how we think monetary conditions

Chart 1
New Zealand's CPI Inflation, 1970 to 1996

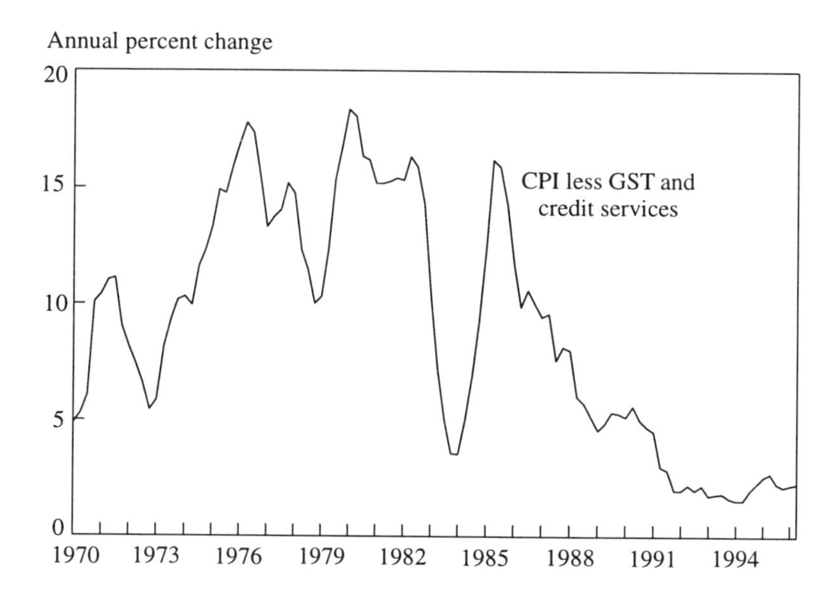

affect inflation. Hence when actual conditions move, that provides us with useful information and a need to reassess our views in the light of that information.

Results to date

As can be seen in Chart 1, the period since the passage of the Reserve Bank Act in 1989 has seen a dramatic improvement in New Zealand's inflation record. We cannot and should not ascribe all of that improvement to the act. Significant progress in the fight against inflation was being made in the years immediately prior to 1989 (the bank had been explicitly instructed to aim for inflation of between 0 and 2 percent at least as early as the beginning of 1988), and we cannot claim that such progress would not have been maintained subsequently without the act. Other countries with poor inflation performances through the 1970s and 1980s have also made the transition to low single-digit inflation without resorting to such dramatic changes in institutional structures as occurred in New Zealand.

I must rely largely on assertion here, but I have little doubt that New Zealand's progress toward long-term price stability has been significantly aided by the passage of the Reserve Bank Act. And I make that assertion for three reasons.

First, the act and the PTA have been instrumental in achieving a clear downward shift in inflationary expectations, and in anchoring those expectations at low single-digit levels. Given New Zealand's inflation and monetary policy history, one might well have expected serious problems in getting price-setting behavior to adapt to a low inflation environment. And though it is by no means the case that general inflation expectations have yet conformed to the 0 to 2 percent target in the PTA, the extent of the adaptation has been considerable. New Zealand's most recent economic cycle has been of large amplitude, with unemployment falling from 11 percent to 6 percent in less than four years. Yet inflation as defined in the PTA (exclusive of certain policy-driven changes in government charges) is expected to peak at no more than 2.6 percent (in the year to September 1996). By our historical standards, this is remarkable, and almost certainly says something about the expectations and behavior of price and wage setters.

Second, the act, and its transparency and accountability provisions, have had a discernable impact on the way the Reserve Bank approaches policy formulation. Given the pressures which even central bankers are always under, the clear and public statement of the acceptable limit to inflation provides a crucial discipline. I have no doubt that hard decisions have been taken earlier and presented more forcefully than would have occurred under our previous charter.

Third, those same transparency provisions have had a discernable impact on the way politicians think about, and comment upon, the objectives and conduct of monetary policy. In particular, politicians apparently perceive a need to ensure that any comments on the stance of monetary policy are firmly grounded within a credible view of the future path of inflation, and none sees electoral advantage in advocating a tolerance of more than low single-digit inflation. The upper limits of that inflation tolerance may vary between 2 percent and something closer to, perhaps, 3.5 percent, but that is clearly a substantial shift from the sort of levels regarded as acceptable prior to 1989.

One striking change in the way the Reserve Bank of New Zealand goes about its task under the new charter is found in the emphasis we now place on public education and advocacy. In our strategic planning, the communications function has assumed an increasingly important role as we have come to recognize that building a broad public constituency for price stability is the single most important challenge the bank faced. To that end, we have devoted considerable, and increasing, resources to public information programs. Such programs take the form of pamphlets and other publications, a very active speaking program (I believe we are currently undertaking upward of 200 speaking commitments annually, throughout the country), production of resource material on inflation and monetary policy for schools, background briefings for each of the major media, and sponsoring a Visiting Professorial Fellowship in monetary economics (appointments thus far have been Bennett McCallum, Ralph Bryant, and, currently, Larry Ball). We proactively target and seek out particular audiences where we discern there to be concerns about the objectives and impact of monetary policy. To date, judging by the indications we receive from a variety of opinion surveys, the communications programs have been beneficial in both lowering inflationary expectations and building a stronger public acceptance of the merits of our price stability target.

Incidentally, the framework established by the act and PTA has produced one other interesting by-product, and that relates to an apparent reduction in exchange rate volatility. We have a floating exchange rate, as mentioned, but we do adjust monetary policy to ensure that the exchange rate stays within bounds consistent with inflation staying inside the inflation target range, and the market has a very clear understanding of this fact. That might be thought of as an exchange rate intermediate target, but using that description can easily mislead: our exchange rate "target" or "comfort zone" is heavily conditional on what is happening to inflation pressures. The net result of approaching monetary policy implementation in this way seems to have been an exchange rate which is relatively stable, in a month-to-month variability sense, but relatively flexible. So far, at least, we have avoided the "excessive" high-frequency variability of entirely unconstrained floating exchange rates and also avoided the problems of unduly rigid targeted exchange rates.

For all the effort and improved structures in New Zealand, staying within our 0 to 2 percent CPI target range has not proved to be a straightforward task. Indeed, while we stayed within the target range consistently from 1991 until June 1995, the outcomes were always in the top half of the target range. Moreover, since June 1995, we have been either just at the upper 2 percent level, or slightly above. As noted, we expect our targeted inflation measure to peak at 2.6 percent for the year to September 1996 before again falling under 2 percent in the first half of 1997.

So how come I still have my job? On two occasions over the past year, the nonexecutive members of my board have conducted a formal review of the adequacy of my performance. On both occasions, the review was sparked by our own projections that inflation would exceed the target range. Those reviews have covered the reasons for the projected inflation excesses, the monetary policy stance being adopted over the year or so prior (that is, during the period when a tighter policy might have been able to avert inflation outcomes above the target range), the rationale underlying the policy stance at that time, the quality of our policymaking processes (including the quality of our inflation forecasting methodologies), and the future outlook for inflation (that is, is there a reasonable expectation that inflation will move back into the target range promptly?).

To my considerable relief, on each occasion, the nonexecutive directors have found in my favor. I have no doubt that the fact that we have been running a demonstrably "tight" monetary policy since 1994, and have been consistently more pessimistic than most other forecasters about the course of future inflation, were important elements in that judgment. Also key was the specification of the PTA which requires me to operate monetary policy "with the intention" of being within the target inflation range: outcomes beyond the target range are not, of themselves, grounds for automatic dismissal.

But I hasten to add that this performance review process is not one that any of the participants takes lightly. In no sense can the nonexecutive directors' review be regarded as "hollow" or essentially "presentational." Moreover, while my nonexecutive directors have found my performance to be consistent with the intentions of the PTA, and the Minister of Finance has been prepared to accept their judgment on that issue, both the minister and the nonexecutive directors have gone on record as indicating that their judgments are conditional on future inflation outcomes being brought back within the target range within a reasonably short period. Note also that the nonexecutive directors' reports to the Minister of Finance, and his responses, are public documents. In this process, as in others associated with the operation of the Reserve Bank Act, transparency acts as a very powerful discipline on all concerned.

Public response to the "new" brand of monetary policy

This is an excellent time at which to make an assessment of the public's response to our new approach to monetary policy. I say that for several reasons.

First, New Zealand has now had more than four years of uninterrupted growth. That makes it one of the longest periods of uninterrupted economic growth in New Zealand since the early 1960s. Moreover, this growth phase has also included some of the most vigorous growth that New Zealand has experienced in recent times. Strong growth, and more particularly growth above the economy's long-term potential output capability, brings monetary policy challenges and the risk of public resentment as monetary policy moves to restrain demand.

Second, New Zealand's monetary policy has been unambiguously (some would say, aggressively) tight for the past couple of years as we have grappled with this strong growth phase. The interest rates on 90-day bank bills rose from around 4.5 percent in January 1994 to over 9 percent in December of that year, and have remained within a range of 8.2 and 10.3 percent ever since. In late November 1994, yields on 90-day bills moved sharply above yields on 10-year bonds, and have remained there since. The trade-weighted measure of the exchange rate has increased by 15 percent since January 1994 (and by 23 percent since the trough in January 1993), while the New Zealand dollar has moved up even more sharply against the U.S. dollar over the same period.

Third, we are just over one month out from an election—the first to be held under a new German-style proportional representation system. Elections tend to bring any public criticisms to the fore, and maximize the likelihood of public criticism of a firmly anti-inflationary monetary policy. Inevitably, those who perceive themselves to be hurt by policy are more outspoken than those who are benefiting, or who can see benefits coming.

Given that environment, is there public criticism of the Reserve Bank Act, and the single-minded pursuit of price stability? Of course—some of it vocal and emanating from people of significant influence.

What is very gratifying, however, is how strong support for the act and its objectives remains. Market research commissioned by the bank recently suggested that 63 percent of the public were aware that delivering low inflation was the bank's key objective, and 73 percent were in favor of that objective. Other market research, not commissioned by the bank, has suggested that 42 percent of New Zealanders think that the Reserve Bank Act itself has been good for New Zealand, while only 17 percent think it has been detrimental.[1]

Within the political sphere, there are four major parties and three minor ones with some prospect of representation in the new Parliament. Of these, two of the major parties and all three of the minor parties favor retention of the Reserve Bank Act in essentially its present form. The other two major parties, holding combined support in recent opinion polls of about 32 percent, both favor widening the objectives of monetary policy to include economic growth and employment. All but one of the seven parties have also specified, in numerical terms, what their inflation target would be if they became government: most favor retention of the current 0 to 2 percent target, one favors widening the range to -1 to +3 percent (retaining a mid-point of 1 percent), while one favors targeting inflation below 3.5 percent, on the basis that that is the (unweighted) inflation rate in our ten largest export markets. The point which I think is relevant here is that none of our significant political parties is suggesting that price stability is unimportant, and none has found electoral advantage in advocating a wholesale shift away from price stability, in some fairly constrained definition, as the primary objective of monetary policy. This, in itself, reflects, and represents, a substantial transformation of the political landscape in New Zealand over the past decade or so.

Within the business and farming community there are groups who are currently under quite intense financial pressure—from weak commodity prices, increased competition as protective barriers have fallen, and the impact of rising interest rates and rising exchange rates. Certainly, some within those groups question whether we have our policy settings right, and ask whether we can find other, non-monetary, means to assist in the restraint of inflation. However, almost unanimously, those same people are very quick to reject any thought of a return to the days of high and variable inflation.

Summary and conclusions

I am in no doubt that our structure of inflation targeting has yielded New Zealand significant advantages as we tackled a long history of high inflation. Equally, I am in no doubt that the comprehensive nature of reform in New Zealand has been a significant aspect of the country's ability to turn from being a chronic underperformer, to a country which looks to have put itself on a long-term, sustainable, low-inflation growth track. Monetary policy could not do that in isolation.

The institutional structure has been important in the reform of monetary policy. In particular, it has been important to find mechanisms by which the natural incentives on politicians, and central bankers, to opt for the soft decisions could be countered by incentives to confront emerging inflationary pressures. Achieving that in a way that still recognizes the centrality of the democratic political process is no simple feat. After almost seven years' experience with our structure, and having gone through a couple of political cycles, and the tests of both recession and a sustained growth cycle, I think we can safely say that the New Zealand structure is proving constructively and positively robust to all of those pressures.

Fundamental to every aspect of that outcome has been transparency: transparency in the establishment of the inflation target, transparency in the formulation and implementation of monetary policy, transparency in regard to accountability for the outcome. The fact that financial markets very largely implement policy for us is demonstrative of the power of that transparency.

Endnote

[1]New Zealand Insight, Vol. 5 (4), April 1996, UMR Insight Limited.

Israel's Experience with Inflation

Jacob Frenkel

Thank you very much. Listening to Donald Brash convinced me that, for many countries, there is a long way to go to achieve price stability. In addition, there is some sense of envy and gratification. As he explained, New Zealand's inflation target is above zero because inflation may simply be just measurement errors. I hope that nobody from my government was listening because he would immediately adopt the conclusion that our inflation is measurement errors.

There is also the question of who is responsible for lowering inflation and for omitting or missing the target. In our case, the division is very clear. It is ex post. If you miss the target, the Governor was responsible. If you hit the target, of course, the government was responsible.

Let me provide a brief background about inflation in my country. Israel's experience with inflation has gone through basically three phases since the mid-1980s. Up to the mid-1980s we had hyperinflation. During that period, there was a major stabilization program—the core of which was budgetary restraint and exchange rate anchoring—along the lines that Rudi Dornbusch described. We were then stuck at an inflation rate of 18 to 20 percent for about seven years. Inflation targets then came into the game and now we have about half the rate of inflation we started with.

Thus, what are the lessons and mechanisms that brought about the decline in inflation? Many of you have raised the question of where the exchange rate comes in. And, indeed, initially in the stabilization program, the exchange rate against the dollar was a very important anchor. The question, though, became how do you exit from it? As inflation at home continues, you have real appreciation. And with the real appreciation, competitiveness gets eroded and may hurt the economy after a while (as it did in Israel). With large changes in bilateral exchange rates, Israel moved to pegging to a basket of currencies, then to a band vis-à-vis the basket, then to a wider band vis-à-vis the basket. And from time to time, an adjustment of the band had to take place.

At the end of 1991, the existing system was introduced, which we refer to as the "crawling band," not "crawling peg." The slope of the band is a function of the difference between the inflation target and the expected inflation abroad. That is how the inflation target came into being in the Israeli context. In a way, it was the mechanism by which we got out of a relatively rigid exchange rate regime. And in order to introduce the slope, the inflation target came in through the back door.

Why did we start getting interested in inflation? After all, inflation was about 20 percent and nothing bad happened. Our economy has been very indexed and the illusion that inflation does not carry a cost was prevalent. But after a while, several things happened. First, some public opinion polls showed to the politicians that inflation does matter; in fact, it mattered more than unemployment. Second, as foreign investors started to get interested in the Israeli economy, we found out that one of the first questions that investors asked was, "What is your inflation rate?" Third, the rating agencies came in. In short, that's where the motivation came from. There was initially no motivation to lower inflation. Up to that point, fighting inflation occurred only when your back was to the wall.

When we come to the targets, a few specific technical questions come up. First, who sets the target? In our case, we found that it is essential that the government have a very important say in setting the target—not simply the central bank, but the government with the central bank. There are several reasons. First, it forces the government to put inflation within the spectrum of its own objectives. Second, it assures that inflation is not just the residual that comes out of the budget debate, but that it is done simultaneously. Third, it forces the tradeoff issue. For a long time, when the central bank tried to fight inflation, arguing that we needed to lower inflation, people came back to us and asked, "Who told you? There is a tradeoff—there is unemployment, there is growth. You are not an elected official." The tradeoff involves a political decision. We can always argue whether there is a tradeoff or there isn't. But if the politicians feel that there is a tradeoff, they can translate that feeling into the setting of the inflation target. Once the inflation target has been set, then the independence of the central bank is understood, as far as the user of the policy instrument. It also helps the central bank to explain why it raised or lowered rates: here is the target, we are about to miss it, that's why we have to raise or lower rates.

Should it be a point target? Obviously not, for several reasons. First, typically when you disinflate—in our case, when you go from 20 percent to 10 percent to 8 percent—you also are engaged in financial market liberalization. And that's the period where some of the relations are not as stable. It is good to have a range. And of course, you need to allow for real exchange rate changes and other changes. There is another question, which is, which index should you use? Although it sounds like a technical question, it is actually a fundamental one. Many countries have removed parts of the index from their inflation target. Not the consumer price index (CPI), but the CPI excluding one or more components. In our case, I don't think we have a choice: it is the CPI. The reason why we do not have a choice is that the Israeli economy is very indexed. Many contracts, if not most, are indexed to the CPI: rents are CPI-indexed, mortgages are CPI-indexed, government bonds are CPI-indexed, and wages are CPI-indexed. Thus, the CPI is the index that matters for behavior, which is why it is a very important matter. However, if one decides to exclude some items from the index, one technical statistical test should be made. Any excluded item should be one that may have larger noise, but not a fundamentally different rate of inflation than the average rate of inflation. Otherwise, you are excluding something which is more fundamental.

Should you have a single-year target? We have found that a multiyear target is essential for several reasons. First, monetary policy operates with a lag. By midyear, you are operating as far as the next year's target, so you better know what it is. Second, our politicians, like those in most places, are much more at ease in agreeing on a long-term target than on a short-term target, because the long term is never-never land. It was so easy to speak about the end of the decade; except that today, the end of the decade, the end of the century, the end of the millennium, the end of the term of the existing government are all falling at the same time. The fact of the matter is that we are moving closer. And as we move closer, forcing a long-term target is a very useful way to introduce discipline.

How do we conduct monetary policy? Because of our inflationary heritage, we have had indexed bonds for a long time. Most of the government's debt is indexed. One of the achievements of the disinflation process has been to broaden the base of the nonindexed, or shekel-based, financial instruments. So in the conduct of monetary policy, we make extraordinary use of inflationary expectations as measured from these financial instruments. Since we have indexed and nonindexed for the same maturity and for the same government, we can read inflationary expectations over the next twelve months. And the public knows it. As a matter of fact, when we introduced the inflation targets, a statement was made to the public about the way our Open Market Committee would study the economy. We told the public what variables we are looking at and the inflation rate that is expected from the rate of monetary expansion. In our case, it is M1, which has the most stable relation and has a two- to three-quarter lag to future inflation. In fact, a week before our monetary announcements (which are happening once a month), the financial press is simulating the discussions that will take place. They will report that since they know that the inflationary expectation that the central bank looks at is so and so, and that the rate of monetary expression has been so and so, then it is likely these guys will do so and so. And occasionally they are right, which is OK.

The idea is not to surprise the market, but rather to communicate with the market. So we have found these indexed bonds are a very useful instrument in the conduct of monetary policy.

How fast should you lower inflation? One of the difficulties that we had was that we started with excessive success. In the year after we introduced the inflation targets, inflation was cut by half. As a result, politicians got the idea that reducing inflation was an easy task. Therefore, the next year's target was even more ambitious, but it was missed. As it was missed, a real test for the inflation target strategy was put into place: Are you going to revise the target upward? Or are you going to use tight monetary policy and tough monetary policy? We decided to use tight monetary policy and interest rates went up very significantly. I know that monetary policy was tight, because during that first month, the Governor had to travel with bodyguards.

So as it happened, the decision about the next year's target became much more difficult. It was at this point that the Finance Minister said, "My goodness, if I have a tight target next year, this crazy central bank will start raising rates and they will take us seriously. After all, we're only politicians; why should we be taken seriously?" And that's where the debate took place. Everyone agreed, therefore, on a long-term target. We all want to be in paradise, but not yet. The issue, therefore, is how quick is quick?

What is the role of preconditions? How are we going to reduce inflation? And what is the interaction between the budget on the one hand and monetary policy on the other? And when I remarked this morning in reference to Larry Summers' point about the business of coordination, it was not just an analytical insight but rather a bitter experience. We have made some deals with the government, just as the G-7 has made deals with the United States about the budget. The fact is, it is very easy for governments to make a commitment. But it is much more difficult to either pass it through Congress, or once passing it through Congress, to implement it. So, we have an exchange with the government, in which they say they have already made their fiscal reduction. How do they know? Well, they have announced it. Therefore, you need to make your monetary expansion. And how do they know that we have not done it yet? Because interest rates are still high. So before long, monetary expansion is already taking place. And once monetary expansion is taking place, there is no need to fight unemployment anymore, because policies are already expansionary, so there is no need to cut the budget any more. Before long, it's over. So at least in our case, we have been very explicit. We coordinate, but we make it very clear that coordination means that monetary policy will take into account government actions, not government announcements.

And this brings, therefore, the question of how do you make sure that everyone recognizes that there are two guys on the block, not only one—there is fiscal policy and there is monetary policy. When we speak about inflation reports, we have insisted and (it has not been adopted, but it is in the process) that twice a year there should be a cabinet meeting in which the Governor presents the inflation report. If we are missing the inflation rate, we explain what it means for monetary policy. And the government understands it. At the same session, there is also a fiscal report. The Finance Minister reports to the government where the budget stands relative to the plan. If the budget plan is not being met, the government decides what actions should be taken in order to deal with it. Thus, we do not have a mechanism that leads to an overburdening of monetary policy. In the late 1980s, many countries suffered because monetary policy was overburdened—not because of ill design or ill will, but because of poor management of the budget.

What are the necessary preconditions that are needed? First, of course, you need to have the capacity to change interest rates. But if your capital markets are open to the world, then raising interest rates as you fight inflation means that capital flows in. And as capital inflow comes in, you have an appreciation of your currency. If you only worry about inflation, you celebrate. But you are not allowed to celebrate because exporters and the government remind you that something is happening to the real exchange rate and that you better do something to the nominal rate. And before long, you find yourself worrying about interest rates for inflation, and exchange rates for competitiveness. You see that you don't have two heads to have these two hats. And that's exactly where the next issue comes in.

In many of the countries that have used interest rates to fight inflation, while maintaining open capital markets, capital inflow came in. These countries have then found it necessary that after the maximum appreciation that could be sustained politically or otherwise took place, the central bank had to intervene in the foreign exchange market. But if you intervene in the foreign exchange market, you better make sure that you have financial monetary instruments to sterilize the monetary injections that occur as you buy the foreign exchange.

All of this means that you cannot do it for too long. Ultimately, the real exchange rate is the story of government spending and the budget; the nominal exchange rate and inflation is the story of the monetary authority. The division of labor between real exchange rates, budget deficits, nominal exchange rates, inflation, and monetary policy, must be made explicit.

And we found ourselves against an extraordinary lobby. In contrast with Donald Brash, where everyone wants low inflation, in our case, exporters want high inflation. Since high inflation means higher costs, why would exporters want high inflation? Exporters understand that high inflation means that the Governor will not need to have high interest rates because the Governor must have agreed to high inflation. And if we don't get the high interest rate, then the exchange rate will not be so appreciated. And thus it comes back to the exporters. They don't understand fully that it is the budget deficit that effects the real exchange rate, not monetary policy. Thus, they come and say that they want high inflation. There must be the recognition that the interest rate that deals with inflation is higher than the interest rate that contributes to exchange rate stability, that is still higher than the interest rate that gives a boost to the short-term capital markets. And that's where we are in the transition. And somebody asked how we get out of the transition. And let me remind you that Jacob Viner once said that a transition period is the period that lies between two transition periods.

In conclusion, we have found that inflation targeting has been an extraordinarily important and useful mechanism to explain what the central bank is doing. There are inevitable conflicts when we try to accomplish too much. Our central bank law was drafted in the 1950s, when everyone thought that one could simultaneously be young, beautiful, rich, healthy, and all the rest. So our central bank, like the Federal Reserve in the United States, is supposed to take care of prosperity, growth, the standard of living, and inflation and price stability. So against this background, having an inflation target has proven to be useful.

But, the real test will be when we are going into a downturn. Since the beginning of this decade, we have grown over 40 percent; 50 percent in the business sector. So growth has been very, very high. Given this background, tight monetary policy that lowered inflation from 20 percent to 10 percent was not viewed as an extraordinary thing. But the test will come when a slowdown, I wouldn't call it a recession, inevitably comes. And that's when the Phillips curves will come out from under the carpet.

Like Rudi Dornbusch, I agree that when you start from hyperinflation, inflation targeting or monetary targeting is the wrong thing to do. You must break inertia; you must really press on the brakes. And that's where either exchange rate or some other system will do the job. But you must realize that an exit policy is part and parcel of that system. In this way, when you exit, you are not viewed as having lost credibility. Rather, you are viewed as having graduated to the next stage. And once you are in the next stage, then you look at Donald Brash with envy and you hope to be there.

The key is that if you are going to adopt inflation targets, make sure it goes side-by-side with budgetary targets. Furthermore, make sure that the decisions and the discussions about the inflation report are joined with the decisions and discussions about the budget report. In this way, you will not become the orphan that is the residual of all the evils in the system.

Disinflation in the Czech Republic: Looking Both Backward and Forward

Josef Tosovsky

I am delighted to be invited to this symposium where so many of you have found the time in your busy schedules to gather and discuss the never-ending story for every central banker, which is price stability. Despite the worldwide dimension of this issue, I hope that taking some lessons from the Czech case may still be rewarding. The Czech Republic (and former Czechoslovakia) is an example of a country which opted for a rapid transition from a command to a market-oriented economy. During the transition we gathered some empirical evidence that there are consequences, on both the plus and minus side, of the radical approach for monetary affairs in the economy and for disinflation efforts of monetary authorities.

Let me emphasize two general features of a country undergoing a rapid transition. First, such an economy should be seen as a unique mix of market-oriented reforms on the one hand and built-in non-market inertia on the other. This peculiar coexistence of market and nonmarket structures gives rise, on both macro- and microeconomic levels, to some nonstandard or even strange economic phenomena that are easier to explain ex post than to anticipate ex ante. But more importantly, the composition of the mix is exposed to constant change in which the transition features wither away and economic agents become more experienced with the basics of free market behavior. Under such circumstances, the key issue for policymakers is to appropriately track this systemic shift from transition frictions to the regularities of an internationally integrated market economy and this entails reconciling previously autonomous decisionmaking with the loss of a degree of freedom.

Second, just as a supersonic aircraft may produce annoying sound waves, similar waves from a fast movement ahead are sure to be expected in a rapidly transforming economy.[1] As a consequence of this background phenomenon, the transition from a command to a market-type economy can be, to the discomfort of a central banker, pretty bumpy and challenging in terms of looking for various shock absorbers.

Early transition policy mix

Reforming programs elaborated for transition economies attach a great importance to preventing an accelerated inflation that could be otherwise easily triggered by the price and foreign trade liberalization. The debate how to achieve this goal was frequently structured as finding an anchor, that is, a variable whose stability should be the most conducive to containing inflationary pressures. Several arguments were put forward showing that the nominal exchange rate is well-suited to perform this role.

First, during the transition, the degree of monetization of the Czech economy grew sizably, and as a consequence, the velocity of money declined. But in advance, the speed and extent of these changes were difficult to predict. This notorious instability of money demand in transition economies made it difficult to rely exclusively on monetary aggregates' targeting.

Second, the Czech economy has been traditionally open, with the share of imports and exports in GDP both around 40 percent. In view of this large openness, the stability of the exchange rate was of great importance to economic agents, as it reduced exchange rate uncertainty and allowed them to make sufficient long-term decisions.

Finally, an argument about the low credibility of the central bank at the inception of economic reform implies the need to base the stabilization program on a nominal variable that could be easily observable to the general public who can thus quickly judge about the commitment of monetary authorities to financial stability.

The paradigm of the exchange rate anchor thus became the backbone of the stabilization program as it was designed and applied in the Czechoslovak economy. There was, however, the other side of the coin, in the sense that the more devalued the initial level of the exchange rate, the higher the chances for a longer-term survival of the anchor. On the other hand, too large a devaluation could lead to a sharp increase in import prices, which, in turn, should spread into the whole economy. These considerations were further complicated by the uncertainty about the size of the initial price jumps. A certain degree of assistance was also perceived necessary in order to shield the domestic business sector, which was exposed to a deep process of restructuring, privatization, and exodus from collapsing CMEA markets. So-called "protection through the exchange rate" thus gained official support, partly enforced as well by a relatively low tariff protection.

The credibility of the fixed exchange rate regime also requires a certain minimum level of foreign reserves that would allow the central bank to intervene, if need be, to support the chosen level. In fact, foreign reserves in the former Czechoslovakia shortly before the introduction of a fixed exchange rate regime were dangerously low, covering less than one month imports (partly due to a mistaken view to allow the policy decision on the right depth of devaluation to become a nationwide dispute). With this respect, financial assistance provided by the International Monetary Fund (IMF) under the stand-by program played a crucial role.

A thorny issue of selecting a more balanced exchange rate level was resolved in practice by the series of opening devaluations which totaled 96 percent against the U.S. dollar. A substantial part of this, however, was simply a pre-reform move toward a more reasonable exchange rate rather than devaluations in the true sense, bearing in mind that the exchange rate was one of the most distorted prices in the previous planning system. This shock-type change created an important cushion which provided a competitive edge to exporters and discouraged imports (in conjunction with a temporarily levied and later gradually phased out 20 percent import surcharge), at the cost of a one-off price jump of 56.6 percent in 1991. Of course, a substantial part of the price increase (we estimate 50 to 70 percent) must be attributed to other price shocks: sweeping price liberalization, eliminating subsidies, and switching to world prices for payment of Russian oil imports and other raw materials.

The unexpectedly high initial price jump created another cushion in the form of a radical decline of real wages by 26 percent during the first year of economic reform. To some extent, the drop of real wages was seen as an unavoidable belt-tightening policy during the transition and negotiated with trade unions. But such a pronounced drop of real wages, however, came as a surprise, which, for the benefit of price stability, was only gradually undone by subsequent wage demands. It helped that the general public seemed to suffer from a money illusion. The outspoken criticism regarding the price rise was soothed by payrolls which were, in nominal terms, growing, although in real terms declining. Incomes policy was also put in place penalizing the wage increase above legally approved regulatory limits.

The two cushions which came into existence at the very start of economic reform raised the implicit question about minimizing the speed of their flattening. In other words, a reasonably low real exchange rate appreciation was required on the part of the first cushion and temperate wage increases on the part of the second. At this point, prudent monetary management proved to be a key precondition for keeping inflation on a leash. Initially, we orchestrated a restrictive monetary policy. Later, we projected a neutral stance of monetary policy, but even then, we might have effectively, although unintentionally, practiced some restriction due to an underestimated decline of money velocity.

Proper credit should be given to administrative controls. Credit ceilings, interest rate ceilings, and even moral suasion contributed to the outcome that, in an environment crowded with discontinuities and institutional reforms, credit extension and the growth of the money supply did not get out of the hands of the monetary authorities. Their widespread usage makes sense when the role of interest rates in the transmission mechanism of monetary policy is unpredictable due to badly functioning financial markets. Moreover, there was little help in insisting that interest rates be strictly positive in real terms because high interest rates would only provoke the moral hazard phenomenon instead of encouraging efficient allocation of credit. At the same time, negative real interest rates did little harm to savings as countervailing precautionary motives encouraged the propensity to save. This, however, was only temporary. To sum up, in the above corset which allowed no escape from a tight control of the money supply, one can find one of the secrets of successful disinflation in the Czech transition economy.

Last but not least, fiscal policies were tight or neutral but never expansionary. The coordinated anti-inflationary actions of the central bank and government stemmed from a shared philosophy that high inflation would not be conducive to progress with reforms and that it would increase the costs of transition while simultaneously delaying its benefits.

It is true that the application of tight monetary and fiscal policies was followed by a steep decline in output (by around one-fourth between 1990 and 1993). Many commentators even drew parallels with the Great Depression of the 1930s. But that view was misleading as it mixed up the cyclical reasons for the latter with the structural and institutional factors of the former. It also neglected the severe external shocks that hit the bloc of Central European countries at the time. Let me recall, for example, the collapse of trade between the former CMEA countries, German reunification, the wars in Yugoslavia and the Persian Gulf, and the specific disintegration disturbances from the dissolution of Czechoslovakia. After all this, the economy did a marvelous job in absorbing the shocks without undermining the general consensus on the objectives of a radical reform.

With the benefit of hindsight, we can say that the Czech heterodox approach—I would call it the strategy of a padded exchange rate anchor inserted in the money supply corset—has been reasonably successful. Within a half year following sweeping price liberalization, monthly inflation settled down to average levels not far above single-digit yearly figures and kept staying on these levels, disregarding temporary blips caused by the adjustment of administratively regulated prices and the introduction of the VAT tax reform.

Coping with external sector deregulation

Determining the point of time beyond which an economy ceases to be a transition one seems a matter of convention. Critical observers would expect to cross the point rather later; incumbents might be biased toward seeing it earlier. Whatever set of criteria we use, the fact is that around the middle of 1993 the Czech economy entered a new economic landscape. While in the previous stage, liberalization and deregulation measures were to a large extent superimposed by the rigidities of institutional reforms, in the subsequent phase, these frictions waned and the wheels of a market-based economy started to turn round more and more smoothly. The national economy climbed out of the transformation recession and showed the first signs of a robust recovery, interrupted by the breakup of Czechoslovakia.

A major systemic change can be seen in the rapid capital account liberalization and the firm heading toward full convertibility of the Czech currency. Both of these processes had already been entrenched in the initial package of the so-called internal convertibility that guaranteed domestic businesses free access to hard currencies needed to meet demands associated with trade-related transactions. The arrangement was also designed to create a friendly environment for foreign investment.

In the second half of 1995, the opening of the Czech economy was, to a large extent, completed. On October 1, 1995, the Czech Republic accepted the obligations of Article VIII of the IMF, meaning that the Czech currency became free of any restrictions for current account transactions. The new Foreign Exchange Act went even further by lifting some capital restrictions. Thus, in the space of five years, the Czech Republic succeeded in opening up its economy to a degree of capital mobility that took most industrial countries several decades to realize. This rapid opening reflected, however, not only the rapid pace of economic reforms in the country, but also the radically different conditions in today's world financial markets that make capital controls far more difficult and costly to maintain.

Increased openness of the economy created the possibility of large capital inflows, while progress with privatization, structural reform, and improving macroeconomic indicators (reflected in the upgrades of ratings by major rating agencies) supplied necessary incentives for foreign investors. As a result, the Czech economy became one of the favorite targets of capital inflows.

A more liberal environment also made more visible the conflict with the so-called uncovered interest rate parity condition. The point was that prevailing interest rate differentials, having their origin predominantly in the inflation differential, became fundamentally inconsistent with the regime hitherto of a fixed exchange rate. Economic agents, spared from taking account of exchange rate risk, tried to exploit lower interest rates abroad. This incentive was particularly strong for domestic firms, thus making foreign borrowing the largest item in the structure of capital inflows, and true as well for the short-term speculative capital. It took some time for the inconsistency among fixed exchange rate, interest rate differentials, and capital mobility to develop openly, but once it developed, the Czech Republic received a massive capital inflow which peaked in 1995. In that year the share of net capital inflow in GDP reached a world record level of 18.4 percent. During this period of inflow, the official external reserves witnessed an unprecedented increase from almost zero at the beginning of 1993 to $14 billion (U.S.) at the end of 1995. The share of the change in net foreign assets as a part of the change in the money supply doubled from 45 percent in 1993 to 80 percent in the last quarter of 1995.

Describing the disinflation efforts of the time boils down to a description of the techniques we used to sterilize capital inflows. The first reaction was to close the window for central bank refinancing facilities and switch government-owned deposits from banks to the central bank. A substantial role was then given to open market operations in order to mop up excess liquidity from the commercial banking sector. We also increased reserve requirements and experimented with a sort of "throwing sand into the wheels" measure by limiting the nonresident short-term open positions of commercial banks.

Sterilized interventions to support a fixed exchange rate pose policy dilemmas, and this was no different in the Czech Republic. The massive sterilization prevented interest rate differentials from diminishing and so enticed even larger amounts of foreign borrowing and speculative capital. At the same time, it did not eliminate, but only postponed, the upward pressure on prices since the stock of short-term securities held by banks in their portfolios acted as standby liquidity for credit formation which was drawn once banks started to dispose of the papers by selling them back to the central bank. Last but not least, there were considerable costs to the central bank's profit and loss statement.

The policy of sterilized interventions may thus reach a point beyond which benefits from maintaining an exchange rate anchor are completely undone by mounting inflationary pressures through excessive capital inflows. The Czech Republic thus can add one more piece to the already extensive evidence that a fixed exchange rate is not, in itself, sufficient to reduce inflation to levels achieved in the industrial countries. The underlying logic of this assertion should, however, be properly understood. The main reason is the coincidence of two events: first, the growing openness of a transition economy which gradually destroys the previous corset of autonomous monetary policy, and second, the occurrence of this opening at a time when the economy has not yet succeeded in realigning its fundamentals with those of industrial countries, inflation rate differentials being one of the most pervasive disturbances. The higher inflation then creates problems both for the current and capital accounts of balance of payments. In the former case, it leads to an excessive real exchange rate appreciation, while in the latter, to an excessive increase in liquidity through capital inflows. Both reasons make the fixed exchange rate arrangement vulnerable to a potential confidence crisis.

In the second half of 1995, the time was ripe for rethinking the exchange rate regime. The change came in February 1996 when the five-year-old arrangement was modified by adopting a horizontal wider band: 7.5 percent in both directions from the unchanged central parity. Whether, and how long, it will be possible to maintain this more flexible exchange rate regime depends on many factors. Among the most prominent is the speed with which it would be possible to use the newly regained—though only partial—freedom of monetary policy to reduce excess liquidity in the economy, and how fast continued restructuring will result in productivity growth, justifying exchange rate appreciation.

The episode of skyrocketing capital inflow served as a final exam testing our capability to manage monetary affairs primarily by market instruments, considering that administrative controls—credit and interest rate ceilings—were already phased out. We learned that linkages between money stock, exchange rate, and interest rates became more established once financial markets grew out of their infancy and started to communicate with the external environment. The Czech National Bank policies seemed to pass the test because inflation kept declining, although, at the present time, the further reduction of inflation is becoming increasingly more difficult. These policies also had to cope with a less cooperative mood of fiscal policies, which were partly infected by the contagion of the political cycle.

Challenges of further disinflation

Where are we now and where are we heading? A succinct answer could be that we successfully accomplished the rougher part of disinflation by getting the annual price increase slightly under 10 percent. Compared with other post-communist countries this result looks satisfactory. On the other hand, the result is less impressive from the point of view of new benchmarks flashing in the form of inflation levels achieved in European Union countries. From this perspective, further disinflation in the Czech Republic still remains an overriding concern. We feel, however, that the difficulty of our job resembles a vacuum pump: while it is relatively easy for this device to exhaust the first 90 percent of the air, most of the effort is spent exhausting the remainder.

A major problem common to all post-transition economies lies in the compatibility of pushing inflation down with a robust economic growth. Facing this tradeoff, our comparative advantage within the group of formerly command economies consists in a tradition to value price stability. The tradition stretches back as far as to the 1920s when Czechoslovakia avoided hyperinflation that plagued all other neighboring countries and even central planners more or less followed suit. Despite this favorable setup, however, disinflation remains a sensitive issue. I would not claim that our problems are unknown to other central bankers in other times. But the still nonstandard economic environment with surviving rigidities does not offer straightforward hints and solutions. Let me go through a short list of issues we are debating and pondering the right policy responses.

First of all, two structural features are going to make disinflation difficult or even painful. The first is connected to the fact that a major part of the CPI (up to 60 percent) is composed of administered prices subject to a long-term deregulatory timetable and agricultural prices dependent on weather and other external factors. (It should be noted that the CPI is a narrow sample of consumer prices, so the share of regulated prices included in it considerably underestimates the true extent of price liberalization reaching, itself, about 95 percent.) This means that we are faced primarily with a supply-shock driven inflation which the general wisdom usually recommends accommodating in a piecemeal fashion. The alternative is to instigate a sort of Big Bang to get rid of the inflation frozen in regulated prices through a one-off price jump probably accompanied by a social compensation scheme.

Secondly, our research confirms different propensities to inflate in the tradable and nontradable sectors (7 percent against 14 percent in 1995). This gap is quite understandable as it reflects softer market conditions for firms oriented toward domestic outlets as opposed to firms that must compete internationally. The consequence, however, is that tightening of monetary policy tends to hit firms in the two sectors differently, because the same nominal borrowing interest rates represent a lower real burden for those firms whose output prices are growing at a faster rate.

As far as operating procedures are concerned, some observers would argue that we gave up the old anchor in the form of the fixed exchange rate. So should we look for a new one? Needless to say, our exchange rate anchor has not been completely abandoned, only its chain has been loosened. In other words, we opted for a wider but horizontal band with the old central parity, unlike many countries in similar conditions which operate with a crawling peg or diagonal band. Putting aside the gyrations caused by short-term capital movements, the exchange rate may thus continue to perform its disciplinary role, which substantially increased after the cushion from the initial devaluations was eroded by the steadily appreciating real exchange rate.

A delicate issue arises whether we could even afford some nominal exchange rate appreciation to fight inflation. This idea has been constantly provoked by calculations of an exchange rate based on purchasing power parity (PPP), which suggests a still high undervaluation of the Czech currency. Some Czech economists even infer from the gap between the PPP and market exchange rates a kind of "hands-off approach" for monetary policy, arguing that fiddling with monetary tightening will not bring forth sustainable disinflation but only prolongs the time needed for domestic prices to catch up with the world level. On the other hand, should we believe in a substantial undervaluation on the background of prevailing current account deficits (4.1 percent of GDP in 1995 with a worsening outlook for 1996)? Are not the trade deficits rather a sign of currency overvaluation? In that case, triggering exchange rate appreciation for the sake of lower inflation may prove an overkill which is certain not to do any good.

A growing number of countries resort to inflation targeting as an alternative procedure for central bank disinflation policies. We are also carefully analyzing what could or could not be accomplished by this approach. Some observers maintain that we should cash in on our, so far, sound anti-inflationary track record and use inflation targets for breaking inflation inertia. The point, however, is whether the credibility we have accumulated up to now is strong enough to persuade the public that there will be a penalty paid for diverting inflation from its desired downward trajectory so that the public itself will opt deliberately for only tolerated price increases. I would claim that if the public is not educated in this respect through central bank rhetoric and, if that is not enough, through persuasive tightening measures, inflation targeting may become an easy way to lose credibility.

A key condition is the cooperative attitude of other economic policies. Up till now, there were no serious rifts in the concerted dialogue with the government. We hope that this feature will be preserved even if inflation proves more persistent and stubborn than we previously expected.

Endnote

[1]Let me give some examples:

(a) A full-speed attack on distortions inherited from a planned economy, including sweeping price liberalization, elimination of enterprise subsidies, fear of mass layoffs, and so on, gives birth to many uncertainties which are matched by prudential savings of the household sector at the expense of consumption. This deflationary adjustment is conducive to nascent price stability. Later, however, depressed consumption will spur a consumption wave; the stronger position of higher income groups will tend to encourage demands, particularly for imported goods.

(b) A scheme of rapid privatization often induces short-sighted behavior on the part of incumbent managers who react by shrinking investment expenditures. Lower investment demand then contributes to the current price stability. Later, however, deferred investment plans join forces in an investment wave which pushes wages and prices up or fuels the current account deficit.

(c) A program for bold external sector deregulation quickly removes barriers to capital mobility that, in conjunction with higher profit opportunities in a transition economy, is followed by a wave of capital inflow.

(d) Privatization and demonopolization of state-owned companies, as well as a boom of small and medium enterprises, lead to the monetization of many formerly intrafirm transactions. This structural feature may result in an underestimation of the decline of money velocity. Later, when institutional changes slow down and the pace of financial innovation accelerates, the trend in velocity seems to pick up. The consequences of this so-called velocity wave for monetary management are far-reaching. While on the downward slope of the wave, the politically more palatable neutral character of monetary policy may actually mask the restrictiveness; being situated on the upward slope implies that an unpopular tightening of monetary policy may prove "too little, too late."

(e) This list of "supersonic" waves can be completed with a fifth one: the expansion-consolidation pattern in the banking sector. I will not pursue this line of argument which is a topic for a separate symposium.

General Discussion:
How Have Central Banks Reduced Inflation? —Practical Issues

Chairman: Gordon Thiessen

Mr. Thiessen: Thanks very much, Josef. I won't make any comments, but I will open the floor for discussion. There is a question back there.

Mr. Barnes: Donald Brash quoted falling bond yields as an indicator of declining inflation expectations, and clearly this has occurred in every industrialized country. However, if you look at the standard deviation of bond returns, you see that bond volatility has been extremely high in recent years. I don't think it is plausible to say that is simply fluctuations in real rates. Clearly, bond investors are the real skeptics in terms of believing that price stability is close at hand and I wondered if the experience in New Zealand sheds any lights on this. Has bond volatility declined in line with declining bond yields? Or are they still high as in other industrialized countries?

Mr. Thiessen: Let's gather a few questions, and then let the panel comment. One right at the back.

Mr. Darby: This panel reminds us of the variety of monetary experience. And Donald Brash's remarks particularly brought us back to the charming situation of a subset of countries in which we are worried about the bias in measures of price inflation. That is our problem compared to some of our fellow countries. This morning, Chairman Greenspan emphasized, particularly with his examples in the medical and software areas, the bias in measures of inflation. That illustrates one of the important things about biases—they are not constant. They change. Lynne Zucker and I have examined, for example, movements in where our science is working—what fields. In the recent National Research Council report compared to the one from a dozen years ago, we see a vast movement of our scientific input toward the biological sciences, precisely areas where any advances are not measured. We still have the hospital day problem for that whole side as we begin to talk about curing cancer, curing AIDS. Those are not counted as productivity increases or output increases. So not only do we have a problem of a bias, but particularly a changing bias—in this case an increasing bias in the CPI. So I think that is another issue to lay on the table. Not only do we need to estimate that bias, but we need to deal with the changes in it.

Ms. Gronkiewicz-Waltz: I have shared the experience of Jacob and Josef for the past years. I have a question for Josef. I haven't noticed that much flexibility in your bank, and I wanted to ask why, because when we started to be more flexible, some of our problems disappeared.

Mr. Hale: In analyzing the capital inflows that you referred to last year, do you distinguish in your policy decisionmaking between foreign direct investment and portfolio capital flows? And could you elaborate perhaps on the composition of them? And for Don Brash: Could you explain to us why you think New Zealand's index-linked bonds yield almost 6 percent, compared to a 3 to 4 percent range for Britain, Canada, Australia, and Sweden?

Mr. Sinai: I have one question for Jacob and then one for the entire panel. How is Israel responding to the generic issue, at least for inflation targeting purposes, of shocks—if there have been shocks, whether from the demand side, supply side, or exchange rate side—where most recently the financial shock or problem or crisis of the Provident Funds difficulties, whether it was a central bank response that may or may not have deviated with the inflation targeting goals. And, as a related central bank question really for all, when there is a crisis shock in Orange County, a stock market crash, exchange rate crisis, Mexican government default risk, financial fragility, and any of these kinds of things happen, is the way to treat it on a case-by-case situation? Or is there some general approach of dealing with the generic issue of shocks that you would offer up?

Mr. Thiessen: Let's let our panelists respond to that group of questions; then if we have time, we will go back for another set. Josef, why don't we start with you?

Mr. Tosovsky: I will start with the question which was directed to me from Hanna Gronkiewicz-Waltz. Concerning our exchange rate policy, I would say we are flexible in using the band. In fact, we introduced a band when the expectations on appreciation and devaluation were more or less balanced. I would say we surprised the market, because it was done just before the elections and nobody expected us to make a move at that time. We haven't intervened in the market for at least two or three months. Now the supply and demand for foreign exchange is quite balanced in our country. Inflow is just consumed by deficits on the current account. My third comment is that there is a small tendency to appreciation and it accelerated yesterday. We are now in the revaluation part of the band—4.5 percent from the center parity. We didn't want to intervene up to now, because once the central bank intervenes, we show our cards. We would give the signal of the level we would like to defend. We want to create the Damocles' sword for potential speculation at least by rhetoric that we will use the whole band—7.5 percent—up or down, because our interest rate differential between our money market and especially the money market in deutsche marks is about 8.5 percent. Hence there is still potential for speculation on interest rate differential should there be low exchange rate risk. The second question was from David (Hale). David, we have been analyzing the inflow of capital very carefully. We have been analyzing when buying permanently, intervening on the market, and buying excess foreign exchange from the market, and our reserves were growing. We were basically making calculations of what are our reserves and what are our borrowed reserves. And, of course, we had specific details of direct foreign portfolio investment. The majority of the money came from long-term investors that made some huge investments. For example, Czech Telecom represented 17 percent of the inflow of capital and that percentage amounted to $1.3 billion (U.S.). And there were other examples. So we took this into consideration. I could even evaluate the proportion of short-term hot money, because once we widened the band, we surprised the market and some investors started immediately to liquidate their portfolios. So within the first three days after the introduction of the band, we lost $660 million from $14 billion. This is probably the size of the short-term speculative capital which was in our reserves. In other words, we don't think we are exposed too much or in too fragile a position in this respect.

Mr. Thiessen: Jacob Frenkel.

Mr. Frenkel: Concerning the question Allen Sinai asked about difficulties for monetary control or for monetary policy when there is capital market turmoil—in particular, when holders of Provident Funds want to cash in. In the last two months, the name of Alan Greenspan was mentioned in the Israeli press more than any other time, because everyone said, "Well, last time it happened in 1987, Alan Greenspan did so-and-so." At the Bank of Israel, we have announced that we will provide the necessary liquidity for Provident Funds, if they need to mobilize resources in order to repay the holders of Provident Funds. At the same time, we have announced that we have the monetary instruments to reabsorb all of the monetary injections that may result from it. It was very important that the two announcements be made simultaneously—one to calm capital markets and the other to avoid the message that inflation might be at risk. And, indeed, both of them have been made. I want to discuss a question that David Hale raised, which was about the composition of capital inflow. When you raise interest rates significantly, of course, it induces capital inflow, which is a problem if you do not allow your exchange rate to vary. If you do not allow your exchange rate to vary, then you basically give a sure bet of interest rate differentials that everyone can use to come in and make a killing. Again, this is the reason why in the Israeli case we allow the exchange rate to vary fully within the band—literally up to the boundaries of the band, so as to manifest whatever maximal risk premium that can come up in order to make sure that it is not just interest rate differentials that cause it. Last year about two-thirds of our capital inflow was the short-term variety and one-third was foreign direct investment. This year the proportions have switched—four-fifths are real investment and only one-fifth is short-term.

Mr. Brash: Several points have been raised relevant to New Zealand. First, does our experience with bonds tell us anything about the question of bond volatility and the relationship with inflationary expectations? Unfortunately, I don't think it does because the bond rates in New Zealand today are largely a function of what is happening on Wall Street. If U.S. bond rates move, ours tend to move to a similar extent after adjusting for the somewhat higher holding costs because of much higher short-term interest rates and some additional risk premium. So we don't learn much independently by looking at the New Zealand market. On the question of why indexed bonds are yielding close to 6 percent at the moment, I think there are two reasons why they are yielding markedly more than, for example, in the United Kingdom. I think the principal reason is the difference in tax treatment. In the United Kingdom, as I understand it, the inflation increment in the indexed bonds is not subject to tax; in New Zealand it is, as indeed it is in Australia. And for that reason, yields in New Zealand and Australia are similar. The Australian yields are lower, but there is not nearly as much difference as there is between the New Zealand yield and the U.K. yields. I must say, I was very keen on having the inflation increment not taxed. I thought there should be an instrument which was effectively yielding a post-tax real return. I was finally persuaded by the Treasury that the tax-avoidance opportunities raised by exempting the principal adjustment made it difficult to proceed that way. The difference in tax treatment is the main reason for the difference in yields. I think the second reason is frankly we have a very small history of issuing. I think we have had only four tenders to date, and there is a significant illiquidity premium as well. Mr. Chairman, if I could just make two other comments. First, about handling shocks. We were one of the few central banks which in 1987 did not ease in response to the share market fall, and we were subject to very severe criticism in New Zealand for that. I think it illustrates Mervyn King's point that when you are in a very early stage of disinflation, you have much less flexibility to respond to these kinds of shocks than you have when you have a long track record as the Fed has. So, for better or worse, we did not show much flexibility at that time. My final point on the exchange rate: I guess we would all have to accept that if you get strong capital inflow, you almost certainly are going to get an appreciation of the real exchange rate one way or the other. And, it seems to me, you either get that through an increase in the nominal exchange rate with the domestic inflation rate held low, or you get it typically by trying to hold the nominal exchange rate down with consequential increases in domestic liquidity and domestic inflation, unless you are very successful indeed in sterilizing that capital inflow. In New Zealand we clearly preferred the rise in nominal exchange rate with low domestic inflation. But undoubtedly if the capital inflow becomes volatile, you push your real economy around in a way which is less than fully desirable.

Mr. Thiessen: I don't want to try and summarize the sessions this morning, but I think there are some interesting themes that come through. Certainly, from a practicing central banker's point of view, the use of targets to control inflation has made most of us who have those targets feel that monetary policy does indeed work better. It makes it easier to explain what you are doing and why you are doing it. It does not avoid having to make some difficult decisions about how you respond to shocks, how quickly after you have been pushed off your targets you should go back. But keeping the focus of monetary policy on long-term price stability, on the inflation-control targets that you have defined, I think, on balance, gives you the right kind of response over time. The other interesting issue that a number of people have mentioned is the focus on transparency. Since we all want to make our monetary policy objectives more credible and the responses in markets more appropriate, I think the focus on transparency is an interesting one, and one that is quite widespread in central banks now. I'm struck by the major change that has occurred over the last ten years or so in terms of central banks wishing to make clear—as Don Brash was saying—what they are doing and why they are doing it. While I think that whole process has been working reasonably well for us, I don't think it really deals with the hard question that Alan Greenspan raised for us—which is the issue of defining your price stability more precisely than most of us have felt comfortable with up until now. He and perhaps others of you have mentioned that challenge. I think that is an issue we need to deal with in the period ahead.

Lessons From the Stabilization Process in Argentina, 1990-1996

Domingo Cavallo

Hyperinflation exploded in 1989. It was the final stage of a chronic inflationary process that began in 1945 and lasted forty-five years. From the beginning of the century until the end of World War II, Argentina had been characterized by stable prices. Internal prices only reflected fluctuations related to events in the world economy, such as the two world wars and the Great Depression of the 1930s.

After 1945, the combination of industrial protectionism, redistribution of income based on increased wages, and growing state intervention in the economy touched off the inflationary process shown in Table 1. After so many years of inflation, there is a general consensus among economists about the mechanics of this process. A persistent fiscal deficit, increasingly financed by monetary emission, caused more and more frequent devaluations of the local currency. The acceleration of inflation resulted from the demonetization of the economy as the public tried to avoid the inflation tax.

During the last decade of this period of chronic and growing inflation, the social and economic costs of inflation became evident. In the 1980s, the economy, increasingly disoriented by inflation, declined at a rate of 1 percent per year. Employment continued to grow 1.6 percent per year but the 2.6 percent average annual decline in the productivity of the employed was the clearest evidence that only unproductive activities were expanding. This was especially

Table 1
Argentine Inflation by Decade
(Annual rates of change in the consumer price index)

Period	Average	Maximum	Minimum
1920-1929	-1.7	17.1	-15.9
1930-1939	-0.3	13.0	-13.9
1940-1949	10.6	31.1	-0.3
1950-1959	30.3	111.6	3.7
1960-1969	23.3	31.9	7.6
1970-1979	132.9	444.0	13.6
1980-1989	750.4	4,923.3	87.6

Source: INDEC

the case of the public sector but it also existed in the private sector, which continued to be strongly protected from foreign competition and involved in financial speculation. Government expenditure during the 1980s represented, on average, 33 percent of GDP, while the fiscal deficit was about 5 percent of GDP.

In spite of the fact that the currency was strongly undervalued during the whole decade, exports grew at a rate of only 3 percent annually and imports contracted at a rate of approximately 7 percent annually.

The year 1989 was catastrophic. Government expenditure reached 35.6 percent of GDP and the fiscal deficit climbed to 7.6 percent of GDP. From December to December, inflation almost reached 5,000 percent; at the peak of March 1989 to March 1990, it was over 20,000 percent. Gross domestic product fell more than 6 percent and imports fell 21 percent that year. The government could not ignore the strong public demand for the price stability that had been absent for forty-five years.

The stabilization plan

In 1990, the government began to completely overhaul the organization of the Argentine economy. It included (a) comprehensive liberalization of foreign trade and capital movements, (b) the privatization of public enterprises and the deregulation of the economy, (c) reduction of the bureaucratic apparatus of the public sector and the reconstruction of the tax system, and (d) the creation of a new monetary system.

Government expenditure fell drastically from 35.6 percent of GDP in 1989 to 29.8 percent in 1990, and continued to fall to 27 percent of GDP by 1995. The fiscal deficit also decreased sharply from 7.6 percent of GDP in 1989 to 2.3 percent in 1990, and from 1991 onward, it fluctuated around 0 percent, accompanying the economic cycle.

The prices of goods and services began to be freely determined in competitive and open markets. As of April 1991, the public could freely choose the currency used in all financial and commercial transactions. Among the alternatives was the convertible peso, which came with the transformation of the central bank into a virtual currency board. The central bank must back each peso in circulation with an equivalent amount or gold or foreign exchange, permitting holders of pesos to exchange, at any moment, one peso for one American dollar.

The same law that created this monetary system included the prohibition of indexation clauses or any other monetary alterations in the terms of contracts. Wage agreements resulting from collective bargaining had to be accompanied by agreements on productivity.

The disinflationary process was continuous and sustained: Inflation fell from 1,344 percent in 1990 to 84 percent in 1991, 17.5 percent in 1992, 7.4 percent in 1993, 3.9 percent in 1994, 1.6 percent in 1995 and 0 percent in the twelve-month period between June 1995 and June 1996.

Table 2

The Argentine Stabilization in Numbers

(decade of the 1980s and 1989 through 1996)

	80 to 89	89	90	91	92	93	94	95	96
Annual Inflation rate	750.4	4,923.3 (20,266)[1]	1,343.9	84.0	17.5	7.4	3.9	1.6	0.0
GDP growth (annual %)	-0.9	-6.2	0.1	8.9	8.7	6.0	7.4	-4.4	3.0[2]
Export growth (annual %)	3.0	4.9	29.0	-3.0	2.1	7.2	20.8	32.4	4.0[3]
Import growth (annual %)	-6.7	-21.0	-3.0	103.0	79.7	12.8	28.6	-6.8	7.0[3]
Current Account of the Balance of Payments (% of GDP)	-2.4	-1.7	3.3	-0.2	-2.4	-2.7	-3.3	-0.9	-0.9
Public spending (% of GDP)	33.1	35.6	29.8	29.3	28.7	28.4	27.2	27.0	27.0
Budget deficit (-) (% of GDP)	-5.8	-7.6	-2.3	-0.3	0.2	1.2	0.1	-1.0	-2.0
Foreign reserves (billions of dollars)	3.1	3.8	6.4	9.0	12.4	17.4	17.9	18.5	20.0[4]
Employment growth (%)	1.6	1.0	1.1	4.3	2.7	1.3	-0.2	-2.6	0.0
Productivity per person employed (Index 1980=100)	100[5]	76.6	74.2	79.5	85.6	89.9	97.9	95.2	99.3
Share of household below the line of poverty (Total Greater Buenos Aires)		26.2[6]	29.0	29.5	19.0	14.4	13.3	13.0	17.2

[1] March 1989 with respect to March 1988

[2] Second quarter of 1996 with respect to same period of 1995 First six months of 1996 with respect to same period of 1995

[3] First six months of 1996 with respect to same period of 1995

[4] As of June 30, 1996

[5] Corresponds to the year 1980

[6] Average for years 1988 and 1989

Sources: Secretaría de Programación Económica, B.C.R.A

Table 3
The Recession After the Mexican Crisis

	1994	1995				1996	
		1Q	2Q	3Q	4Q	1Q	2Q
Inflation (annual percent)	3.9	4.4	3.7	2.2	1.6	0.2	0
GDP growth (annual percent)	7.4	3.2	-4.6	-8.1	-7.7	-3.2	3.0
Export growth[1] (percent)	20.8	48.5	47.7	23.9	13.9	4.3	3.3
Import growth (percent)[1]	28.6	6.6	-10.3	-12.9	-9.0	-4.9	19.3
Trade balance (billions of dollars)	-4.2	-0.3	1.9	0.7	0	-0.3	0.6[3]
Current Account of the Balance of Payments (Billions of dollars)	-9.4	-1.8	0.9	-0.2	-1.3	-1.4	
Foreign reserves (billions of dollars)	17.9	12.5	15.0	15.2	18.5	18.8	20.0
Bank deposits (billions)	47.2	41.1	42.1	43.4	45.2	49.3	52.2
Unemployment (percent)	12.2[2]		18.4		16.4		17.1
Persons employed ('000)	10,609		10,307		10,348		10,343

[1]Change from the same period of the previous year

[2]October 1994

[3]April-May 1996

Sources: Secretaría de Programación Económica/B.C.R.A.

The new monetary system encouraged a strong increase in the external reserves that back the monetary liabilities of the central bank. Reserves went from $3.8 billion at the end of 1989 to $17.9 billion at the end of 1994. This trend was reversed when the fall in the level of confidence following the devaluation of the Mexican peso led to capital flight from Argentina: by the end of March 1995, reserves had fallen to $12.5 billion. But the policies adopted to face the crisis reestablished confidence. By the end of June 1996, reserves had already surpassed $20 billion.

Between 1991 and 1994, GDP grew at an average annual rate of 7.7 percent. However, due to capital flight, after the second quarter of 1995 the economy entered a period of recession. The recession lasted a year and in the second quarter of 1996, the economy was already showing signs of a recovery at an annual rate of 3 percent.

Exports, virtually stagnant in the previous decade, grew vigorously during the period of the stabilization. Imports, which had grown much more than exports until 1994, shrank during 1995 with the onset of the recession.

Despite the strong increase in the GDP, employment grew relatively slowly, and suffered a decline during the recession that began in 1995. The poor performance of the economy in relation to employment is explained by the substantial increase in worker productivity, which by mid-1996, had reached the level of 1980. The rapid growth of the economy during the period permitted the transformation of numerous low-productivity or unproductive activities that had been artificially created during the decade of the 1980s into productive efforts. However, this was not sufficient to employ all of the growing labor force. Thus, beginning in 1992, the unemployment rate increased and reached a peak of 18.4 percent of the active population in May 1995. Since then, there has been a slight decrease in unemployment. The survey of May 1996 recorded a rate of 17 percent, still three times higher than that of the 1980s.

The percentage of households below the poverty line (an average of 26 percent in the late 1980s, which had risen to 29 percent in the period of hyperinflation) fell to 13 percent in 1994 but went up to 17 percent during the recession of 1995.

In July of 1996, with the appearance of a fiscal deficit during the first half of the year that was greater than had been expected (approximately 2 percent of GDP), a discussion began about measures to contain government expenditure and increases in some taxes in order to reach a balanced budget during 1997. The reappearance of the fiscal deficit in the second half of 1994 was caused by automatic increases in social security expenditure, as well as in the elimination or reduction of economically distorting taxes, especially payroll taxes, that had been implemented to encourage increased productivity and employment.

Beginning in early 1995, facing the risk of running out of financing, evident since the onset of the Mexican crisis, the government was able to limit social security expenditure. In July 1996, these restrictive measures were reinforced, limiting family allowances and the expenses of the health system for the elderly. Regarding taxes, the April 1995 increase in the value added tax from 18 percent to 21 percent to face the Mexican crisis was maintained. Recently, a proposal to increase tax collection by eliminating exemptions from several taxes has been presented to Congress.

But beyond these fiscal adjustments, the reduction and eventual elimination of the deficit will result from economic recovery. This has already been demonstrated by the effect on tax revenue in July 1996 of the 3 percent increase in output between the second quarter of 1995 and the second quarter of 1996. In fact, in July 1996, the highest historical level of tax collection for any July was attained (also the third highest monthly level of tax collection on record).

Finally, a strong reduction in expenditure and the fiscal deficit of the provinces is already being observed due to the adjustments that they were obligated to carry out in response to the flight of deposits that affected provincial state banks since the beginning of 1995. Those institutions had continued to provide financing to their respective governments, running counter to the restrictions imposed by the Convertibility Law on the central bank and the national treasury. Forced by the lack of financing and encouraged by the conditional support of the federal government, most of the provinces decided to privatize their banks and public companies, as well as to reform the social security systems for their employees.

The combination of the sharp increase in bank deposits that occurred after the effects of the Mexican crisis had subsided and the accumulation of contributions to the new pension funds reflect an increasing trend in domestic savings that is already being transformed into medium- and long-term credit offered at moderate interest rates. Mortgage credits for housing, absent for decades in Argentina, promise to become the driving force for the construction sector. This could touch off a substantial increase in employment, as in Chile after 1984.

Lessons of the Argentine experience

The main lesson of the Argentine stabilization experience is that the elimination of inflation is possible even when an economy has been flogged by that disease for decades. It is not true that in Latin American economies it is necessary to accept annual inflation rates of around 10 percent, even after many years of searching for stability.

Another important conclusion of the Argentine experience is that the fiscal adjustment, understood as a reduction of the government expenditure, as well as the reduction and the elimination of budget deficits are the keys to stabilization after decades of instability, the origins of which are mainly found in the monetary financing of persistent fiscal deficits.

For a society in economic chaos due to inflation, the imposition of basic discipline on both the private and public sectors is of special importance. External and internal competition—achieved through the opening of the economy, deregulation, and the privatization of public companies—is an excellent disciplining mechanism for the private sector. The budget is the disciplining mechanism for the public sector. In order to achieve the transparency necessary for the markets and the budget to function efficiently, the monetary system is the key.

The success of stabilization in Argentina is neither due to the quantitative control of the national currency, nor due to fixing its value in terms of the dollar because, in a strict sense, these two monetary policy rules were not applied. What the government offered the public was freedom to choose the currency to be used in its transactions and for its savings. In practice, the choice was given between the American dollar, that the public had already transformed into its currency during hyperinflation, and the convertible peso that began to be offered by the central bank. In accordance with the Convertibility Law, this currency should be at least as stable as the dollar. For this reason, from the outset its creation was limited to the quantity that could be backed by the gold and foreign currency reserves in the central bank. Freedom of choice of the currency to use, not necessarily limited to the peso and the U.S. dollar, sustained the prohibition on monetary corrections or indexation clauses in contracts. This was very important to the elimination of all vestiges of inflationary inertia in the system.

Stability in the value of the peso in relation to the dollar was not an obstacle for a healthy expansion of exports, much greater than that of the previous decade when the Argentine currency had been grossly undervalued. And it was not necessary to devalue the peso in order to reduce the deficit in the current account of the balance of payments, which, in 1994, reached 3.3 percent of GDP but fell drastically to just 0.9 percent in 1995.

The stability of the peso was vital to encouraging public officials as well as private entrepreneurs to pay greater attention to the real determinants of external competitiveness: economically distorting regulations and taxes, as well as factor productivity.

The increase in the rates of investment and productivity explain the impressive economic growth during the stabilization period. The increase in the unemployment rate could not have been avoided by allowing higher inflation. With the exception of the year of recession, aggregate demand was constantly expanding and tending toward an overheating of the economy. The causes of unemployment can be found in the institutional rigidities in the labor market and the low levels of productivity of the 1980s. In the case of both problems, the transparency attained with price stability creates a much more adequate environment conducive to improving the quality of the public policy debate and of the labor negotiations that are necessary to overcome them.

Author's note: Sonia Cavallo contributed to the preparation of this paper.

General Discussion:
Lessons from the Stabilization Process in Argentina

Chairman: Thomas M. Hoenig

Mr. Hoenig: Since we are short on time, we will take just one question.

Mr. Lipsky: Mr. Cavallo, Argentine interest rates rose significantly following your recent resignation as Minister of Finance, suggesting that at least some investors are worried about the sustainability of the fixed peso/dollar rate under the Convertibility Plan. In such circumstances and considering the theme of this seminar—is there any policy action that the central bank could undertake in order to enhance the credibility and sustainability of the plan and thus lower interest rates? Or rather, is the bank essentially a passive captive of the actions of financial market participants and of the fiscal authorities?

Mr. Cavallo: There is nothing that the central bank can do to increase credibility, except perhaps one thing that Pedro Pou, the new president of the central bank, can do—and that is not to get involved in borrowing for the government. That is one thing that I particularly dislike from recent events. I was told that yesterday Pedro Pou went to New York instead of the Secretary of the Treasury or the other Secretary of Finance to borrow for the government. It is not good if the central bank, which is responsible for keeping the reserves and backing the currency, borrows for the government. That is the only thing that he can do—perform according to the law as the head of the central bank and take care of convertibility. Let the government worry about financing the budget. That is the only advice I can give to the central bank. Now, the government can do a lot to bring down interest rates and reduce the currency risk. Particularly, it has to clarify what kind of policies it wants for the future. The appointment of Roque Fernandez as the new economic minister suggests that President Menem and the government want to continue exactly the same rules of the game and the same policies. That is the way the market read this decision the first week. Since the re-election of President Menem, let's say since May of last year, there has been a two-tier attitude in relation to the government. One attitude was evident in the speeches of President Menem and my actions and my proposals. And the other was evident in the decisions by the Peronist party in Congress and in suggestions made by the trade unions. It was argued that the attitude of the trade unions and of the Peronist party via the Congress was because of my personality, my political ambitions, and so forth. If that were true, it is perfectly good for Argentina that I am out of office. So the problem has been removed from the scenario. I am very happy to have helped resolve the problem. But now, that must be reflected in the attitude of the Peronist party through the Congress and the trade unions. If they continue to push the government for increased spending and changes in policies, that will be very bad for the country. It will be reflected in higher interest rates that will provoke another recession. If, on the contrary, President Menem does what I think he will finally do, because he is a very smart politician and he is a real political leader and a statesman, he will work hard to discipline his party and to have the Congress support the proposals by the Economy Ministry and the executive, of course, and not pay attention to what the trade union leaders have to say, because they are clearly defending vested interests. They have a crazy system of monopolies that generates a lot of corruption and a lot of inefficiencies, and they are just defending the system. So, if the government continues in the same line and there is support in Congress, interest rates should go down and the price of bonds should go up. If I were to bet on that, I would purchase Argentinian bonds, but you know that depends on everyone's confidence in the future.

Mr. Hoenig: Thank you very much, Domingo.

How Should Monetary Policy Respond to Shocks While Maintaining Long-Run Price Stability?—Conceptual Issues

John B. Taylor

This paper takes as given the principle that long-run price stability should be the central goal of monetary policy. The purpose of the paper is to discuss conceptual issues pertinent to the task of maintaining price stability once achieved.

Price stability—which because of an upward bias in measuring inflation may be defined as 1 or 2 percent measured inflation—directly raises economic well-being by increasing the efficiency of the monetary system and by reducing uncertainty about the future. There are also macroeconomic benefits of price stability. Cross-country evidence shows that countries with lower rates of inflation tend to have higher long-term economic growth rates. Moreover, a low and steady inflation rate improves cyclical performance: since the high and volatile inflation was ended in the early 1980s and a more credible and systematic monetary policy was put in place, cyclical stability has improved in the United States. From 1982 to the present, there have been two historically long economic expansions separated by a relatively short national recession. Hence, it appears that price stability yields benefits both in higher economic growth and greater output and employment stability.

In order to examine the question about how price stability should be maintained in the future, the paper first reviews some of the mistakes of the past. In particular, it examines the history of the late

1960s and 1970s in the United States when price stability was not maintained.

The paper then goes on to review what macroeconomics tells us about how monetary policy should be conducted to maintain long-run price stability. It examines how monetary policy should react to shocks and other developments in the economy such as changes in the rate of growth of potential GDP.

Learning from the past

The rise of inflation in the late 1960s and 1970s in the United States—sometimes called the Great Inflation—was an unusual historical event. It was the only major peacetime abandonment of the goal of price stability in U.S. history. As this episode fades into the distant past, it is useful to review and document the events that led to the rise in inflation and to seek lessons from them.[1] The failure of monetary policy to maintain price stability in past episodes like this should provide lessons about how monetary policy should be designed to maintain price stability in the future.

Why was price stability not maintained in the United States and many other industrialized countries during this period?

Price shocks

Some macroeconomic accounts of the 1970s point to price shocks—in particular oil price shocks—as the main source of the rise in inflation. However, in a recent paper documenting this period, economic historian Brad De Long (1996) concludes that price shocks could not have been a cause of the rise in inflation during this period. To establish the case, De Long shows that the rise of inflation was well under way before 1972 when the oil price shocks began. "The baseline inflation rate was some 5 percent per year in the early 1970s *before* there were any supply shocks...Thus I would tentatively conclude that the supply shocks of the 1970s were in large part sound and fury," De Long argues.

De Long's timing argument is convincing. It suggests that there must be other reasons for the failure to maintain price stability. Although the price shocks had temporary effects on the inflation rate—jumps in the price level—they did not have a lasting effect on the underlying inflation rate.

Time inconsistency

In another review of the Great Inflation, Michael Parkin (1993) uses the idea of "time inconsistency" to explain the rise in inflation. Without some mechanism for the central bank to establish credibility, or consistency over time, Parkin argues that the inflation rate chosen by the central bank will be too high—an inferior equilibrium in which the inflation rate exceeds what is optimal for the economy. According to the time inconsistency theory, as developed by Finn Kydland and Edward Prescott (1974), the amount by which the inflation rate exceeds the optimal rate is higher if the natural rate of unemployment is higher.

Parkin argues further that during the 1970s in the United States, there was an increase in the natural rate of unemployment and that in the 1980s and 1990s the natural rate has come down again. Hence, according to the time inconsistency theory we should have seen an increase in inflation in the 1970s and a decline in the 1980s, a rise and fall that would roughly match a rise and fall in the natural rate.

In my view, however, the time inconsistency argument is not persuasive in explaining the failure of monetary policy to maintain price stability. It would seem too easy for society to figure out the time inconsistency problem; that is, to see that the central bank's choice of the inflation rate is excessive and to fix the problem with legislation or other social arrangements. Moreover, the time inconsistency argument fails to explain why inflation rose and then fell in much of Europe during roughly the same period even though, by most estimates, the natural rate of unemployment continued to rise throughout the 1980s, rather than fall as in the United States.

Fears of another Great Depression

In rejecting the price shock explanation, De Long argues that the main reason for the Great Inflation was the memory of the Great Depression of the 1930s and people's fear of a return to high unemployment. In other words, he argues, policymakers and the public were willing to let inflation rise because, having recently experienced the Great Depression, they feared that maintaining price stability would lead to much greater unemployment.

However, there is a problem with De Long's explanation. If the experience of the Great Depression conflicted with the goal of price stability, then why was the price level so nearly stable during the 1950s and early 1960s—a period nearly as long as the Great Inflation itself? We should have seen the inflation rate rise much earlier. In this case, the timing seems off in De Long's explanation. While it is possible that the Great Inflation was just an "accident waiting to happen"—about which no one can explain the timing, I think there is a better explanation which fits the timing of the events just about perfectly.

Misleading economic theories

In my view, the rise of new macroeconomic theories and their application in practice provides much of the explanation of the abandonment of price stability in the late 1960s and 1970s. The idea that there is a long-run Phillips curve tradeoff began to appear in textbooks, newspapers, and even the *Economic Report of the President;* the inflation costs of an overheated economy according to this theory was simply a higher rate of inflation, not rising inflation. There were also the estimates indicating that the full-employment unemployment rate (now usually called the natural rate of unemployment or the NAIRU) was as low as 4 percent, although there was little evidence that price stability was consistent with this number without changes in the operation of labor markets.[2] Today most estimates of the natural rate of unemployment in the 1960s and 1970s are much closer to 6 percent than 4 percent.

I think it is clear that the Phillips curve and the low estimate of the natural rate of unemployment helped lead to the appointment of policymakers with less concern about pursuing price stability. It also probably led to monetary decisions—such as delays in raising interest rates when faced with inflationary pressures in the late 1960s and 1970s—which were inconsistent with price stability.

At first the Friedman-Phelps accelerationist revision of the Phillips curve—which was being absorbed into thinking and models by the mid-1970s—did little to change this predilection of existing theories to higher inflation. Once the underlying inflation rate had started rising, the accelerationist model was used to demonstrate how costly it would be to reduce inflation. So the inflation continued throughout the 1970s.

It was not until macroeconomics began to incorporate more reasonable models of expectations and price adjustment—largely through the research started by Robert Lucas (1972)—that the idea that the costs of disinflation might not be so great began to take hold. As this idea began to filter through the economics profession in the late 1970s and as popular opinion polls showed the public's aversion to inflation, we began to see a change in monetary policy. The monetary disinflation of the 1980s—while certainly not costless—was, at least in retrospect, the appropriate policy as the superior cyclical performance of the economy since that time makes clear. Observe that this explanation for the monetary policy mistake gets the timing right, not only for the rise in inflation, but also for the fall in inflation.

Lessons for maintaining price stability

I think there are three key lessons to draw from this brief review of the Great Inflation and its possible causes. First, beware of economists bearing strange new theories! A simple rule of thumb: check any new theory against Adam Smith and David Hume. Second, simply reviewing the history of the Great Inflation—how economic theory influenced decisions, the change in the natural rate and estimates about it, the changes in public opinion, the costs of the disinflation, and so forth—will go a long way to preventing another abandonment of the price stability goal in the future; this period, along with the Great Depression of the 1930s, should be part of the curriculum of any school for central bankers. Third, price shocks—from whatever future source—should not be viewed as a reason to abandon the goal of price stability. If a credible policy aimed at price stability is in place, then such price shocks might cause a jump in the price level, but they should not require a sacrifice in the long-run goal of price stability. The experience with price shocks in Japan in 1979 and in the United States in 1990 shows how little an effect such shocks have on the underlying inflation rate if monetary policy is devoted to price stability.

The macroeconomic setting: two propositions

As the above discussion makes clear, deciding on a monetary policy to maintain price stability requires some basic propositions of how the economy works (and that they be consistent with Hume and Smith!). Two propositions are key to the question of maintaining price stability.

The *first* proposition, about which there is now little disagreement, is that there is no *long-run* tradeoff between the rate of inflation and the rate of unemployment. In other words, over long periods higher rates of inflation are not associated with lower levels of unemployment, and lower levels of inflation are not associated with higher levels of unemployment. Historical experience with inflation and unemployment provides considerable evidence for this view.

A *second* proposition, and there is more disagreement here, is that there is a *short-run* tradeoff between inflation and unemployment. I think that the short-run tradeoff is best described in terms of a tradeoff between the *variability* of inflation and the *variability* of unemployment;[3] that is, in terms of the short-run fluctuations in these variables rather than their levels over time.

To understand this short-run tradeoff, consider a situation where the unemployment rate equals the natural rate of unemployment (or real GDP equals potential GDP) and where inflation is equal to the central bank's target rate of inflation. Now suppose that there is an upward shock to the money supply due to an unavoidable error in measurement. The monetary shock will cause real GDP to rise above potential GDP, though with a lag of several quarters. This rise in GDP will cause the inflation rate to rise above its target. In such a situation the central bank has to decide how much should we "tighten" policy to bring inflation back down.

If monetary policy is tightened sharply with short-term interest rates rising by a large amount, the inflation rate will return to target quickly, but the economy will slow down and perhaps go into recession. Alternatively, if monetary policy does not tighten so much, the inflation rate will return to target more gradually, but there will be a smaller slowdown in real GDP. One policy reaction results in more inflation stability and less real GDP stability. The other policy reaction results in less inflation stability and more real GDP stability.

The money supply shock is just an example. Other shocks would give rise to the same decision. For example, the monetary response to an unanticipated change in velocity or in potential GDP growth would determine the size of the fluctuations of inflation versus output or employment.

Price stability and inflation targets

The first proposition implies that central banks should choose a target, or a target range, for inflation and then maintain the target. A low inflation target is to be preferred to a high inflation target because higher inflation has higher costs and there are no benefits because the unemployment rate will be no lower according to the proposition.

The first proposition also implies that the central bank should not set a long-run target for the unemployment rate (or for the deviation of real GDP from potential) because according to the proposition, neither the unemployment rate nor the GDP gap can be affected by monetary policy in the long run; hence setting a target for these is beyond the scope of monetary policy.[4]

What time frame: months, quarters, years?

In reality, of course, the inflation rate would not equal the target exactly. The actual inflation rate would tend to fluctuate around the target, due to various shocks as the economy changed over time. Only on average would the inflation rate equal the target. But if one is monitoring the performance of monetary policy, over how long a time period should the average be taken?

The answer depends very much on the volatility of the inflation measure and is not the same in all countries. For example, requiring that the monthly consumer price index (CPI) inflation rate be within a narrow range of plus or minus 1 percent would not be a good policy. According to the second proposition above, it would lead to poor monetary performance because the central bank would constantly be taking corrective action which would affect the performance of real GDP. More generally, if the average is taken over too short a period of time, then the inflation rate will always be missing the target and policy will have to react too much. If the average is taken over too long a period, then large and persistent fluctuations in inflation will reduce the credibility of the policy.

For the United States, I find that a yearly measure works well in the sense that if a four quarter moving average of the inflation rate is above the target, then some corrective action should be taken.[5]

The inflation target should not be a maximum for inflation; deviations below the target are just as bad as deviations above the target.

Price level versus inflation rate

There is a subtle distinction between targeting a fixed price level versus targeting a zero inflation rate. For example, if the target price level is 100, and the price level jumps from 100 in year 1 to 103 in year 2 because of a price shock, then price level targeting requires that the central bank take corrective action to reduce the price level back to 100 in year 3. But, if a zero inflation target is the policy, then the central bank will aim to keep the price level at 103 in the third year and no new corrective action is required. (Though as the inflation rate rose to 3 percent, most prescriptions for monetary policy would require some tightening.)

If there were no short-run tradeoff, then the corrective action would have no effect on the economy and price level targeting would be a better policy. However, if proposition two holds, then the corrective action taken to return the price level to 100 may reduce output stability.

For the same reasons that trying to keep the inflation rate within too narrow a band would not be good policy, in my view, targeting a fixed price level rather than maintaining a zero inflation rate would not be a good policy either. To be sure, the answer depends on empirical magnitudes of the short-run tradeoff, but historical experience suggests to me that a zero inflation target (perhaps adjusted for measurement error) would be preferred.

How should monetary policy react to shocks?

A long-run target, or a target range, for inflation does not imply any particular policy to achieve that target. There are a whole range of policies which will give the same average target rate of inflation. The long-run average rate of inflation is determined by the long-run average rate of money growth, but there are two broad classes of policies—those that focus on monetary aggregates and those that focus on short term interest rates—that will lead to a particular long-run path for money growth.

Money growth policies

One simple money growth policy is the constant growth rate rule for the money supply put forth by Milton Friedman. According to the quantity theory of money (not a new idea), the average long-run rate of inflation will equal the average money growth rate minus the long-run growth rate of real GDP plus the velocity growth rate. Hence, as long as one knows the trend growth of velocity, one can use money growth policies to maintain any long-run rate of inflation—and price stability in particular.

There are extensions of Friedman's constant growth rate rule to allow for contingencies. For example, an alternative money growth policy would have money growth responding to real GDP or to inflation. Money growth would average the Friedman k-percent rate, but would be increased when real GDP dropped below potential GDP and decreased when real GDP rose above potential GDP. And McCallum (1988) and Meltzer (1987) have examined money growth policies which automatically adjust to shifts in velocity.

How do money growth policies react to *shocks*? One might argue that there is no reaction, but constant money growth rules imply an important automatic adjustment of interest rates to shocks as described below. First, consider a money supply policy which calls for constant growth rate of the money supply. In its most simple form, the demand for money is a demand for real money balances—the money supply divided by the price level—which is a function of real GDP and the short-term interest rate. If money growth is fixed, then there must be a relationship between the price level or its percentage change (the inflation rate), real GDP and the short-term interest rate.

In other words, the interest rate depends on the inflation rate and on real GDP. For a fixed money growth policy, a higher level of real GDP raises the interest rate as does a higher level of inflation. Thus, constant money growth policies entail an automatic adjustment of interest rates to shocks in a generally stabilizing direction: when there is an upward shock to inflation, the interest rate rises which tends to reduce spending and bring back down the inflation rate.

Interest rate policies

Interest rate policies have received much more attention than money supply policies in recent years. But there is a similarity between how money supply policies and many interest rate policies respond to shocks. The interest rate policy I have proposed, for example, (see Taylor, 1993, and discussion in the next section) has the same properties as the money growth policy discussed above: a rise of real GDP has the central bank raising the interest rate as does an increase in the inflation rate.

I think this close connection between how money growth policies and interest rate policies respond to shocks is useful for maintaining price stability. The similarity in how they react to shocks suggests that both have a role as a consistency check on the other when deciding how monetary policies should respond to shocks in order to maintain price stability. They give two reinforcing recommendations for monetary policy. And if interest rate policies become unreliable—perhaps because inflation gets very high or very low—then money supply policies can be brought into play.

Responding to real GDP

This relationship between money growth policies and interest rate policies also helps answer an important question about how monetary policy should respond to changes in real GDP. Proposition one above implies that it is not wise for a central bank to have a long-run target for real output or unemployment as it should for an inflation rate. But should real output be a factor in interest rate decisions? In general, non-target variables can play an important role in policy reactions. We know that real GDP plays a role in moving interest rates when the central bank keeps money growth fixed; this is one of the attractive features of money supply rules, because the interest rate changes help moderate booms and slumps in real GDP and thereby help stabilize both inflation and real GDP.

For the same reason, real GDP should appear in interest rate policies: the increase in the interest rate in response to a rise in GDP helps moderate the boom and stabilize inflation.

Supply-side changes in potential GDP growth

How should monetary policy respond to a change in the growth of potential GDP, perhaps due to an increase in the trend growth of productivity after a change in tax or regulation policy?

To answer this question I will focus on interest rate policies and use a little algebra. (For a money growth policy, an increase in the growth rate of potential GDP will lead to a lower inflation rate according to the quantity theory of money equation, unless the money growth rate is increased by the amount that potential GDP growth rises. When choosing the k in the k-percent money growth policy, one needs to have an estimate of the long-run growth rate of the economy. Mistakes in the estimate of potential growth are translated into mistakes on inflation).

Consider the following policy for setting the interest rate:

$$i = \pi + gy + h(\pi - \pi^*) + r^f \quad (1)$$

where y is real GDP measured as a percentage deviation from potential GDP, i is the short-term nominal interest rate measured in percentage points, and π is the inflation rate measured in percentage points. The parameters π^*, r^f, g, and h are all positive. Thus the interest rate responds to deviations of inflation from a target π^* and to the deviations of real GDP from potential GDP. When inflation rises, the nominal interest rate rises by more than the inflation rate. When real GDP rises relative to potential GDP, the interest rate also rises. The intercept term r^f in this relationship is the implicit real interest rate in the central bank's reaction function.

Suppose first that the long-run average value of the real GDP deviation y is 0 and let the long-run real interest rate be r^* so that in the long run $i - \pi = r^*$.

Suppose now that there is an increase in the growth rate of potential GDP; that is, rather than averaging the constant 0, the central bank's perceived gap variable is actually growing so that $y = a + bt$ in the long run. Plugging these values into the policy rule and solving for the equilibrium inflation rate yields

$$\pi = \pi^* + (r^* - r^f)/h - g(a + bt)/h. \tag{2}$$

This equation implies that if the central bank chooses a monetary policy with wrong estimates of the parameters that the steady state inflation rate π will not equal the target inflation rate π^*.

If potential GDP growth rises and the Fed does not take this into account, then the Fed's error would eventually show up in less price stability (inflation below the target). Eventually the Fed would adjust so that any negative effects on real GDP would be temporary. For the same reasons that there is no long-run tradeoff between inflation and unemployment, a policy of underestimating potential GDP growth on the part of the monetary authorities would have short-term effects on growth but not long-term effects.

But a much better policy response to an increase in potential GDP growth would be to adjust the estimate of potential GDP in monetary policy decisionmaking. This would prevent the inflation rate from deviating from its target—and thus be a policy of maintaining price stability. To the extent that there is a short-run tradeoff (proposition two), this policy would prevent a shortfall of the economy below the now higher potential GDP growth path.

Conclusion: the choice of policy rules

I have tried to discuss the appropriate monetary polices for maintaining price stability in general terms without taking a position on whether these policies should be formulated with policy rules or guidelines. But I think that the discussion makes clear that most of the issues of how policy should react to shocks are really questions about alternative policy rules which describe how policymakers should react to different contingencies.

I think that there are several reasons to use policy rules to recommend how policy instruments should respond to shocks. First, and the most commonly cited academic reason, is the time inconsistency problem discussed earlier. Second, if people are forward-looking, one needs to stipulate future as well as current policy actions in order to evaluate the effects of policy. Third, policy rules can reduce uncertainty about policy actions. Fourth, policy rules can be useful as a way to instruct policymakers about actions to take to achieve their goals. Fifth, policy rules can make it easier to teach students and educate the public about monetary policies. Sixth, policy rules provide a way to increase the accountability of policymakers.

I recognize that some events may require that the central bank depart from the rule, and that some discretion is still necessary in working with a rule. But with a policy rule, the analysis of policy—including showing that a deviation from the rule is needed—will emphasize discretion less and the rule more.

Author's Note: This research was supported by the Center for Economic Policy Research at Stanford University.

Endnotes

[1]Papers in the volume, *Price Stabilization in the 1990s,* Kumiharu Shigehara, ed., 1993, provide a useful review of the inflation episodes in the United States, Canada, Europe, East Asia, and Latin America during the 1970s.

[2]It was not until 1976 that the outgoing Ford Administration's Council of Economic Advisers, chaired by Alan Greenspan, raised the estimate to 4.9 percent and they were criticized for doing so.

[3]Or the fluctuations in the deviations of real GDP from potential GDP, because these are highly correlated with deviations of the unemployment rate from the natural rate.

[4]Recall that a higher inflation rate can lower the growth rate of potential GDP, so that price stability is the best monetary policy for potential GDP growth.

[5]Using a forecast of inflation rather than the actual inflation rate is another form of averaging, because most forecasts are close to weighted averages of past variables.

References

De Long, J. Bradford. "America's Only Peacetime Inflation: The 1970s," in D. Romer and C. Romer, eds., *Monetary Policy and Low Inflation.* National Bureau of Economic Research, 1996, forthcoming.

Kydland, Finn, and Edward Prescott. "Rules Rather than Discretion: The Inconsistency of Optimal Plans," *Journal of Political Economy*, (1977), pp. 473-92.

Lucas, Robert E. Jr. "Expectations and the Neutrality of Money," *Journal of Economic Theory,* vol. 4 (April 1972), pp. 103-24.

McCallum, Bennett. "Robustness Properties of a Rule for Monetary Policy," *Carnegie-Rochester Conference Series on Public Policy,* 29, 1988, pp. 173-204.

Meltzer, Allan H. "Limits to Short-Run Stabilization Policy," *Economic Inquiry*, vol. 25 (1987), pp. 1-13.

Parkin, Michael. "Inflation in North America," in Kumiharu Shigehara, ed., *Price Stabilization in the 1990s,* 1993, pp. 47-83.

Taylor, John B. *Macroeconomic Policy in the World Economy: From Econometric Design to Practical Operation.* New York: W.W. Norton, 1993.

Commentary: How Should Monetary Policy Respond to Shocks While Maintaining Long-Run Price Stability? —Conceptual Issues

David W. Mullins, Jr.

Thank you Mr. Chairman. It's a great pleasure to be here and a special honor to appear on so distinguished a panel.

The Great Inflation

John Taylor has produced a comprehensive and insightful paper. He begins by reviewing what he calls the "Great Inflation," the period of the 1970s and early 1980s. Following Brad De Long's observation that by the early 1970s, well before the oil shocks, baseline U.S. inflation was already in the 4 percent to 5 percent range, John Taylor rejects the hypothesis that the oil price shocks of the period were the main source of the rise of inflation. While De Long's observation does suggest that shocks were not the sole source of the inflation of the 1970s, in my view, one cannot conclude that shocks were not important contributors to the inflation of the 1970s. Concurrent with shocks, the 4 percent to 5 percent inflation of the early 1970s accelerated to above 9 percent in the mid-1970s and again in the late 1970s and early 1980s. So I think it is reasonable to suggest that these oil price shocks, though not the sole source, were a significant contributor to the inflation of this period, both directly and especially indirectly through the interaction of shocks and policy mistakes. Shocks put policy under pressure and provide enhanced opportunities for policy mistakes. For example, the overestimation of the cost of disinflation in the presence of these shocks likely combined to contribute to the higher inflation of the period.

After absolving shocks of blame, John Taylor concludes that the prime cause of the inflation of the 1970s and early 1980s was policy mistakes. I do agree that policy mistakes played a significant role in the Great Inflation. This raises the question as to how one can explain these policy mistakes. In reviewing this issue, John Taylor rejects the argument that time inconsistency problems produced these policy mistakes. He does so by appealing to the proposition that society—and presumably society's agents, politicians—that politicians are simply much too rational and farsighted to be misled by short-term, myopic considerations. Instead, they are wise enough to look through short-term considerations and focus on the longer term. I think this is a particularly courageous argument to make in the United States in years divisible by four. In fairness, I should add that he also presents somewhat more convincing arguments with respect to the inadequacy of this hypothesis to explain the European inflation experience.

As a result, John Taylor assigns the bulk of the blame for the inflation of the 1970s and early 1980s squarely on the shoulders of the economics profession in general and economic theorists in particular. Perhaps he overstates their influence. I do not precisely recall that professors were so firmly in control of the policy apparatus during this period. I must say that I was relieved for my colleagues who remain in the academic community, that John Taylor did not extend his analysis to suggest attaching financial liability to economic research, requiring professors to pay compensation to the hapless victims of their mischief. Interestingly, he does suggest attaching warning labels to new economic research requiring that new theory should be taken only with large doses of traditional remedies such as Adam Smith and David Hume.

Continuing in the academic vein, John Taylor does recommend a study of the Great Inflation as part of the required curriculum in the training of central bankers. I would suggest extending this to shocks. Shocks cannot be anticipated with respect to timing, but some types of shocks seem to recur periodically. Oil price shocks might be an example. One concrete suggestion for the practical training of policymakers is that I think it would be useful for central bankers to examine explicit case histories of prominent shocks, perform economic autopsies to assess actual policy responses, and contemplate alternative policy paths. Candidates for this exercise include the oil price shocks of the last several decades, the German reunification, and the stock market crash of 1987. With respect to the latter incident, it is interesting to note that the 25 percent decline in stock prices in one day in October 1987 is considered a shock. But, an increase of almost 50 percent in U.S. stock valuations during the last year and a half is not noted as a shock. Other episodes worth examining include the deflating of the Japanese asset price bubble, the collapse of the exchange rate mechanism (ERM), and the impact of the Mexican crisis on other emerging economies to name a few.

Practical issues associated with shocks

As an addition to the conceptual approach presented by John Taylor, there are a few practical points worth noting with respect to shocks. Shocks, by their nature, are destabilizing, producing volatility, which alone can be damaging. I think, perhaps, the first principle of response is to do no unintended harm and respond with caution to avoid unnecessarily amplifying instability. One wants to avoid monetary authority actions which represent an additional source of volatility. So therefore, it would be useful to respond in a manner which engenders confidence.

Perhaps a corollary principle is that one should not underestimate the self-equilibrating capacity of economies and financial systems, their inherent ability to respond to and absorb shocks. It is at least plausible that recent developments have enhanced the capacity of economies to absorb shocks. An example in the United States would be the continuing process of a relatively rigid, institutionalized financial system evolving toward a more flexible, responsive market system. While the rapid transmission of shocks through markets might itself entail risks, market rates and asset prices respond with a force and speed, often in a counter-cyclical manner, which, in effect, may do some of the work for policymakers. A nonfinancial example of this possibly increased capacity of economic systems to respond to shocks is the advances in information technology inherent in point-of-sale information systems. Such systems allow production, distribution, and inventory managers to respond quickly to shifts in supply and demand, dampening the amplitude and muting the force and economic significance of traditional inventory cycles.

Another issue is the increased interconnection among international economies. Because of this, global shocks might be expected to engender coincidence responses from many monetary authorities. The cumulative impact of these responses might be more forceful than anticipated by one central bank focused on its own economy. So in a global economy, somehow monetary authorities in responding to shocks must take into account the likely response of other monetary authorities as well.

Price stability, deflationary shocks, and negative real interest rates

John Taylor does not address one particular concern associated with shocks noted in Stanley Fischer's paper. Consider a monetary authority successfully pursuing either price stability or a very low inflation rate. The result would be a very low interest rate environment. The concern is that since nominal interest rates are bounded from below by zero, will such a monetary authority have the capacity to respond to a sharp deflationary shock? In such an environment, for example, it would seem quite difficult to engineer negative real interest rates as a response.

Some would suggest that a policy of reducing interest rates to zero, flooding the economy with liquidity, would ultimately be effective. This is consistent with John Taylor's suggestion that at very low or very high inflation, it might be useful to go to quantity-based policies as opposed to interest rate policies. To gain insight into these issues, it might be useful to examine episodes such as the recent experience in Japan. However, I suspect the recent Japanese experience has unique aspects concerning the severe problems within that financial system. Moreover, I think it is also accurate to recall that this situation would not represent unchartered policy territory for the United States. Indeed, U.S. inflation and nominal interest rates were quite low in the 1950s and early 1960s through several economic cycles without memorable policy problems, and it could be instructive to examine this period as well. I would, however, highlight this problem because we need a convincing analysis to refute those who would argue that a little bit of inflation is a good thing.

Shocks under different monetary policy objectives

With these points in mind, what about the primary issue at hand? I very much agree with the main thrust of John Taylor's paper. How should monetary policy respond to shocks? In my view, the answer is straightforward, at least conceptually. Policymakers' response should be derived rigorously and consistently from the objective pursued by the central bank. However, this could result in quite different policy responses and economic outcomes depending upon differences in the objectives of monetary authorities.

To illustrate, I would like to focus for a moment on one issue which John Taylor discussed briefly in his paper; that is the distinction between two leading candidates for the objective of monetary policy. The first is strict adherence to the objective of price stability, that is, stabilizing the price level through time; and the second is pursuing a target of low inflation or zero inflation, stabilizing the inflation rate through time.

I do think these are conceptually quite different policy objectives. With price level stability, market participants and other economic agents have a commitment, a promise from the government in the form of the central bank to stabilize the price level. With inflation rate targeting, there is simply no such commitment. With a zero inflation target, there is a promise not to systematically and intentionally devalue the purchasing power of the currency. But since such a policy, in effect, forgives and forgets the impact of price shocks and policy mistakes, the monetary authority essentially takes no responsibility for the actual path of the price level. With inflation rate targeting, the actual price level will, of course, drift as a function of the cumulative incidence of shocks and policy mistakes, their frequency, direction, and magnitude. The monetary authority's lags in adjusting to these shocks and policy mistakes will also influence the price level.

What distinguishes the objective of price stability from zero inflation is only the impact of shocks and policy mistakes. The objectives are isomorphic and produce identical results unless shocks knock the economy out of line with policy or policy mistakes knock policy out of line with the economy. In practice, even with a zero inflation target, the actual price level can, through time, exhibit large departures from price level stability. Market participants will assess the risk of such large departures and incorporate an appropriate risk premium for the possibility of departures from price level stability. The potential for price level instability should also influence the decisions of other economic agents as well.

Whether this conceptual distinction has any economic significance depends upon the expected future incidence and nature of shocks and policy mistakes and how monetary authorities adjust to these departures from target. Standing at the end of what John Taylor calls the Great Inflation, a period characterized by both severe shocks and policy mistakes, at such a time it is certainly plausible that market participants and other economic agents would view a commitment to price level stability as substantially different from a zero inflation target, a difference motivated by the potential for poor price performance driven by shocks and policy mistakes inherent in the zero inflation target approach.

It is less clear that the deficiencies in inflation rate targeting would be economically significant in today's environment. John Taylor, in his analysis, considers the period following the Great Inflation as a relatively enlightened period of policymaking, characterized by success in handling shocks. Still, in 1990, when the Iraqis invaded Kuwait, the resulting oil price shock contributed to a U.S. consumer price index (CPI) inflation rate in 1990 of 6 percent. As John Taylor notes, this did not get into the underlying inflation rate. As you recall, we immediately descended into recession and experienced a bout of what I think now is called opportunistic disinflation. The 6 percent inflation shock of 1990 did, however, remain in the price level and, in my view, was incorporated in market assessments, as indicated by generally stubbornly high long bond rates during the early 1990s. Indeed, in the six years within the 1990s (1990-95) the U.S. price level has increased 24 percent. At this inflation rate, prices double every two decades. Departures from price stability of this magnitude should be expected to alter the decisionmaking of market participants and other economic agents.

So the goal of targeting inflation, even zero inflation, has the potential for much poorer price performance as opposed to the direct commitment to price level stability as an objective.

But, of course, there is more to the distinction between these two objectives than simply price performance. There should also be a substantial difference in the economic variability associated with the monetary authority's response to shocks under price stability compared with a target inflation objective. For example, consider an inflation shock of 4 percent. With a zero inflation target, the monetary authority's response need only produce disinflation from 4 percent to zero. Depending upon the timing of the policy response, the price level might rise by 6 percent to 10 percent, a measurable departure from price stability.

In contrast, with strict adherence to price level stability, it would be necessary not just to produce 4 percent disinflation, but it would also be necessary to produce a symmetric period of deflation, an actual decline in prices necessary to bring the price level down to the initial target level. Thus, with the objective of price level stability, the monetary authority's response to a shock should produce substantially greater variability in economic performance compared to the result with an inflation target.

So the general conclusion is that pursuing price level stability promises the economy the advantages of stable prices, but at a cost of greater economic instability in response to shocks and policy mistakes. In contrast, pursuing a low inflation target, even a zero inflation target, runs the risk of substantially poorer price level performance, but has the advantage of producing less economic instability in response to shocks.

I have ignored the possibility that economic stabilization appears directly in the monetary authority's objective function (as suggested, for example, by the Humphrey-Hawkins Act in the United States). Adding this modification would change the response to shocks under both policy objectives, but should not change the general pattern of the result that targeting price stability produces greater instability in economic activity associated with shocks. The reason, of course, is that price stability as an objective, requires reversing price shocks, and seems to inherently involve increased economic volatility in comparison to a target inflation rate policy.

Market participants may incorporate a risk premium under inflation rate targeting to account for the possibility of price level instability. Similarly, under a price stability objective, it is possible that market participants and other economic agents adversely affected by volatility, will asses these risks and incorporate an appropriate risk premium or otherwise alter their behavior, to account for the greater economic volatility under price level targeting.

The choice of monetary policy goals

How then, should one choose between the objectives of price stability and zero (or low) inflation as a target? John Taylor simply makes a judgment call, concluding that in his judgment, the increased economic variability associated with price stability as an objective outweighs the advantages of better price performance. Therefore, John Taylor, in his paper, prefers an inflation rate target. This answer may be sufficient for use in the current U.S. policy context, where over the past ten years through July 1996, the U.S. consumer price level has increased by fully 46 percent and indeed in 1996, year-to-date CPI inflation is running at roughly a 3.5 percent annual rate. Perhaps in such an environment, our policy energy should be focused on continuing to reduce inflation, rather than arguing about or fantasizing about which goal we should select after inflation is eliminated.

But I do hope that this answer is not sufficient in the future. As more and more central banks are successful in reducing inflation, increasingly they will confront the question of where to stop—at low inflation, zero inflation, or price level stability. And I think this question of the distinction among these objectives will emerge as a central issue of importance to practitioners of monetary policy. The reason is that these different objectives have the potential of producing very different responses and very different patterns of economic outcome.

Ultimately, how should the choice be made? While this is certainly not the topic of this session, I would like to conclude with a few thoughts on this issue. I would note two approaches. First, some argue that central banks are simply creations of the political system and policymakers should be dutiful technocratic servants, obediently following the dictates and goals of society expressed though the political system. Some argue that central bankers should look to public opinion polls for goals. I must admit that this approach is not entirely satisfactory to me. It conflicts with the observation that the monetary authorities do not seem to act simply as agents. More generally, I question whether it is useful to exclude those professionals most experienced and knowledgeable on these issues from a proactive role in the selection of a monetary policy objective. At the other extreme is perhaps a tendency in some central banking circles simply to assert the validity of price stability as an article of blind philosophical faith. This approach is equally unsatisfactory.

In my view, economists and central bankers in their first analysis of the appropriate monetary goal, should begin by ignoring the approaches mentioned above. Instead, I think we should address the question of the appropriate goal of monetary policy as an issue of objective of economic science. Which goal produces the best results in terms of social welfare? Do the benefits of moving from low inflation to zero inflation to price stability outweigh the costs?

This issue is an important topic for research, and there has been recent research activity focused on the issue. I would question the research focus on the downward rigidity of nominal wages (Akerlof, Dickens, and Perry (1996), Lebow, Stockton, and Wascher (1995)). In my view, the focus should not be on nominal wages, but on nominal compensation.

In the United States, benefits account for close to 40 percent of compensation. Moreover, benefits include a heterogeneous bundle of complex contingent claims (for example, insurance, medical benefits) some with long horizons (for example, pensions). Unlike wages, these benefits are quite difficult for workers to value precisely. It should not be difficult to reduce nominal compensation through difficult to value reductions in benefits without workers perceiving any noticeable discontinuity as the change in total compensation passes through zero. Indeed, with the substantial reining in of benefits during the past several years in the United States, (for example, medical, insurance, switch from defined benefit to defined contribution pension plans), we have likely experienced a significant incidence of reductions in nominal compensation, even with rising wages.

Chairman Greenspan mentioned another approach to changing compensation—altering the nature of the job, the quantity of work. Again, in view of the widespread job restructuring activity in the United States, one might suspect this has also led to reductions in nominal compensation with rising wages as workers have been asked to do more.

These two degrees of freedom, adjusting benefits and the quantity of work, should provide ample grease for the wheels of the labor market. Why should one expect employers to have to reduce wages, the most visible component of compensation? In my view, the infrequency of reductions in wages says very little about the frequency of reductions in nominal compensation.

Moreover, as Gordon Thiessen noted, learning is important here. It takes time to get used to an environment of low inflation, to build confidence in stable purchasing power, and to accept the implications for nominal income. It is true even in a moderate inflation environment, those employed in industries that have experienced pervasive deregulation (for example, airlines) have gotten used to lower nominal wages. More generally, U.S. workers in the lower segments of the income distribution have experienced declining wages for the past decade or so. Therefore, before reaching even tentative conclusions on the downward rigidity of nominal compensation, I think we need evidence on more than just the most observable component of compensation.

In my view, the real challenge to zero inflation is not the evidence to date on the downward rigidity of nominal compensation, because I think there is very little persuasive evidence on this issue. Nor is it the concern about the inability to produce negative real rates. We experienced and prospered in a low rate environment in the past.

The real challenge to zero inflation is implicit in John Taylor's paper and in Stanley Fischer's paper as well. Simply put, what is wrong with 2 percent inflation, properly measured? To put it even more bluntly, isn't 2 percent inflation close enough for government work?

My response would be: why abandon the scientific approach that got us here? At low inflation rates, why dissolve into gesticulation? Instead, we should, in an objective and rigorous manner, examine the evidence on the costs and benefits of going from 2 percent inflation to zero inflation to price stability. Under the U.S. tax system, very low inflation rates translate into relatively significant and costly distortions. Interesting research into this issue has recently been presented by Martin Feldstein (1996) who argues that the lasting benefits of price stability outweigh the one-time cost of establishing it. It is encouraging to see active research on these topics, and in my view, more research is needed to provide definitive insight into this important issue.

Conclusion

Even after convincing evidence is assembled, of course, central bankers and economists still face the not insubstantial task of gaining support in the political system for the best objective. The main point of my discussion is that once this objective function is rigorously defined, many, if not most, of the conceptual issues associated with how monetary authorities should respond to shocks are also determined. The question of how to respond to shocks collapses into the more fundamental question of what is the best objective for monetary policy. I agree with John Taylor that the best approach for monetary authorities confronting the challenges of shocks, is to stay focused on sound longer-term objectives of monetary policy.

Commentary: How Should Monetary Policy Respond to Shocks While Maintaining Long-Run Price Stability? —Conceptual Issues

Lars E.O. Svensson

Having admired John Taylor's work for about two decades, it is a great pleasure for me to comment upon his paper, especially at this distinguished conference. Being a discussant of his paper is both easy and difficult, though. It is easy to be inspired, but it is very difficult to find something to seriously disagree with.

I find John Taylor's review of the mistakes of the past very inspiring, but I am not willing to write off time-consistency problems as easily as he does. In some European countries, strong labor movements seem to have imposed unrealistically high employment goals on fiscal and monetary policy. These movements seem to have done their best to block any reform and deregulation of labor markets and wage setting, which might lower the natural rate of unemployment, and have instead preferred to assign responsibility for lowering unemployment to fiscal and monetary policy, even though these cannot deliver. John Taylor believes that time-consistency problems can easily be fixed with legislation or other social arrangements. As we all know, there is a very strong case, both theoretically and empirically, for a monetary policy arrangement with a legislated price stability mandate, operational (instrument-) independence, and accountability for the central bank. (See Fischer, 1994.) In practice, though, the politics of such reforms are far from easy. Only recently have a number of countries undertaken such reforms, but reforms are still blocked in some countries, often by labor movements (my own country being a prime example). This is ironic, since labor governments should have more to gain from central bank reform, because they most likely have a larger credibility problem to start with.

Let me get to John Taylor's recommendations for how monetary policy should be conducted to maintain price stability. The points I would like to discuss are (1) inflation targeting implies inflation *forecast* targeting, (2) target rules vs. instrument rules, and (3) price level targeting vs. inflation targeting.

Inflation targeting implies inflation forecast targeting

I completely agree with John Taylor that having an explicit inflation target is the best way to maintain price stability, price stability here meaning low and stable inflation. (I will get to the issue of price *level* targeting later in this commentary.) I will extend on some implications that follow from explicit inflation targeting.

A serious problem in inflation targeting is the imperfect control of inflation due to lags, supply and demand shocks, and model uncertainty. As I have argued elsewhere (Svensson, 1996a), I believe there is a very good solution to this problem, namely to consider the inflation forecast for the control lag as an explicit intermediate target.[1] In his paper at this symposium, Charles Freedman also emphasizes that the inflation forecast should be thought of as an intermediate target for countries with explicit inflation targets. From this general insight follows some very explicit and useful results.

A simple model

Let me start from the stylized fact that both inflation and aggregate demand react with a lag to changes in the central bank's instrument, and that the lag for inflation is longer than for aggregate demand. This can be captured by two equations. The first describes a so-called accelerationist Phillips curve, where the change in inflation depends on output with a lag of one year,

$$\pi_{t+1} = \pi_t + \alpha y_t + \varepsilon_{t+1}. \quad (1)$$

Here π_t is inflation between year t-1 and year t, y_t is (the) output (gap), ε_t is a serially uncorrelated (negative) supply shock with zero mean, and α is a positive constant. The natural output level (consistent with constant inflation) is normalized to zero.

The second equation describes an aggregate demand/IS curve, where output depends on previous output and the real interest rate with a one-year lag,

$$y_{t+1} = \beta_1 y_t - \beta_2(i_t - \pi_t) + \eta_{t+1}. \quad (2)$$

Here the nominal interest rate i_t is the central bank's instrument (for instance, the federal funds rate in the United States, a repo rate in several other countries), η_t is a serially uncorrelated demand shock with zero mean, and β_1 and β_2 are positive constants. If current inflation is taken as a proxy for expected inflation, $i_t - \pi_t$ is a proxy for the real interest rate. The model with these two equations is similar to that used by Taylor (1994), with the addition of an explicit one-year lag in the aggregate demand equation. (The average real interest rate is normalized to zero.)

Thus, an increase in the federal funds rate will lead to a fall in output in one year, and a fall in inflation in two years,

$$i_t \uparrow \Rightarrow y_{t+1} \downarrow \Rightarrow \pi_{t+2} \downarrow. \quad (3)$$

Due to the control lags and the demand and supply shocks that may occur during these lags, control of inflation and output will be imperfect. Inflation and output can only be predicted with some uncertainty. Given inflation, output, and the federal funds rate in year t, the two-year inflation forecast (predicted inflation for the period beginning in one year and ending in two years), $\pi_{t+2|t}$, will be given by

(4) $$\pi_{t+2|t} = \pi_t + \alpha(1+\beta_1)y_t - \alpha\beta_2(i_t - \pi_t).$$

Actual inflation in year $t+2$ will differ from the forecast because of the supply and demand shocks that occur in year $t+1$ and $t+2$,

(5) $$\pi_{t+2} = \pi_{t+2|t} + (\varepsilon_{t+1} + \alpha\eta_{t+1} + \varepsilon_{t+2}).$$

John Taylor recommends a long-run inflation target for the central bank. Let π^* denote this long-run inflation target (for instance, 2 percent per year). Let the central bank's preferences over short-run fluctuations of inflation and output be captured by the quadratic loss function

(6) $$L_t = (\pi_t - \pi^*)^2 + \lambda y_t^2,$$

where $\lambda \geq 0$ denotes the weight on output stabilization around the natural output level relative to inflation stabilization around the long-run inflation target. In line with John Taylor's recommendation, there is no long-run output target separate from the natural output level. If the weight λ is zero, there is a *single goal* for monetary policy in that only inflation enters in the loss function. If the weight is positive, there are *multiple goals* for monetary policy, in that output enters beside inflation in the loss function.

A rule for the inflation forecast

What does the optimal monetary policy look like? We can find it by minimizing the expected discounted sum of future loss functions. The appendix reports the details.

The case of a single goal, when the weight on output stabilization is zero, is easiest to examine. Then a necessary and sufficient condition for the optimal monetary policy is that the two-year inflation forecast equals the inflation target,

(7) $$\pi_{t+2|t} = \pi^*.$$

Thus, the central bank should take the two-year inflation forecast to be its intermediate target, and it should adjust the instrument so as to always make the forecast equal to the inflation target. If the inflation forecast is above (below) the inflation target, the central bank should increase (decrease) the federal funds rate to make the forecast equal the target.

Ex post, due to the shocks, some deviations of actual inflation from the inflation target are inevitable. The best the central bank can do to minimize deviations from the target is to assure that the inflation forecast is right on target.

The case of multiple goals, when the weight on output stabilization is positive, also has a simple and intuitive interpretation (although, as the appendix demonstrates, it is a little more complicated to derive). Then, instead of adjusting the two-year inflation forecast all the way to the inflation target, the central bank should let it return gradually to the long-run inflation target. More precisely, the two-year inflation forecast should be a weighted average of the long-run inflation target and the one-year inflation forecast, $\pi_{t+1|t}$, according to

$$\pi_{t+2|t} = c\pi^* + (1-c)\pi_{t+1|t}, \tag{8}$$

where the coefficient c, the rate of adjustment toward the long-run target, is between zero and one. (The one-year inflation forecast is predetermined; it is determined by previous policy and the shocks that have occurred, and therefore, beyond the control of the central bank.) We can interpret this as implying a variable short-run target for the two-year inflation forecast.

The intuition for this is that adjusting the two-year inflation forecast all the way to the long-run inflation target, regardless of the one-year inflation forecast, may require considerable output fluctuations. If there is a positive weight on output stabilization, a gradual adjustment of the two-year inflation forecast toward the long-run inflation target is better, since it requires less output fluctuations.

The higher the weight on output stabilization, the slower the adjustment of the inflation forecast toward the long-run inflation target (the smaller the coefficient c).

The optimal policy is thus a steady leaning toward the long-run inflation target, very different from the so-called opportunistic approach to disinflation discussed in Orphanides and Wilcox (1996) and in Rudebusch (1996).

An ideal intermediate target

Thus, the above analysis implies that the central bank should consider its inflation forecast for the control lag as an intermediate target, and adjust the instrument so that the inflation forecast is either always on the long-run inflation target (when there is a zero weight on output stabilization) or gradually approaches the long-run inflation target (when there is a positive weight on output stabilization). As I have argued more fully elsewhere in Svensson (1996a), the inflation forecast is indeed an ideal intermediate target. It is the current variable that by definition has the highest correlation with the goal, future inflation. It is easier to control than the goal, since various supply and demand shocks enter in the latter. It is easier to observe than the goal, since it depends on current variables, whereas one has to wait some two years to observe realized inflation. The principles of inflation forecast targeting are highly transparent and intuitive, which I hope the above discussion has demonstrated. Also, inflation forecast targeting is incentive compatible, in the sense that it gives the central bank strong incentives to learn how to control inflation, by improving its modeling, forecasting, and information collecting. With transparency and openness by central banks toward the public, the public then has the best possibilities to understand, evaluate, and monitor monetary policy. The increasingly informative *Inflation Reports* regularly issued by inflation-targeting central banks are examples of such improved transparency.

Response to shocks

How should monetary policy react to shocks? The conventional wisdom is that monetary policy should neutralize aggregate demand shocks, since these move inflation and output in the same direction. With regard to supply shocks, the conventional wisdom is that the response depends on the weight on output stabilization. With a positive weight, it is optimal to partially accommodate supply shocks, since they affect inflation and output in opposite directions. With a zero weight, the supply shock effect on inflation is neutralized, even though this enhances the effect on output.

When lags are taken into account, the conventional wisdom must be modified. First, because of the lags, the central bank cannot affect the first-round effects on inflation and output of supply and demand shocks. Second, the lagged monetary policy reaction to demand and supply shocks are more symmetric. Third, the reaction to both shocks differ with the weight on output stabilization. With a zero weight on output stabilization, regardless of how the shocks have affected the one-year inflation forecast, the two-year inflation forecast is brought in line with the long-run inflation target. Hence, shocks are not allowed to let the two-year inflation forecast deviate from the long-run target. With a positive weight, the two-year inflation forecast is adjusted due to the shocks. The effect of these shocks on future inflation is only gradually eliminated.

Target rules vs. instrument rules

Setting the instrument to make the inflation forecast equal to the inflation target is an example of a *target rule* which, if applied by the monetary authority, would result in an endogenous optimal reaction function expressing the instrument as a function of the available relevant information. This is different from an *instrument rule* that directly specifies the reaction function for the instrument in terms of current information. I interpret John Taylor's discussions of instrument rules as advocating instrument rules rather than target rules.[2]

Setting the instrument so as to fulfill the target rules (equations 7 or 8) results in an endogenous instrument rule corresponding to inflation targeting. Since the current information in the model is inflation and output, the instrument rule will be of the same type as discussed by John Taylor in the references I cite of his work,

$$i_t = \pi_t + h(\pi_t - \pi^*) + gy_t. \tag{9}$$

The above target rule in equation 8 depends only on the parameters in the Phillips curve and the central bank's loss function. The single-goal target rule in equation 7 depends on the long-run inflation target only. In contrast, the instrument rule also depends on the aggregate demand function. (The appendix shows that the coefficients g and h depend on all the parameters of the model.) Therefore, the target rules (equations 7 or 8) are less complex and more robust than the instrument rule in equation 9. In the real world, much different information is relevant to forecast inflation; the instrument rule is, in principle, a complicated function of all such information, not just a few macrovariables.

I consider a commitment to a target rule to be a more advantageous arrangement than a commitment to an instrument rule. A target rule focuses on the essential, that is, to achieve the goal, and allows more flexibility in finding the corresponding reaction function. More specifically, with new information about structural relationships, such as changes in exogenous variables, a target rule implies automatic revisions of the reaction function. A commitment to an explicit instrument rule either requires more confidence in the structural model and its stability, or frequent revision that may be difficult to motivate and hence less transparent. Target rules are inherently more stable than instrument rules, and easier to identify, motivate, and verify.[3]

Price level targeting vs. inflation targeting

Let me refer to a monetary policy regime as *price level targeting* or *inflation targeting*, depending upon whether the goal is a stable price level or a low and stable inflation rate, where the latter allows base drift of the price level. Base drift in the price level implies that the price level becomes non-trend-stationary, and the variance of the future price level increases without bounds with the forecast horizon. This is obviously rather far from literal price stability.

In the real world, there are currently several monetary policy regimes with explicit or implicit inflation targeting (see Haldane, 1996, and Leiderman and Svensson, 1995), but there are no regimes with explicit or implicit price level targeting. Whereas the gold standard may be interpreted as implying implicit price level targeting, so far the only regime in history with explicit price level targeting may have been Sweden during the short but successful period 1931-33. (See Fisher, 1934, and also Jonung, 1979.)

Even if there are no current examples of price level targeting regimes, price level targeting has received increasing interest in the monetary policy literature. At the Federal Reserve Bank of Kansas City's Jackson Hole symposium in 1984, Robert Hall argued for price level targeting. Several recent papers compare inflation targeting and price level targeting, some of which are collected in Bank of Canada (1994). Some papers compare inflation and price level targeting by simulating the effect of postulated reaction functions. Other papers compare the properties of postulated simple stochastic processes for inflation and the price level (see, for example, Fischer, 1994). A frequent result, emerging as the conventional wisdom, is that the choice between price level targeting and inflation targeting involves a tradeoff between low-frequency price level uncertainty on the one hand and high-frequency inflation and output uncertainty on the other. Thus, price level targeting has the advantage of reduced long-term variability of the price level. This should be beneficial for long-term nominal contracts and intertemporal decisions, but it comes at the cost of increased short-term variability of inflation and output. The intuition is straightforward: In order to stabilize the price level under price level targeting, higher-than-average inflation must be succeeded by lower-than-average inflation. This should result in higher inflation variability than inflation targeting, since base level drift is accepted in the latter case and higher-than-average inflation need only be succeeded by average inflation. Via nominal rigidities, the higher inflation variability should then result in higher output variability.

Applying postulated monetary policy reaction functions, instrument rules, evokes the issue of whether these reaction functions are optimal for reasonable objective functions of the central bank. Also, such reaction functions may not be consistent with the realistic situation when the central bank acts under discretion because commitment to an optimal or a simple second-best rule is not possible. Similarly, applying postulated stochastic processes for inflation and the price level evokes the issue of whether these are consistent with a reasonable equilibrium.

In Svensson (1996c), I compare price level and inflation targeting, but I depart from the previous literature on price level versus inflation targeting by applying a principal-agent approach: the decision rules considered are the *endogenous* decision rules that result when society (the principal) assigns (delegates) an inflation target or a price level target to a central bank (the agent) acting under discretion. The reaction functions are hence endogenous, given central bank objectives and constraints, including available commitment technology.

Output and employment are, realistically, considered to be persistent. The degree of persistence in employment is indeed crucial for the results: Without persistence, a trivial tradeoff between long-term price level variability and short-term inflation variability arises. With at least moderate persistence, counter to the conventional wisdom, there is *no* tradeoff between price level variability and inflation variability. Price level targeting then results in *lower* inflation variability than inflation targeting. This result is due to the endogenous decision rule that results under discretion for different targets. Under inflation targeting, the decision rule is a linear feedback rule for inflation on employment. Then the variance of inflation is proportional to the variance of employment. Under price level targeting, the decision rule is a linear feedback rule for the *price level* on employment. Then inflation, the change in the price level, is a linear function of the *change* in employment. The variance of inflation is then proportional to the variance of the change in employment. With at least moderate persistence, the variance of the change in employment is less than the variance of employment.

In addition, a price level target has the advantage of eliminating any inflation bias that results under discretion if the employment target exceeds the natural rate of employment. It is replaced by a harmless price level bias. Indeed, with at least moderate persistence, even if society prefers to minimize inflation variability rather than price level variability, it will be better off by assigning a price level target to the central bank rather than an inflation target. The variance of inflation will be lower, there is no inflation bias, and with expectations incorporating price level targeting, employment variability will be the same as under inflation targeting.

I believe these results show that the relative benefits of price level targeting and inflation targeting are far from settled. However, I believe that inflation targeting is a sufficiently ambitious undertaking for central banks as of now. Once central banks have mastered inflation targeting, in perhaps another five or ten years, it may be time to increase the ambitions and consider price level targeting. By then we should know more about which regime is preferable.

Author's Note: I thank Christina Lönnblad for secretarial and editorial assistance.

Appendix

The model is described by the equations

(A1) $$\pi_{t+1} = \pi_t + \alpha y_t + \varepsilon_{t+1}$$

(A2) $$y_{t+1} = \beta_1 y_t - \beta_2(i_t - \pi_t) + \eta_{t+1},$$

where ε_t and η_t are i.i.d. disturbances.

The intertemporal loss function is

(A3) $$E_t \sum_{r=0}^{\infty} \delta^r L(\pi_{t+r}, y_{t+r}),$$

where δ ($0<\delta<1$) is a discount factor, the period loss function is

(A4) $$L(\pi_t, y_t) = (\pi_t - \pi^*)^2 + \lambda y_t^2,$$

and $\lambda \geq 0$ is the relative weight on output stabilization.

One-year control lag

In order to solve the model it is practical to first study the simpler problem

(A5) $$V(\pi_t) = \min_{y_t} \left[(\pi_t - \pi^*)^2 + \lambda\, y_t^2 + \delta E_t V(\pi_{t+1})\right]$$

subject to

(A6) $$\pi_{t+1} = \pi_t + \alpha y_t + \varepsilon_{t+1},$$

where output y_t is regarded as a control variable and there is only a one-year control lag for inflation.

The indirect loss function $V(\pi_t)$ will be quadratic,

$$V(\pi_t) = k_0 + k\,(\pi_t - \pi^*)^2\,, \tag{A7}$$

where the coefficients k_0 and k remain to be determined. The first-order condition is

$$2\lambda y_t + \delta E_t V_\pi(\pi_{t+1})\alpha = 2\lambda y_t + 2\delta\alpha k\,(\pi_{t+1|t} - \pi^*) = 0, \tag{A8}$$

where I have used equation A7 and $\pi_{t+r|t} = E_t\pi_{t+r}$. This can be written

$$\pi_{t+1|t} - \pi^* = -\frac{\lambda}{\delta\alpha k}\,y_t\,. \tag{A9}$$

The decision rule for output fulfills

$$\begin{aligned} y_t &= -\frac{\delta\alpha k}{\lambda}\,(\pi_{t+1|t} - \pi^*) \\ &= -\frac{\delta\alpha k}{\lambda + \delta\alpha^2 k}\,(\pi_t - \pi^*)\,, \end{aligned} \tag{A10}$$

where I have used that by equation A6

$$\pi_{t+1|t} = \pi_t + \alpha y_t\,. \tag{A11}$$

Then the equilibrium inflation forecast fulfills

$$\begin{aligned} \pi_{t+1|t} = \pi_t + \alpha y_t &= \pi^* + \left(1 - \frac{\delta\alpha^2 k}{\lambda + \delta\alpha^2 k}\right)(\pi_t - \pi^*) \\ &= \pi^* + \frac{\lambda}{\lambda + \delta\alpha^2 k}\,(\pi_t - \pi^*). \end{aligned} \tag{A12}$$

In order to identify k I exploit the envelope theorem for equations A5 and A7 and use equation A12, which gives

$$V_\pi(\pi_t) = 2k\,(\pi_t - \pi^*) = 2\,(\pi_t - \pi^*) + 2\delta k\,(\pi_{t+1|t} - \pi^*)$$

$$= 2\left(1 + \frac{\delta\lambda k}{\lambda + \delta\alpha^2 k}\right)(\pi_t - \pi^*)\,. \tag{A13}$$

Identification of the coefficient for $\pi_t - \pi^*$ gives

$$k = 1 + \frac{\delta\lambda k}{\lambda + \delta\alpha^2 k}\,. \tag{A14}$$

The right-hand side is equal to unity for $k=0$ and increases toward $1 + \frac{\lambda}{\alpha^2}$ for $k \to \infty$. We realize that there is a unique positive solution that fulfills $k \geq 1$. It can be solved analytically:

$$k^2 - \left(1 - \frac{\lambda(1-\delta)}{\delta\alpha^2}\right) k - \frac{\lambda}{\delta\alpha^2} = 0,$$

$$k = \frac{1}{2}\left(1 - \frac{\lambda(1-\delta)}{\delta\alpha^2} + \sqrt{\left(1 - \frac{\lambda(1-\delta)}{\delta\alpha^2}\right)^2 + \frac{4\lambda}{\delta\alpha^2}}\right)$$

$$= \frac{1}{2}\left(1 - \frac{\lambda(1-\delta)}{\delta\alpha^2} + \sqrt{\left(1 - \frac{\lambda(1-\delta)}{\delta\alpha^2}\right)^2 + \frac{4\lambda(1-\delta)}{\delta\alpha^2} + \frac{4\lambda}{\alpha^2}}\right)$$

$$= \frac{1}{2}\left(1 - \frac{\lambda(1-\delta)}{\delta\alpha^2} + \sqrt{\left(1 + \frac{\lambda(1-\delta)}{\delta\alpha^2}\right)^2 + \frac{4\lambda}{\alpha^2}}\right) \geq 1.$$

(A15)

Two-year control lag

After these preliminaries, consider the problem

$$\min_{i_t} E_t \sum_{r=0}^{\infty} \delta^r L(\pi_{t+r}, y_{t+r}) \tag{A16}$$

subject to equations A1 and A2. We realize that this can be formulated as

$$V(\pi_{t+1|t}) = \min_{y_{t+1|t}} \left[(\pi_{t+1|t} - \pi^*)^2 + \lambda y_{t+1|t}^2 + \delta E_t V(\pi_{t+2|t+1})\right] \tag{A17}$$

subject to

$$\begin{aligned} \pi_{t+2|t+1} &= \pi_{t+1} + \alpha y_{t+1} \\ &= \pi_{t+1|t} + \alpha y_{t+1|t} + (\varepsilon_{t+1} + \alpha\eta_{t+1}), \end{aligned} \tag{A18}$$

where $y_{t+1|t}$ is regarded as the control, and where the optimal federal funds rate can be inferred from

$$i_t - \pi_t = -\frac{1}{\beta_2} y_{t+1|t} + \frac{\beta_1}{\beta_2} y_t. \tag{A19}$$

This problem is analogous to the problem in equation A5 subject to equation A6. Thus, in analogy with equation A9, the first-order condition can be written

$$\pi_{t+2|t} - \pi^* = -\frac{\lambda}{\delta\alpha k} y_{t+1|t}, \tag{A20}$$

and the reaction function will fulfill

$$\begin{aligned} i_t - \pi_t &= -\frac{1}{\beta_2} y_{t+1|t} + \frac{\beta_1}{\beta_2} y_t = \frac{\delta\alpha k}{\lambda\beta_2} (\pi_{t+2|t} - \pi^*) + \frac{\beta_1}{\beta_2} y_t \\ &= \frac{\delta\alpha k}{\lambda\beta_2}\left[\pi_t - \pi^* + \alpha(1 + \beta_1) y_t - \alpha\beta_2 (i_t - \pi_t)\right] + \frac{\beta_1}{\beta_2} y_t \\ &= h(\pi_t - \pi^*) + g y_t, \end{aligned} \tag{A21}$$

where

$$h = \frac{\delta\alpha k}{\beta_2(\lambda + \delta\alpha^2 k)} \text{ and } g = \frac{1}{\beta_2}\left(\frac{\delta\alpha^2 k}{\lambda + \delta\alpha^2 k} + \beta_1\right), \tag{A22}$$

and where I have used

$$\pi_{t+2|t} = \pi_t + \alpha(1+\beta_1)\, y_t - \alpha\beta_2(i_t - \pi_t), \tag{A23}$$

and where k will obey equation A15.

Since by equation A1 we have

$$y_{t+1|t} = \frac{1}{\alpha}\left(\pi_{t+2|t} - \pi_{t+1|t}\right), \tag{A24}$$

we can eliminate $y_{t+1|t}$ from equation A20 and get, after some algebra,

$$\pi_{t+2|t} = c\pi^* + (1 - c)\pi_{t+1|t}, \tag{A25}$$

where

$$0 < c = \frac{\delta\alpha^2 k}{\lambda + \delta\alpha^2 k} \leq 1. \tag{A26}$$

The coefficient $\frac{\lambda}{\delta\alpha k}$ in equation A20 will be (i) increasing in λ and (ii) decreasing in α. Then c in equation A25 will be (i) decreasing in λ and (ii) increasing in α. To show (i), consider

$$z = \frac{k}{\lambda} = \frac{1}{2}\left[\frac{1}{\lambda} - \frac{1-\delta}{\delta\alpha^2} + \sqrt{\left(\frac{1}{\lambda} + \frac{1-\delta}{\delta\alpha^2}\right)^2 + \frac{4}{\lambda\alpha^2}}\right]$$

$$= \frac{1}{2}\left[w - A + \sqrt{(w + A)^2 + 4ABw}\right], \tag{A27}$$

where

$$w = \frac{1}{\lambda}, A = \frac{1-\delta}{\delta\alpha^2} > 0, B = \frac{\delta}{1-\delta} > 0. \tag{A28}$$

It is straightforward to show that $\frac{\partial z}{\partial w} > 0$, hence that $\frac{\partial(k/\lambda)}{\partial\lambda} < 0$, and $\frac{\partial(\lambda/k)}{\partial\lambda} > 0$. To show (ii), consider

$$v = \alpha k = \frac{1}{2}\left[\alpha - \frac{D}{\alpha} + \sqrt{\left(\alpha + \frac{D}{\alpha}\right)^2 + 4\lambda}\right], \tag{A29}$$

where

$$D = \frac{\lambda(1-\delta)}{\delta} > 0. \tag{A30}$$

It is sufficient to show that $\frac{\partial v}{\partial \alpha} > 0$. Thus,

$$2\frac{\partial v}{\partial \alpha} = 1 + \frac{D}{\alpha^2} + \frac{2(1+\frac{D}{\alpha^2})\alpha(1-\frac{D}{\alpha^2})}{2\sqrt{(\alpha+\frac{D}{\alpha})^2 + 4\lambda}} = (1+\frac{D}{\alpha^2})\left(1 + \frac{\alpha - \frac{D}{\alpha}}{\sqrt{(\alpha+\frac{D}{\alpha})^2 + 4\lambda}}\right)$$

$$= \left(1 + \frac{D}{\alpha^2}\right) + \frac{\sqrt{(\alpha+\frac{D}{\alpha})^2 + 4\lambda} + (\alpha - \frac{D}{\alpha})}{\sqrt{(\alpha+\frac{D}{\alpha})^2 + 4\lambda}} > 0. \tag{A31}$$

It follows that c decreases monotonically from 1 toward 0 when λ goes from 0 to infinity.

Endnotes

[1]Similar ideas about inflation targeting are independently expressed in Haldane (1996). Some additional issues, including model uncertainty, are examined in Svensson (1996b).

[2]In several papers, for instance, McCallum (1990) has argued for an instrument rule in the form of a monetary base rule.

[3]In Svensson (1996a), I extend on how the public can monitor the target rules for inflation targeting.

References

Bank of Canada. *Economic Behavior and Policy Choice under Price Stability*. Ottawa, 1994.

Fischer, Stanley. "Modern Central Banking," in Forrest Capie, Charles Goodhart, Stanley Fischer, and Norbert Schnadt, *The Future of Central Banking*. Cambridge: Cambridge University Press, 1994.

Fisher, Irving. *Stable Money,* 1934. Published in Britain under the title of *Stable Money: A History of the Movement*. London: Allen & Unwin, 1935.

Freedman, Charles. "What Operating Procedures Should Be Adopted to Maintain Price Stability? — Practical Issues," in *Achieving Price Stability*, proceedings of a symposium sponsored by the Federal Reserve Bank of Kansas City at Jackson Hole, Wyoming, August 29-31, 1996.

Haldane, Andrew G., ed. *Targeting Inflation*. London: Bank of England, 1995.

____________. "Some Thoughts on Inflation Targeting," Working Paper, Bank of England, 1996.

Hall, Robert E. "Monetary Strategy with an Elastic Price Standard," in *Price Stability and Public Policy*, proceedings of a symposium sponsored by the Federal Reserve Bank of Kansas City, 1984, pp. 137-59.

Jonung, L. "Kurt Wicksell's Norm of Price Stabilization and Swedish Monetary Policy in the 1930s," *Journal of Monetary Economics* 5, (1979) pp. 459-96.

Leiderman, Leonardo, and Lars E.O. Svensson, eds., *Inflation Targets*. London: CEPR, 1995.

McCallum, Bennett T. "Targets, Indicators, and Instruments of Monetary Policy," in William S. Haraf and Phillip Cagan, eds., *Monetary Policy for a Changing Financial Environment*. Washington, D.C.: The AEI Press, 1990.

Orphanides, Athanasios, and David W. Wilcox. "The Opportunistic Approach to Disinflation," Finance and Economics Discussion Series No. 96-24, Federal Reserve Board, Washington, D.C., 1996

Rudebusch, Glenn D. "Is Opportunistic Monetary Policy Credible?" Federal Reserve Bank of San Francisco *Economics Letters*, no. 96-28 (October 4, 1996).

Svensson, Lars E.O. "Inflation Forecast Targeting: Implementing and Monitoring Inflation Targets," NBER Working No. 5797 (1996a), forthcoming in *European Economic Review*.

____________. "Inflation Targeting: Extensions," Institute for International Economic Studies, Working Paper (1996b).

____________. "Price Level Targeting vs. Inflation Targeting," NBER Working Paper No. 5719 (1996c).

Taylor, John B. "Discretion versus Policy Rules in Practice," *Carnegie-Rochester Conference Series on Public Policy* 39, 1993, pp. 195-214.

____________. "The Inflation/Output Variability Tradeoff Revisited," in Jeffrey C. Fuhrer, ed., *Goals, Guidelines, and Constraints Facing Monetary Policy Makers*. Federal Reserve Bank of Boston, 1994.

__________. "How Should Monetary Policy Respond to Shocks while Maintaining Long-Run Price Stability?—Conceptual Issues," in *Achieving Price Stability*, proceedings of a symposium sponsored by the Federal Reserve Bank of Kansas City at Jackson Hole, Wyo., August 29-31, 1996.

__________. "Policy Rules as a Means to a More Effective Monetary Policy," Discussion Paper No. 449, Center for Economic Policy Research, Stanford University, 1996.

General Discussion:
How Should Monetary Policy Respond to Shocks While Maintaining Long-Run Price Stability? —Conceptual Issues

Chairman: Andrew Crockett

Mr. Crockett: Thank you very much, Lars. We have had from the discussants and the papers, one or two of the elements of the consensus that seemed to be emerging yesterday questioned. It is now time for the discussion period. First is Mike Darby.

Mr. Darby: An excellent session, an excellent discussion on an excellent paper. So my comments are in the form of a series of quibbles, primarily about the history of the 1960s-1970s—the onset of the Great Inflation. I think that, John, you gave insufficient allowance for the dynamics of the money growth. It was not immediately reflected in the price level during the catch-up period that Dave Mullins referred to. You had to have more inflation to get the price level up to the $P*$, as it sometimes was called in the Fed. On the other hand, in work with Jim Lothian, Anna Schwartz, and others, we saw a very direct relationship between what was happening in money and inflation in the United States and Europe because of the Bretton-Woods system. So I think your using Europe as a way of getting out of that one point was maybe a little too facile, because Europe was basically, until 1973 or at least until 1971-73, so much influenced by U.S. monetary policy. And, just one comment for Dave (Mullins): As I recall, Bob Solow went to the Council of Economic Advisers right after writing a very persuasive paper which he presented at the American Economic Association meetings with Samuelson on the Phillips curve. I suspect he was as persuasive in Washington as he has been with the rest of us. Thanks.

Mr. Crockett: Bob Heller.

Mr. Heller: I enjoyed the paper, as well. Let me add two items on the discussion of the Great Inflation. Mike Darby started talking about personalities already. First of all, Arthur Burns was the Chairman of the Fed during most of the period of most of the high inflation, and I don't think that he has ever been accused of being a neo-Keynesian. Arthur Burns also has never been accused of abandoning the goal of price stability; and if you read any of his speeches and papers, that is always goal number one of the Fed during the period. So what went wrong with all these good intentions? Second, I do not think we have talked about the abandonment of the gold standard, which happened right at the beginning of that period of Great Inflation. Yesterday we said that one of the good ways to bring down high inflation rates in a country like Argentina—or any other country—would be to adopt an external anchor for the currency. In the early 1970s, the United States got rid of gold as its external anchor. If Argentina got rid of its external parity tomorrow, you would see an acceleration of inflation. Well, maybe that is what we were seeing in the United States in the 1970s as well.

Mr. Crockett: John Makin.

Mr. Makin: Actually David Mullins almost made me hesitate to bring these points up, but I do want to suggest a topic for a future conference, which comes out of the discussion of these papers. And it is: Having Achieved Price Stability, What Next? When one looks around the G-7, I think six of seven, or maybe all seven, have inflation rates reliably within the 1 to 3 percent inflation range. Having achieved price stability puts central banks in an awkward position. Because if they have what they said they wanted, they are forced to be reactive rather than preemptive. It is very awkward to keep saying, "We want price stability." Suppose inflation is in the 1 to 3 percent range. The central bank sees a shock coming down the road that it knows is going to be trouble. It is very difficult to step out and do something in advance of the actual appearance of inflation. I have one country particularly in mind, but I will not mention which one it is.

Second question: What do you do if you get deflationary shocks? Again, here running the experiment about price-level targeting and inflation targeting becomes very interesting. If you have price-level targeting and you get a deflationary shock, you have to have a period when you run inflation faster than probably you would like to do. This could be awkward. I think that when we are this close to being where we want to on the inflation front, central banks probably ought to start thinking about what they are going to say to the public when and if a deflationary accident occurs. One form of deflationary action, of course, could be incipient fiscal stringencies, such as is planned in Europe and Japan today. If we look at the stated fiscal plans that are present there and look at the state of demand growth now, we could actually see, I think, some deflationary behavior in those countries. Japan has been mentioned frequently as a case where we have already seen a deflationary accident occur. In my own view, the deflationary action in Japan last year at this time was close to a disastrous deflationary accident.

My third point is that we are all so used to running the dynamic experiment in an accelerating inflation environment, I suggest a little bit of practice in thinking about accelerating deflationary environments—definitely something we want to avoid. Thank you.

Mr. Crockett: Ben McCallum.

Mr. McCallum: John did not explicitly mention his proposed policy rule in his talk, but it was clearly present in his discussion, and I wanted to report on a use of his formula in thinking about a case that keeps cropping up in our discussion—namely, the case of Japan during the last few years. Yesterday it was suggested that this case is an example of the danger of setting an inflation target too low, and that low interest rates might interfere with the application of monetary stimulus when it is needed. Well, I have in the past thought, on the basis of my own favorite indicators, that Japanese monetary policy was very tight during 1990 through 1994. So I checked this last night with John's formula, and it agreed. It said that interest rates should have been considerably lower than they were during those years. Now I don't know, possibly it is true that the low-by-absolute-standards interest rates kept the Bank of Japan from being more aggressive. But in 1995, they finally did lower rates even more, in April and again in September. This did lead to a major pick-up, a major increase, in the growth rates of narrow money, and then, in the last quarter of the year and the first quarter of this year, a pick-up in GDP growth rates. Now this seems to me to indicate rather clearly that the low inflation rates in Japan did not keep monetary stimulus from working nicely in the classical way when applied. The example seems to me to work against the argument that low inflation targets should be avoided.

Mr. Crockett: Stephen Axilrod.

Mr. Axilrod: John, I am not sure whether I have an extended footnote or a contrast to your explanation of the Great Inflation. I think I have a contrast, but I could see how you could interpret it as an extended footnote. In any event, from a worm's eye policy viewpoint—which was mine—I would say it came about because of an interaction of a culture of extreme policy caution and a number of unanticipated changes in the economic environment. That is, in the culture of the time the policy instrument, say, the funds rate, was adjusted very carefully—slowly and in small increments. Under those conditions, when you have a curve, to use a metaphor that is now prevalent—which it is hard for me to interpret but it seems to represent the economic environment and attitudes—when you have a curve that is moving and you do not even know it is moving, you are in deep trouble. Sometimes the curve moves and you know it, but you do not know the pace and extent. There were a number of things happening in that period where the curve moved and we did not fully grasp its extent. One was military spending in the late 1960s. Personally, I felt in a way responsible. Estimating government expenditures was part of my job at that time as head of the government finance section. We could not get timely, adequate data on the amount of military spending. So, the policymakers never really knew how the curve was moving in terms of spending.

Secondly, in the mid-1970s, depositors were beginning the shift away from M1 as a result of structural changes under way in banking and finance. It took us as a staff a rather long time to make sure what was happening, and to quantify it with any certainty for interpreting M1 policy objectives. And it takes an even longer time to convince the policymakers. By the time we had convinced them—if they ever got convinced, you never can be sure—maybe a year or so had passed. So we had a curve that moved in that sense, and no one was reacting to it or even could in the policy atmosphere of the period, until it was too late.

A third unanticipated exogenous factor in the 1970s was, of course, the huge oil price shock. I just do not think it was tolerable in the political and social atmosphere of the time to contemplate an extended period of unemployment as a response to keep inflation very low. It just did not seem practically possible to keep the oil price rise from showing through into the overall inflation rate or to have a one-time increase in the price level and then go back to a much slower rate of inflation. I am not sure how much real debate there was. In practice, we split various differences in a very cautious way that permitted a rise in the rate of inflation but did not keep the employment rate from also rising.

In that context, you can think about the policy approach of 1979-82 as an effort to break the culture of excessive policy caution. There were a lot of reasons for the 1979-82 policy shift, but I would interpret it very importantly as an effort to break with the old culture and restore the central bank's credibility.

Now if you think of the about fifteem years since 1982, policy has been both very fortunate and very shrewd. I do not think the Fed has been faced with the kinds of exogenous shocks faced during the Great Inflation period that made it so difficult to control inflation in a culture of policy cautiousness. I think policy is probably less cautious now, but it is still fortunate that the so-called curve does not shift about so violently as it earlier did.

Mr. Crockett: We will have maybe three or four more brief comments and then allow responses. I think Stan Fischer was asking for the floor.

Mr. Fischer: Thanks. Just a couple of observations and then two questions for John. First let me defend the model of dynamic inconsistency. It implies that a society gets more inflation than is socially optimal because of pressures to push output beyond the natural rate. That model seems to me to capture an essential insight. Look around at the inflationary pressures from legislatures, governments, and populists and think about how that works through into inflationary pressure: that's the insight, and it's something we should carry around in our heads as a way of thinking about the world. Even though there are ways of getting around these pressures, such as independent central banks, the pressures are still real. So we should not dismiss the model. On the issue of price level versus inflation targeting—the subject for our conference in ten or fifteen years—we really have to ask what adjustment inflation is helping implement when it takes place. We cannot answer whether you should undo the inflation that happened after a shock, without asking what adjustment took place as a result of that rise in the price level. Were the costs optimally distributed? Or should they be reversed? That's the way to answer the question of whether you want to go back to the original price level path, or just forget about what happened and assume those are one-time costs that were borne more or less optimally. A third observation, and then two questions: On Japan, I don't have any doubt that the fact that nominal interest rates are getting down to zero has inhibited Japanese monetary policy. Now, the two questions. John, on supply shocks, I could not figure out what you actually want to happen. When there is an oil price shock and it has no permanent impact on potential output growth, but potential output is going to be lower for two years, what should the Fed do? And, the other question, when you favor policy rules, do you want them publicly announced or do you just want the Fed to have them and to have good econometricians figure out what they are doing? Or should the Fed announce them and then explain why it is deviating when it deviates? Thanks.

Mr. Crockett: At the back.

Mr. Kudlow: A couple of points. First, on the issue of price-level stability, there is a period of American history that might be worth looking at. More or less from the Civil War to the beginning of World War I, the dollar (the Greenback) was tied to gold and silver. It was not a perfect period, but it was a commodity price rule and it was a period of extraordinary economic growth with price stability. And, in fact we had periods of deflation; the economy still expanded nicely; and interest rates behaved themselves. Second point: to John Taylor and, I think, to David Mullins, I fully agree with the importance of clarity and simplification in policymaking and also accountability. I think all branches of government need to be accountable and central banks are no exception. That leads me to my third point, which is, today's market setting strikes me as odd. Short-term interest rates appear to be steadier than long-term interest rates. Or put another way, the long end of the market is more volatile than the short end. I raise that because it strikes me if participants and economic agents—not just professional traders or even professional investors, but just ordinary people—were convinced that the United States was embarked in a credible, long-term price stability program, then long-term rates ought to be much less volatile, since, after all, inflation is the primary determinant of long-term rates. The business cycle bobs up and down; real rates may bob up and down; and, hence, short-term rates may bob up and down. But why would a holder of a 30-year bond be concerned that more people are working or building houses or even, perish the thought, buying houses. So, if the business cycle is heating up, I would expect to see rising short-term rates, but relatively steady long-term rates, if—*if*—long-term inflation expectations are truly anchored by a policy that is both credible, simple, easily understood, and in tune with real-world events. My concern with some of the dialogue is that we are debating price-level stability versus an inflation target. I tend to lean more toward the price-level stability. But we really do not have, at the moment, in the United States any real targeting, either long-term or intermediate-term. And, I think, despite the good inflation performance—it has been an excellent low-inflation performance in recent years—I think markets have nagging doubts which appear in these risk premiums and these volatility measures, particularly in the long end of the curve, which I think would run counter to what we might expect if the credibility was really there.

Mr. Crockett: I am afraid we have run out of time. With apologies to those whom I nodded to but did not get around to calling on, let me now ask John and then the two discussants if they would very briefly give their reactions to the points that have been made and answer the questions. John first.

Mr. Taylor: I will focus on a number of things. The price level versus inflation targeting has been raised by a number of people. I agree this is something we need a lot more research on. I do not disagree with that at all. I basically was asked in the paper to give an opinion on it. My opinion is that where we are currently, if there is a focus on price targeting, we may face some unfamiliar instabilities. In any case, I agree with everyone that we have a ways to go before we have the inflation goals in mind, especially with the questions of what the measurement bias is, and things like that. But it is a judgment call at this point. And I made a judgment. The issue, which Lars raised and David also mentioned, targeting an inflation rate versus the rules for the instruments, is a very big issue. In other words, Lars, for example, is indicating that he would prefer to have a target rule for the inflation rate and leave the instrument settings up to the central bankers. It seems to me that we want a target for inflation; we agree to that; but then, it also seems to me that we would like to have some description of what policymakers should do to achieve the target. The rules for the instruments are basically that. They are basically trying to describe what central bank policy ought to be in order to achieve an inflation target. So they are not contradictory. I have a preference for stating the rules in terms of instruments, because ultimately that leads to more accountability. The inflation rate itself adapts with a lag; therefore, it is not as good for accountability purposes. I used the example of teaching. I could be held accountable for the success of my students, but we do not know their success for twenty years after I teach them. So ultimate success is not a very good accountability measure. And the same is true with inflation. Forecasts of inflation are better in that respect, because they respond more rapidly to the actions that policymakers take. Bob Heller mentions the abandonment of the gold standard and Bretton-Woods as another candidate for the explanation of the Great Inflation. I think that is certainly a possibility. I tend to think that occurred because of the abandonment of price stability, which began for other reasons, and we just could not stay on the Bretton-Woods system at that point. So, it was abandoned, and there were other reasons that it was abandoned as well, but it just was not consistent at that point. On John Makin's question about the deflation shock: I think of inflation targets not simply as a lower bound by any means. Especially if you are below the target, it is bad policy; if you go above it, it is bad policy. So, if your target for inflation is zero, adjusting for measurement, then deflation is a bad policy and should be corrected. Then, regarding Ben McCallum's point: I personally think that when you are in a situation where there is deflation or hyperinflation, that interest rate rules have a lot of problems. Therefore, that is why I emphasize the similarity between money rules and interest rate rules. When you move into these regions which are incredibly unstable—deflation or hyperinflation—you need to look at quantities again. And, I think in Japan it would have been useful to bring the quantities back into play when the nominal interest rate got so low as to be not a very good guide for policy. I thought Steve Axilrod's points are very important to make. I think we should have more study of this period. The data on military spending, the reasons for that could have been very well based on views in decisionmakers not releasing the data about this tradeoff, about the Phillips curve, about monetary policy. So I think that needs to be studied more carefully. But, I think appointments, actions, relationships between the central bank and the government are things to study during that period. Just two more things: Stanley Fischer mentions we should keep time inconsistency in mind. I agree. I certainly teach that to all my students. I just question, is it more of a technical point—taken literally, the model leaves something to be desired as positive economics. As a metaphor for the legislative issues you indicate, it is fine. It does indicate the pressures that are put upon monetary policy. With respect to price shocks versus supply shocks, again, to me, a supply shock is the change in potential GDP. To the extent you can measure those through looking carefully at productivity, the central bank—whether it is using money growth targets or interest rate targets—should accommodate those changes in the growth rate of potential GDP. They are hard to measure. We had discussions about that yesterday. But, it seems to me, that is how you should view the supply shocks, so to speak. With respect to the oil price shocks, I think you can look and see to what extent those are temporary, coming out of the system; then it is certainly a reason to look carefully at a policy rule. In looking at the policy rule that I proposed, and how it applied in the case of the oil shock of 1990, it seemed to me there was evidence from futures markets that was temporary and could very well therefore have called for an adjustment of the policy rule. And finally, Larry Kudlow's point about the volatility of long-term rates: I think there are still questions in financial markets about the long-term viability of price stability. We should be happy that we are making the progress we are; but in terms of establishing that as a principle for four years, five years, ten years, twenty years, thirty years—what, effectively, long-term interest rates are affected by—I think we need to be working hard to make sure the price stability goal is embedded in our system.

Mr. Mullins: First, I think Steve Axilrod raised a good point. This is another type of shock when these dependable relationships change. I very much agree with Stan Fischer on the plausibility of the time inconsistency hypothesis. It is consistent with what it feels like being a Fed official in the early 1990s testifying before Congress. This has a certain ring of truth to it. John Makin, on worrying about the specter of fiscal stringency: This is perhaps a problem for Japan and Europe, but I think we are safe here in the United States. And finally, Larry Kudlow's point: I think the problem is that we are on the cusp of a regime shift. For ten years beginning in the early 1980s, we had 4 to 5 percent inflation. Now, we have had three or four years with inflation coming in around 3 percent. The opportunity for a sustainable downward shift in the inflation regime comes along once in a decade. The market is uncertain as to whether we are going to reverse the rise in long rates from the 1970s. In October 1993, the long bond rate was 5.78 percent; November 1994, 8.25 percent; December 1995, a little below 6 percent; now, a little above 7 percent. So this is an important crossroads, and the market is very uncertain in this long-term outlook where we are going to settle down; the low-inflation, low-interest regime of the 1950s and early 1960s or the higher rate environment of the 1970s and 1980s. If we were for some reason to revert to the 4 or 5 percent inflation range for a couple of years, then I think it will be awhile before we get back to this stage. Thank you.

Mr. Crockett: Lars.

Mr. Svensson: I would like to reiterate the point about basing accountability on the instrument rule. I think it is in the nature of instrument rules that they will be very temporary. Whenever the bank re-estimates its model, it wants to revise the coefficients in its instrument rule, so there will be frequent revisions. Occasionally, there will be new variables added, new information taken into account. Therefore, instrument rules will be inherently unstable and I think it will be problematic to base accountability on them. Therefore, I am more in favor of basing accountability on target rules, which are likely to be much more stable over time.

Mr. Crockett: Thank you very much.

What Operating Procedures Should Be Adopted to Maintain Price Stability?—Practical Issues

Charles Freedman

In this paper I provide a broad-brush examination from a practitioner's point of view, of some of the issues relating to the maintenance of price stability. I focus mainly on a framework in which the centerpiece of policy is an explicit target range for inflation control, of the sort that has been used in recent years in New Zealand, Canada, the United Kingdom, Sweden, Finland and a number of other countries.[1] However, I also make reference to systems that rely upon a monetary aggregate as an intermediate target, such as those used by Germany and Switzerland. While the experience over the past few years has largely been directed to bringing down the rate of inflation toward price stability, some of the lessons from that experience are equally relevant to the task of maintaining price stability, once it has been achieved.

One of the themes that recurs throughout this paper is the importance of the credibility of the monetary authorities in determining the response of financial markets and of the public to various shocks, and consequently, the appropriate reaction by the authorities themselves to such shocks. This raises the possibility that, over time, as price stability is maintained and central bank credibility gradually increases, there may be changes in the way the monetary authorities respond to economic shocks.

The paper begins with a discussion of the definition of price stability, focusing on the use of the consumer price index (CPI) in setting the target for policy, and possible biases in that measure. The second section deals with the central role of the forecast of inflation in the conduct of policy under an explicit target for inflation control and the appropriate policy response to a variety of shocks in circumstances with different levels of credibility. While this section deals with the response to shocks in a qualitative way, the subsequent section discusses how the central bank decides upon the size of the adjustment to very short-term interest rates in response to a shock to the system that results in a change to the forecast of inflation. It also examines the speed with which inflation should be brought back to the target if it should move away from it (in either direction), and possible tactical problems in achieving a desired path for monetary conditions. In the fourth section, I discuss a number of issues related to achieving and maintaining price stability, including the effect on the behavior of inflation of different specifications of inflation expectations formation, how monetary conditions can be eased when interest rates are already very low, and some of the differences between targeting monetary aggregates and explicitly targeting measures of inflation. The fifth section emphasizes the importance of transparency of policy and the way in which policy goals and policy actions are communicated to the financial markets and the public.

The analysis is directed to countries operating under a flexible exchange rate regime. It is thus relevant both for small open economies, such as Canada and New Zealand, and for very large countries, such as the United States, Germany, and Japan. The analysis does not apply to a small economy which has fixed the value of its currency to that of a larger country since the maintenance of price stability in such a country is based on the maintenance of price stability in the larger country to which it is tied and on reasonable stability in the real exchange rate vis-à-vis that country.

It is important to distinguish between two concepts of price stability. The first focuses on an ex ante achievement of a given rate of inflation (for example, the bias in the measure of inflation used) but does not require correction of the price level ex post for an inflation outcome that differs from the target. Thus, base drift is permitted for the level of prices, but not for the target rate of change of prices. The second focuses on stability in the price level (for example, a constant price level or a price level rising at a rate equal to the bias in the measure of the price index used). A period of positive inflation that resulted in the price level rising above the target would have to be followed by a corresponding period of either negative inflation or inflation less than the bias in the measure, in order to bring the price level back to its target.[2]

Except where noted otherwise, in this paper I treat the price stability target in terms of the first concept and not the second, that is, as the achievement of a target rate of inflation rather than a target price level. This is in line with current views of those central banks that have been using explicit targets for the rate of increase in the CPI to bring down inflation and to maintain price stability.

The definition of price stability for operational purposes

Price stability has been described by Chairman Greenspan in qualitative terms as a rate of inflation so low that it has virtually no influence on economic behavior. For a country aiming at the achievement of price stability by setting an explicit target for prices (whether stated in terms of a level or a rate of increase) it is necessary to have a quantitative measure for price stability. This in turn leads to three questions: first, what measure of inflation should be used as the basis for policy; second, what is the bias in that price measure; third, are there arguments other than statistical bias for targeting a positive rate of inflation?

Measure of prices

There are a variety of consumer and producer price indexes that could be used as the basis for setting policy. While there is no obviously ideal price index, most countries that have chosen to target explicitly on a measure of prices or inflation have used the CPI or a variant of the CPI. Typically, the focus of policy has been on a measure of "core" inflation that excludes very volatile components. In large part, the emphasis on the CPI has been a practical decision, based on arguments relating to the fact that the CPI is the best known by the public of the various price measures, that it is released on a frequent basis, that it is rarely revised, and that it is used in indexing formulas. It has also been argued that as the measure closest to the cost of living for households, the CPI is an appropriate measure for the target for monetary policy, which has as its ultimate aim contributing to a rising standard of living for households.

One argument that has been made against the use of the CPI as the measure of inflation for policy purposes is that it is too narrow, since it focuses only on the prices of currently produced goods and services and does not take into account the prices of future goods and services.[3] According to this line of reasoning, monetary policy should focus on measures of prices that accord some weight to asset prices, not because the latter may be one of many useful leading indicators of aggregate demand pressures, but because such asset prices reflect expectations of future prices of goods and services, which deserve to be included along with prices of currently produced goods and services in the measure of prices being targeted. This approach has not gained favor, however, in part because of difficulties in measuring asset prices (most notably, the price of human capital), in part because there are factors other than the future prices of goods and services that affect current asset prices (such as changes in the real rate of interest and expected shifts in the distribution of income between labor and capital and the resulting effect on profits). There is also the possibility of "bubbles" in asset prices that are unrelated to future developments.[4]

The argument that the price index chosen should reflect the cost of living of households should not be pushed too far. One of the key arguments for a policy of achieving and maintaining price stability is that it facilitates better decisionmaking among investors and savers by reducing or eliminating distortions and uncertainty surrounding price signals. And better investment decisions result in a higher level or rate of growth of productivity and hence higher standards of living. But this suggests that the goal of stable prices should be directed to a broader measure of the prices than the CPI, either a variant of the GDP deflator or a measure of the prices of all transactions in the economy.

Table 1
Correlation Coefficients of Movements in Various Price Measures

A. Quarterly Changes (1971Q2–1996Q1)

	CPI	CPIXFET	PGDP	FWPGDP
CPI	1.00	.82	.85	.87
CPIXFET		1.00	.77	.74
PGDP			1.00	.93
FWPGDP				1.00

B. Four-quarter Changes (1972Q1–1996Q1)

	CPI	CPIXFET	PGDP	FWPGDP
CPI	1.00	.97	.95	.95
CPIXFET		1.00	.95	.96
PGDP			1.00	.99
FWPGDP				1.00

CPI = consumer price index.
CPIXFET = consumer price index excluding food, energy and the effect of indirect taxes.
PGDP = GDP deflator.
FWPGDP = Fixed-weight GDP deflator.

If the different measures of prices moved in very similar way the issue of which measure to use would be less important. However, there can be quite significant differences in inflation movements in the short run, and the levels of different measures of prices can differ importantly even in the long run. The top panel of Table 1 shows the correlations in Canada among quarterly changes in the overall CPI, the core CPI excluding food and energy and the effect of indirect taxes, the GDP deflator, and the fixed-weight GDP deflator over the last twenty-five years, while the bottom panel shows the correlations among the four-quarter growth rates of these same measures. As is clear from the data, the four-quarter growth rates are much more

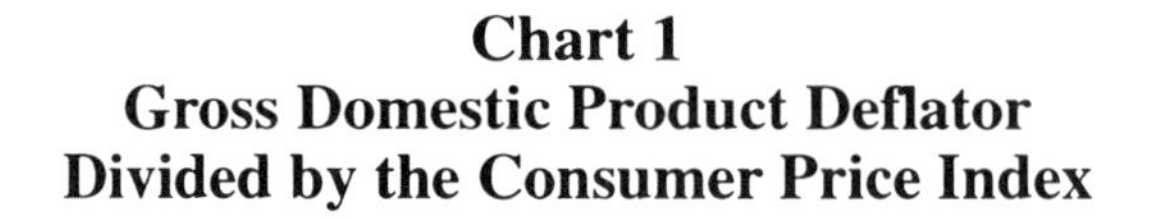

Chart 1
Gross Domestic Product Deflator
Divided by the Consumer Price Index

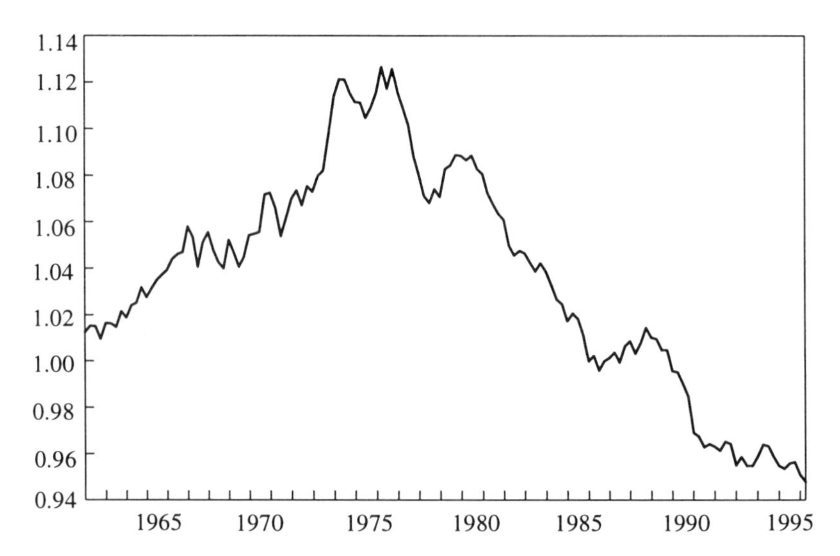

closely correlated than the quarterly movements. The greater similarity of the four-quarter rates of increase of prices suggests that broader inflationary pressures dominate over the longer time periods while special factors affect the various measures over the shorter time periods.

Even over much longer time periods, however, there can be differences in the trend movements of the different price measures. Chart 1 shows the ratio of the GDP deflator to the CPI in Canada over a 35-year period and Chart 2 shows the four-quarter growth rates of the two measures over the same period. Part of the difference in the behavior of the two measures relates to terms of trade developments, with the relative prices of commodities rising in the 1960s and 1970s, and declining on balance subsequently. Since, in Canada, commodities play a more important role in production than in consumption, the GDP deflator initially grew faster than the CPI and

Chart 2
Gross Domestic Product Deflator and the Consumer Price Index

Year-over-year percent change

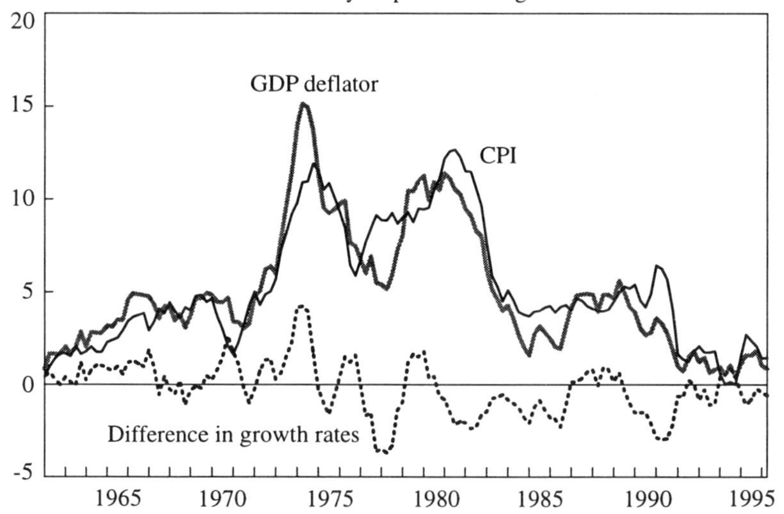

more slowly thereafter. Another factor that has played an important role in the less rapid growth of the GDP deflator than of the CPI over the last two decades has been the downward tendency in machinery and equipment prices, especially computer prices.

In the end, some variant of the CPI measure will probably continue to be the object of policy, largely because of its convenience and its usefulness for communicating with the public.[5] Moreover, as will be discussed in detail in the next section, choosing a particular core inflation measure for operational purposes (such as the CPI excluding certain volatile components) and emphasizing caveats indicating the types of shocks where the first round effects on prices can be accommodated (for example, indirect tax changes) can be important in helping to achieve the objectives of policy. In any case, even though the CPI is used as the centerpiece of the policy framework, close attention should be paid to movements in the broader measures, and different movements in the various measures should be examined for clues as to whether the CPI movements are reflecting underlying trends or special factors.

Biases in the CPI

As is well known, there are five principal sources of bias in the CPI—base weighting, imperfect adjustment for quality changes, new goods, outlet substitution, and formula bias.[6] In most countries, the best estimate of CPI bias is that it is well under one percentage point, although some observers in the United States have suggested that it could be as much as two percentage points.[7]

An obvious way of reducing the bias in the CPI would be to update the consumer basket more frequently. In Canada, for example, such updates are done every four years, on average, while in the United States they are done about every ten years. Evidence from U.S. and Canadian studies indicates that revising the basket less frequently adds between 0.1 and 0.2 percentage points to the annual bias in the U.S. CPI.

A more difficult area to assess is that of quality adjustments. Of course, this is an area that can cut both ways, with overadjustment and underadjustment of prices for quality changes both possible. And while the effect of some quality changes can be quantified fairly directly (for example, using hedonic measures), others may be much harder to capture. Examples would include improvements in the quality of medical care and the increased convenience in accessing financial services through ATMs or home computers.

In the context of targeting on the CPI, considerable efforts should be devoted to reducing the bias in that measure where possible, for example by updating the basket more frequently in those countries where updates are currently infrequent. Since the bias cannot be totally eliminated because of the difficulty in making quality adjustments, measures of residual bias should be estimated and used in the process of targeting on price stability.

What are the arguments other than statistical bias for aiming at a positive rate of inflation?

What measure of inflation is consistent with price stability? If one were certain about the size of the bias in the CPI (say it were equal to b), one could argue that the CPI corrected for bias would be the appropriate measure. Thus, the center of the inflation band would be b, if the authorities targeted the rate of inflation, or the slope of the price level target would be b, if the level of prices were the target.

It has, however, been argued that even though a measured inflation rate of b was consistent with "true" price stability, it would be appropriate to target a band for inflation higher than one centered on b. The arguments in favor of a higher target for the CPI are associated with two possibilities: first, that the costs of a decline in prices are greater than the costs of the equivalent rise in prices and, hence, one should try to minimize those occasions in which the price level is falling; or, second, that rigidities in prices and/or wages make it harder for the system to respond to negative demand shocks near price stability.[8]

Suppose that price stability is defined as the achievement of a rate of inflation equal to b, where b is the measure of bias in the CPI. This will imply a rate of inflation below b about 50 percent of the time, and, if b is relatively small, negative measured inflation from time to time. What are the implications for the economy of such periods of very low or negative inflation?

The first point to note is that use of the term deflation to describe a small decrease in prices lasting a short period, rather than a period of sustained price declines, can be very misleading, particularly for the "person on the street." The term deflation is associated in the public mind with the depression of the 1930s, when prices fell more than 20 percent over a four-year period. Short periods in which the average level of prices fall 0.5 percent or 1 percent are not in any way similar to a situation with an ongoing decline of prices of a substantial amount over a number of years. The kinds of concerns expressed about the latter situation, for example that households will decide to defer consumption expenditures in the expectation that prices will be significantly lower in the future than at present, or that the economy will enter into a debt-deflation spiral, are simply much less important or nonexistent in cases of very small price declines over short periods.[9] The fact that the authorities would be acting to bring the rate of inflation back to its target rate would reduce even further the likelihood that deflationary expectations would take hold in such circumstances.[10]

The second issue that is relevant in this context is whether there are floors to prices and wages such that they are unlikely to decline even if there is slack in the system and the implications of such a situation for the working of the system and for monetary policy. In other words, would aiming at price stability result in outcomes that are costly for the economy?

As far as downward rigidity to prices is concerned, the evidence suggests that many prices, especially those in high productivity industries, can fall. And empirical analysis by Crawford and Dupasquier (1994) and Yates (1995) concludes that the weight of the evidence is against there being significant downward nominal rigidity in prices. Nonetheless, this does not rule out the possibility that there is downward rigidity in some prices, and that relative prices will be significantly affected by a large negative demand shock.[11]

In the case of wages, there are two types of concerns. Would downward rigidity in aggregate wages prevent a needed downward adjustment from taking place in the case of an aggregate demand or supply shock? Would relative wage adjustments be harder to achieve in the case of a shock that reduced the equilibrium relative wages of certain types of labor?

The evidence thus far, although still fragmentary, suggests that wages can and do decline. Thus, Lebow, Roberts, and Stockton (1992) and Crawford and Dupasquier (1994) have assessed macro-level wage data in the United States and Canada, respectively, and have arrived at the conclusion that there is little wage rigidity. On the other hand, Card and Hyslop (1996) have found evidence of wage rigidities in micro-level data. Nonetheless, they concluded that "the overall impact of nominal wage rigidities is probably modest."[12]

In terms of aggregate wage movements, it is worth noting that with positive productivity growth the average wage will normally rise over time. In such circumstances, unchanged nominal wages will enable a decline in the real wage up to the rate of productivity growth to occur, if one is needed. And rigidities to the downward adjustment of wages might well lessen as the public becomes accustomed to price stability.[13] It is the case, however, that the existence of even partial wage rigidities would imply a longer period of disequilibrium in response to shocks that require changes in relative wages than if wages were able to adjust more quickly. The area of price and wage rigidities is one in which the need for further research is very evident.

The forecast of future inflation and its response to shocks

The lags between actions by the central bank in adjusting its policy instrument (the overnight rate or very short-term rate of interest)[14] and the rate of inflation is on the order of one to two years in most countries. Because of these lags, the central bank must take a forward-looking approach in its decisionmaking and focus on the forecast or projected rate of inflation. Indeed, it has been argued with some justification that the forecast rate of inflation (and its relationship to the target band) should be thought of as an intermediate target by countries that have set explicit inflation or price level targets as their ultimate goal.[15]

How does the central bank decide on the instrument settings needed to achieve its price stability goal? The typical decision process in countries with an explicit inflation or price level target has three parts: a forecast or projection of the rate of inflation one to two years out, which is modified in response to shocks to the economy; views on the linkages or transmission mechanism between the adjustment in the policy instrument and the rate of inflation, which determine the size of policy action needed in response to a change in the forecast rate of inflation;[16] and a mechanism for communicating the views of the authorities regarding the reasons for the policy actions. These three elements are the subject of this section and subsequent sections.

Broadly speaking, because of the lags between the policy instrument and the rate of inflation, the response of the monetary authorities to shocks to the economic system depends on the assessment of the effects of such shocks on the projected rate of inflation one to two years out. This requires a judgment as to whether the shock is a demand shock or a supply shock and whether it is persistent or temporary.[17] Moreover, the appropriate response to the shock may depend in part on the degree of credibility of the monetary authorities. This is particularly the case when there is some uncertainty about the nature or duration of the shock, since the room for maneuver for the authorities in such a case (that is, their ability to react less strongly than would otherwise be appropriate until more information becomes available on the nature of the shock) will depend on their credibility. The pre-announced response to contingencies may also be an important factor in determining the action required in response to certain kinds of shocks.

Temporary demand shock

If a demand shock (whether positive or negative) is expected by the authorities to be temporary, its effect on forecast inflation will depend on how the expected rate of inflation changes as the current rate of inflation changes. In circumstances in which monetary policy is lacking in credibility, expected inflation will likely respond strongly to movements in actual inflation and, consequently, even a temporary change in the pressure of aggregate demand would lead to a change in forecast inflation. To bring the forecast rate of inflation back to the target in such a case would therefore require an adjustment in the policy instrument, with interest rates rising in the face of a positive demand shock and declining in the face of a negative demand shock.

If a past history of achieving its target rate of inflation or maintaining price stability had resulted in full credibility for the monetary authorities, expected inflation would be closely linked to the target rate of inflation and would not be much affected by a temporary rise in the actual rate of inflation. Thus, a credible central bank could respond less strongly to a demand shock than one with less credibility, as long as the shock was clearly temporary. The credibility of the authorities thus gives them "room for maneuver," in the sense that they do not have to react as strongly to what appear to be temporary demand shocks.

Persistent demand shock

If a demand shock is viewed as persistent, it will lead to a change in forecast inflation and require a change in the setting of the policy instrument. While a central bank with credibility could take less strong action for a period, relying upon the fact that expected inflation would not immediately follow actual inflation, this would be a very risky strategy. Although the change in demand pressures would initially result in only a moderate change in actual inflation for a limited period following the shock, as the new level of inflation persisted it would begin to affect expected inflation, and the credibility of the authorities would decline in the face of a period of higher or lower inflation than had been targeted.

More formally, one can think of a situation in which monetary policy has very different levels of credibility as reflected in the following type of Phillips-curve relationship (expressed in terms of prices rather than wages).

$$\pi = \pi^e + b\,(y - y^*)$$

$$\pi^e = \pi^T, \text{ full credibility}$$

$$\pi^e = A(L)\pi, \text{ no credibility}$$

Here π, π^e and π^T are actual, expected and target inflation, y and y^* are the logarithms of output and capacity output, and $A(L)$ is a polynomial lag function indicating that expected inflation is tied to current and past rates of inflation.[18] While the equations specify the relationships with full credibility and no credibility, there are also intermediate outcomes with partial credibility, in which expected inflation is linked to a combination of target inflation and past rates of inflation.[19]

With full credibility, the price-output relationship resembles the 1960s-style Phillips curve, with expectations anchored by the target. However, any attempt to exploit the relationship by persistently running output above capacity would lead to a weakening of the linkage between expected inflation and target inflation and to re-establishment of the link between expected inflation and actual inflation that prevailed through the inflationary period of the 1970s and 1980s. In short, while credibility gives the central bank room for maneuver in response to temporary demand shifts, it would crumble if it were used to avoid taking the necessary action to offset a persistent demand shock. In the latter case, action should be taken as quickly as possible in order to avoid inflation moving away from the target for a significant time period and hence leading to entrenched expectations of a rate of inflation inconsistent with the target of price stability.

In this context, I would note that the view that focusing on inflation and price stability makes central banks insensitive to changes in economic activity and unemployment is simply incorrect. In fact, having a target range for price stability with both upper and lower bands results in a monetary policy with stabilizing properties with respect to output in response to unexpected persistent movements of aggregate demand.

Consider a situation in which the measured rate of inflation is within the target band[20] and aggregate demand increases to a level greater than the capacity of the economy to produce goods and services. The rate of inflation will begin to rise toward the upper end of the band. To offset these pressures, the monetary authorities will tighten monetary conditions and hence will provide offsetting restraint to the demand pressures. Conversely, if the measured rate of inflation is initially within the band and demand weakens, there will be downward pressure on the trend rate of inflation and it will move toward the bottom of the band. The monetary authorities will act to ease monetary conditions, thereby providing stimulus to the economy. Thus, by responding to the implications for trend inflation of aggregate demand shocks, monetary policy acts in a countercyclical manner and provides an offsetting influence to these shocks.

The Taylor rule,[21] which links the short-term real interest rate to the rate of inflation relative to its target and the level of output relative to capacity, is often interpreted as one in which the monetary authority has two objectives—inflation at its target rate and output at capacity. However, it can equally well be interpreted as reflecting a situation in which the authorities have as their objective a target rate of inflation, with the forecast rate of inflation as an intermediate target and the current level of aggregate demand relative to capacity as the key indicator of movements in forecast inflation. Of course, a more sophisticated forecast of future inflation would be based on many factors in addition to current inflation and the current level of aggregate demand relative to capacity. Most notably, it would include past movements of monetary conditions which have not yet had their full effect on aggregate demand because of lags in response,[22] known or expected exogenous shocks to demand, such as changes in external demand from developments in the economies of the country's trading partners, anticipated fiscal policy measures, and so forth. Nonetheless, one can treat the implicit forecast in the Taylor rule as a simple way of responding to future inflation pressures.

Supply shocks and other price level shocks

Depending on how the policy framework is structured, there can be a variety of responses to supply shocks. At one end of the spectrum, if the target is based on the overall CPI and is aimed at achieving a price level rather than a rate of increase of prices, a supply shock feeding into prices would have to be completely reversed over time. At the other end of the spectrum, if the policy framework focuses on the rate of increase in prices and does not seek to reverse the once-and-for-all price level adjustments to supply shocks, the emphasis of policy would be on avoiding a feed-through from the price level shock to the ongoing rate of inflation. Such an approach would permit drift in the price level but not in the rate of inflation. It could be facilitated by focusing on an operational definition of inflation that removed the effects of certain types of supply shocks, by explicit assertions by the authorities regarding their responses to certain contingencies, or by some combination of the two. I focus on the latter since it is the approach used in Canada and elements of the strategy appear in the framework used by most of the central banks with an explicit target for inflation control.

Consider a change in a sales tax or value added tax (VAT). The focus in Canada for operational purposes on a target that excludes indirect tax changes (more precisely, the CPI excluding food, energy, and the effect of indirect taxes) gives a clear indication that monetary policy will not aim at reversing the first round or price level effects of a sales tax change.[23] However, both implicitly, by focusing on this measure for operational purposes, and explicitly, in statements about the policy response to such a tax change, the Bank of Canada has made it clear that it will react to any effect of the tax change on the ongoing rate of inflation.

The implication of this approach on the need to adjust the monetary policy instrument will depend on the reaction of the public to the tax change. Consider an increase in taxes. At one extreme, the public is able to distinguish between changes in the level of prices and changes in the ongoing rate of inflation,[24] and there would be no need for tightening actions by the central bank. At the other extreme, if the price effect of the sales tax increase fed directly into the expected rate of inflation (that is, the public was unable to distinguish between once-and-for-all level changes and ongoing inflation pressures, or the public expected the central bank to accommodate whatever inflation pressures result from the tax changes, as was done in some past episodes of tax changes), considerable tightening of monetary conditions might be needed to bring about sufficient slack in the economy to offset the inflation pressures from the tax increase. The greater the credibility of the authorities and the more closely expected inflation is linked to the target rather than to past rates of inflation, the more likely that the reaction to the sales tax change will approach the first case rather than the second. While credibility is being built up, however, the most likely outcome is an intermediate one, in which the tax increase results in some rise in expectations of future inflation but less than would be typical for the same year-over-year advance in prices resulting from an aggregate demand shock. Thus, some tightening would be needed but less than in the second case.

Because it follows an explicit announcement, a tax change is the kind of shock that can be interpreted most easily as a change in price level rather than a change in ongoing inflation. However, a similar approach can be taken to certain supply shocks. For example, food and energy price movements tend to be more volatile than the price movements of the rest of the consumer basket of goods and services. Removing them from the measure of inflation that is treated as the focus of policy for operational purposes (the CPI excluding food, energy, and the effect of indirect taxes) lessens the likelihood that sharp and volatile movements in these components would influence inflation expectations. At the same time, since the target rate of increase of the operational definition of inflation would be adjusted to take into account any longer-term trend difference between food and energy prices and the rest of the CPI, the integrity of the approach is maintained and the importance of the overall CPI as the key variable in the system is reinforced.[25] In fact, over the last fifteen years, this has not been a problem in Canada since the trend of food and energy prices has been similar to that of the rest of the basket.

Another important type of shock that could have significant effects on inflation is a currency depreciation. The cause of a depreciation, in particular whether it is a real depreciation associated with economic weakness or a nominal depreciation associated with inflationary pressures, is a crucial element in determining whether a change in currency value will lead to an increase in the price level or is part of pressures on the ongoing rate of inflation. Hence, the cause of the depreciation will determine the nature of the monetary actions needed in response to it.

Examples might be helpful in illustrating this distinction. In a number of countries (including Canada) there was a sharp downward movement in the real value of the currency in the early 1990s, at a time of considerable slack in the economy. Indeed, in many of these countries, a major element in the decline in the value of the currency was the economic slack,[26] with the financial markets leading a successful speculative attack on currency parities in the expectation that they could not be held in the economic circumstances. In the event, the combined effect of the depreciation and the slack in the economy was a temporary rise in the rate of inflation, but one which was appreciably less than anticipated by most observers based on past episodes of currency depreciation. Furthermore, the increase in the price level directly resulting from the real depreciation did not feed into a rise into expected inflation, in large part because of the offsetting effect of the slack in the economy.[27]

In contrast, persistent domestic inflation pressures, which involve continuing upward movements in domestic prices and wages, will cause similar upward movements in the prices of tradable goods and services through downward pressure on the nominal external value of the currency. In these circumstances, the real value of the currency remains more or less unchanged. Such currency movements are a normal consequence of the inflation process, and not simply a once-and-for-all movement in the price level.

A final type of price level shock in some countries involves changes in the mortgage cost component of housing when the latter is closely linked to current interest rates (for example, if interest rates on mortgages float off the current short-term rate). A common adjustment in such countries is to remove this component from the operational definition of the target. If it were not excluded, interest rate movements aimed at bringing the rate of inflation back to the target could have a perverse effect on inflation expectations. Focusing on a measure that excludes this component should have little or no long-run effect on the CPI since the effect disappears over the interest rate cycle.[28]

The use of "caveats" and wider bands to help deal with supply shocks

Thus far, I have focused on the use of an operational definition for inflation that excludes the effects of certain kinds of supply shocks as a way of minimizing the effects of such shocks on expectations of future inflation and, hence, from directly affecting the ongoing rate of inflation. A similar result can be achieved by establishing in advance that the authorities will not react to certain kinds of shocks, provided that they affect only the price level and not the momentum of inflation. These "caveats" can serve as an alternative to having an operational definition for inflation that excludes such shocks, but they may not be quite as transparent to the public. They can also complement the use of an operational definition that excludes such shocks.

Another approach to achieving the same end would be to widen the target band for inflation, especially after price stability is achieved. The typical band used by central banks in bringing down the rate of inflation has been ± 1 percentage point. In Canada, this band is well below what would be needed to include, say, 95 per cent of inflation outcomes (that is, plus or minus two standard deviations) based on empirical work with historical inflation. The reason for choosing such a narrow band was the importance for communications purposes of focusing on a path that clearly showed a downward trend during the disinflation period, even at a risk of being outside the band at times. A wider band might have left the impression, especially initially, that the authorities were not serious about reducing inflation and would simply aim at maintaining current levels of inflation.

Once price stability has been achieved, the focus changes from achieving a downward trend for inflation to maintaining price stability. While the achievement of price stability and the associated acquisition of credibility are likely to reduce the variability of inflation, the narrow band is still unlikely to include a very high proportion, say 95 percent, of outcomes.[29]

A wider band for target inflation would ensure that more of the price movements resulting from supply shocks remained within the bands. To the extent that movements outside the band have an appreciable effect on expectations, the wider band might lessen the likelihood of supply shocks significantly affecting the expected rate of inflation. Two reservations are in order, however. Such a widening of the band would probably be successful only after the central bank has established a considerable degree of credibility by bringing inflation down to very low levels and would have to be carefully explained. Otherwise, it could be interpreted as a retreat from the commitment to maintain price stability. Second, it should not be used as a way of deferring the taking of action to bring inflation back to the center of the band in response to a persistent demand shock.

How are inflation projections done in practice?

While the above, lengthy discussion of shocks is important in conceptually distinguishing among various elements feeding into the inflation process, in practice there is less clarity about the sources of inflation pressure. Thus, in projecting future rates of inflation it is important to use all relevant available information.

There are a number of approaches to forecasting inflation one to two years out—structural models, reduced-form or vector-autoregression models, surveys of expectations, judgmental forecasts, as well as any of these adjusted to take account of data coming from information variables (especially monetary aggregates and other financial data). Many countries combine a number of approaches in developing their inflation forecast. While the degree of formality of the various approaches may differ from country to country, what is interesting is the central role the forecast has come to play in those central banks with inflation targets.[30] Of course, no one takes the point estimate of such forecasts as more than a best estimate (and one that almost certainly will be revised as new information comes in).[31] Nonetheless, the forecast is the crucial starting point for the analysis of what needs to be done to keep inflation within its band over the policy horizon of one to two years. It also can be used as the basis for simulations that examine the effect on forecast inflation as well as on other variables of alternative assumptions about the movement of exogenous variables or about the momentum of the economy. Such risk analyses can be very useful in assessing the sensitivity of the baseline forecasts to different scenarios.

In assessing the prospects for inflation, it should be clear from our earlier discussion that it is crucial to make a distinction between two types of factors that affect price developments—those that if not offset will lead to a permanent change in the rate of inflation and those that lead to transitory changes in inflation, which are expected to dissipate over time.[32] In the augmented Phillips-curve model of inflation, the fundamental factors affecting the underlying rate of inflation are the path of output relative to capacity and the expected rate of inflation.

It is because of the fundamental role of the path of output relative to capacity in determining the rate of inflation that so much attention is paid (both by the authorities and the financial markets) to information about aggregate demand, especially when an economy is operating near capacity.[33] It should be emphasized that it is not the rate of growth of demand that is crucial, but the *level* of excess demand or supply.[34] However, this emphasis on demand does not mean that the authorities have a target growth rate or target level for output. The estimate of capacity is always very uncertain and neither the level nor the rate of growth of capacity can be determined with precision. This is why there has to be continued re-assessment of the relationship of the path of excess demand or slack in the economy and the rate of inflation. And estimates of capacity (and hence slack) have to be re-calibrated from time to time in response to surprises in inflationary outcomes in either direction.

This way of interpreting inflation developments is of relevance in dealing with the assertion frequently heard in the United States that the Federal Reserve is underestimating the rate of growth of capacity output and preventing the economy from growing at its full potential by maintaining a policy stance that is too tight. If this were indeed the case, the outcome would be ever-increasing slack and a rate of inflation that was both declining over time and always coming in lower than the projection of the authorities.[35] In such circumstances, the estimate of capacity would be adjusted and the policy stance altered in response to the incoming information.

It is also sometimes argued that the emphasis in the policy process on the forecast of inflation and the incorporation of a wide variety of real as well as nominal information in developing the forecast is risky in that it could lead to cumulative one-way errors, as in the 1960s and 1970s, with continuously accelerating or decelerating inflation. However, a crucial difference between the way policy was conducted in earlier years and the way policy is currently conducted is the more central role that the target for inflation plays in the process. Indications that the measure of excess demand or supply is incorrect, or that policy actions are not sufficient to offset the pressures of demand on inflation, lead quickly to an adjustment of the policy instrument.

There is, however, a perceptual problem in this process, in that actions to affect the path of aggregate demand may have to be taken in advance of any direct signs of inflation ("getting ahead of the curve") and policy is sometimes criticized as reacting to nonexisting problems. It is, nonetheless, precisely this early taking of action that is crucial to achieving the desired outcome.

The role of financial variables in forecasting the inflation rate

In addition to focusing on the usual variables that enter into the inflationary process, central banks use information variables or indicators as a cross-check against their structural analysis. Sometimes this is formalized through the use of vector-autoregression models and other types of analysis of information content. Thus, for example, in the case of Canada, the narrow aggregate real M1 is a good leading indicator of real output growth, while M2+, a broad aggregate, serves as an indicator of inflation over the next quarter or two. Moreover, recent work using vector error-correction models suggests that nominal M1 also has useful properties as a leading indicator of inflation over a longer time horizon.[36]

More recently there has been considerable attention paid to the possible use of nominal interest rates, especially in conjunction with the yields on indexed bonds, as a measure of market expectations of inflation.[37] These can serve as a cross-check on the central bank's own medium-term forecasts, as an indicator of the credibility of the policy framework, or as a signal of the interpretation by the market of central bank actions.

The Bank of England has taken the lead among the central banks in the development and use of such measures, in part because of the availability in the United Kingdom of indexed or real return bonds across the maturity spectrum.[38] The difference between the rate on these bonds and on conventional bonds of the same maturity gives the central bank an indication of the average rate of inflation expected over that time horizon. Transformation of the data from a yield-to-maturity basis to a series of forward real and nominal rates of interest and the use of the latter to estimate the expected rate of inflation over these future time periods give a more transparent set of data for interpretation purposes.

Even in those countries that issue indexed bonds, the interpretation of the difference between the real rate and the rate on conventional instruments as a measure of inflation expectations is far from straightforward. Differences in tax treatment and the liquidity properties of the two types of debt can affect the level of the differential, although these factors probably change only slowly. Thus, the tendency is to focus more on changes in the differential as an indicator of changes in the expected rate of inflation, and less on the level of the differential as a measure of the level of expected inflation.

There is another important factor that affects the conventional interest rate but not the rate on indexed debt and that is a risk premium for inflation uncertainty.[39] Thus, for example, an aggregate demand shock that leads to a rise in both the expected rate of inflation and increased uncertainty about the future path of inflation will lead to a rise in the differential that exceeds the change in the expected rate of inflation. And unlike the other two factors affecting the differential, this one can change fairly quickly, making it difficult at times to interpret even the change in the differential.

For those countries without an indexed instrument, there is less scope for use of the term structure of interest rates to derive inflation expectation measures, since some assumption about the real rate (either constancy or relatively small movements) will be needed.[40] However, the empirical tendency for expected real interest rates and inflation expectations to move in opposite directions tends to balance the "noise" that movements in expected real interest rates add to inflation expectations and hence improves the ability of forward interest rates to indicate inflation expectations.[41] Moreover, the forward interest rates can be useful indicators of market expectations of future movements in the policy stance of the central bank as well as of future exchange rate movements. They can also be used to interpret the market's response to central bank actions or to "news" on the economy and inflation.[42]

The appropriate response of policy instruments to changes in forecast inflation

In the framework for inflation control that has been described above, the central bank must adjust its instrument in response to forecasts of inflation because of the lags between policy actions and inflation outcomes. The next issue to be addressed is how much the instruments should be adjusted in response to a given differential between forecast inflation and the target.

Estimating the relationship between interest rate movements and the rate of inflation

Assume that the outcome of the process of forecasting inflation and the related interpretation of leading indicators (and/or market assessments) is that the underlying trend of inflation is very likely to move away from the target and to remain there unless action is taken (for example, as a result of an aggregate demand shock). The response by the authorities would, of course, be to raise or lower the very short-term benchmark interest rate on which the central bank has most influence.

There are a number of factors that have to be taken into account in deciding on the size and timing of the movement of the interest rate instrument. While the magnitude of the links between the instrument and inflation is not known with any precision, the central bank can derive estimates of the relationships underlying this link from both structural and reduced-form models. Unfortunately, in any specific episode there is considerable uncertainty about the responses of the economic participants in virtually every link in the transmission process between the central bank action and the subsequent change in the rate of inflation.[43] That said, the monetary authorities have to take action when pressures on the rate of inflation are likely to push it away from the target in more than a transitory fashion, and that action has to be taken on the basis of the best estimates of the linkages.[44]

A path is therefore laid out for the instrument that would prevent the trend of inflation from moving away from the target or would bring it back to target if it had moved away. However, because of the degree of uncertainty surrounding the estimates of these linkages, there must be a continuous assessment of the effect of the change in the instrument on the various elements in the transmission process and on other variables that can yield useful information about the unfolding process. Thus, close attention is paid to the outcome (relative to the projected outcome) of a wide variety of variables in response to the change in the path of the instrument. Outcomes that differ from projection may be indicating that additional shocks have taken place, or that the initial shock was misinterpreted, or that the strength or timing of the linkages from the instrument to the other variables is different from what was expected. Depending on the interpretation, there may or may not be need for further changes in the path of the instrument variable. This process of continuously responding to the interpretation and re-interpretation of economic and financial developments by adjusting the instrument has been termed a process of "successive approximation."

In assessing the effect of the change in the benchmark interest rate on aggregate demand and inflation, it is important to take into account movements in both market interest rates and the exchange rate. When taking policy actions, central banks do not know the extent to which the effects of their actions will fall on interest rates and the extent to which they will fall on the exchange rate. It is the combined effect of central bank actions on the two variables (termed monetary conditions and encapsulated in a monetary conditions index at the Bank of Canada and in some other central banks)[45] that is crucial for the effect of the policy actions on aggregate demand and inflation.

Thus, for example, while a decline in aggregate demand may clearly necessitate an easing in monetary conditions because of its implications for the future path of inflation, that easing can occur through a decline in interest rates, a depreciation of the currency, or some combination of the two.[46] And it is the markets, rather than the monetary authorities, that determine the "split" of a given change in monetary conditions between the interest rate component and the exchange rate component in the short run. Of course, the relative importance of exchange rate movements and interest rate movements in affecting aggregate demand will differ across countries. In Canada, for example, empirical work suggests that a 3 percent real depreciation has about the same long-run effect on aggregate demand as a one-percentage-point decline in real short-term interest rates. For less open economies, the exchange rate change that corresponds to a one-percentage-point change in interest rates would be considerably larger. Nonetheless, given the potentially large movements in exchange rates that have taken place in recent years, attention to the aggregate demand effects of exchange rate changes is appropriate even for large, less open economies.

The discussion thus far has focused on a change in the desired path of monetary conditions in response to an economic shock.[47] In other circumstances desired monetary conditions may remain unchanged, but actual monetary conditions may change and hence require action by the authorities. Consider, for example, a situation in which the exchange rate appreciates for reasons unrelated to economic developments (for example, confidence in the currency rises in response to a political development). This results in a tightening in monetary conditions, and the appropriate policy response is to reduce the very short-term interest rate so as to bring about a decline in money-market rates. This adjustment is termed a "rebalancing" of monetary conditions.

In sum, central bank actions have to be taken on the basis of projections of inflation, which are based on the interpretation of current and expected movements of aggregate demand and other factors, as well as estimates of the links from policy actions to aggregate demand and from aggregate demand to inflation. While the projections and estimates will at times be incorrect, response to the evolving outcomes and to new information ensures that, at a minimum, the process will not result in cumulative or persistent one-way errors.

How quickly should inflation be brought back to the target if it moves away?

An important operational question is the speed with which the inflation rate should be brought back to the target if it moved away from it following a shock that the authorities were not able completely to offset. The answer to this question may involve a tradeoff between the volatility engendered by a very rapid return to the target, and the damage to credibility if inflation remains away from the target for a period of time, particularly if it remains outside the target band.

Consider, for example, a situation in which an incorrect interpretation of the economic situation (say, an overestimate or underestimate of the level of capacity in the economy or a demand shock that is more persistent than expected) resulted in inflation moving away from its target. Should the authorities try to bring inflation back to the center of the band as quickly as possible or should they aim for a gradual adjustment?

An attempt to engineer a very rapid return minimizes the potential effect on credibility of being away from the target. But it can lead to variability in output and volatility in financial markets, as interest rates and exchange rates swing around sharply to achieve the rapid return to the target.[48] A more gradual response smooths the path of output and may reduce the amplitude of fluctuations in interest rates and exchange rates. But it does risk some loss of credibility and the possibility that a higher or lower rate of inflation than the target rate might get entrenched.

The choice made in the Bank of Canada, based on empirical work regarding the implications of different speeds of return to the target, has been to aim at bringing inflation back to the center of the band over a six- to eight-quarter horizon. To try to minimize possible effects on credibility of pursuing such a policy, the Bank of Canada (1991) made this general approach explicit in the discussion of contingencies in its background statement introducing the targets. It was thus relying upon transparency and a clear understanding by the market of how it proposed to respond to certain shocks to minimize any credibility effects of the gradualist approach.

Tactical problems in achieving the desired path for monetary conditions

Another operational problem experienced at times in Canada has been the difficulty in achieving easier monetary conditions, even when economic developments and the inflation situation clearly call for such an easing. The problem arises from the interactions between markets before credibility is fully established.[49] Consider a situation in which more weakness in the economy than had been forecast indicates to the authorities that inflation is on a downward trend toward the lower end of the band, thus signaling the need for easier monetary conditions. If the markets remain concerned about the commitment of the authorities to price stability, they may interpret the easing as evidence of insufficient resolve on the part of the authorities. In these circumstances, the actions by the central bank to reduce the benchmark short-term interest rate could lead to a sharply declining currency, and, as extrapolative expectations develop in the exchange market, to rises in interest rates further out the maturity spectrum. Thus, the action by the central bank could be counterproductive in these circumstances, and hence, caution and a measured pace of easing, as well as a full explanation by the central bank of the basis of its views, might be required.

This type of concern is especially relevant in circumstances where there are other factors that call credibility into question. In Canada, for example, concerns about the fiscal situation and the political situation interacted with a two-decade history of significant inflation to leave the monetary authorities with limited credibility in spite of a more recent record of very low inflation. This, in turn, resulted in a situation in which the attempted easing by the authorities at times led to the counterproductive outcomes just described. However, more recently, when the fiscal situation improved markedly and the political problems receded, the markets were better able to accept easing monetary actions without the same concern for negative reactions that had been exhibited earlier.

Some issues related to the achievement and maintenance of price stability

The implication of different specifications of expected inflation

As was discussed earlier, with increased credibility, expected inflation may become more closely tied to the target rate of inflation than to past inflation. It is possible, in addition, that this link is stronger when inflation is at or below its target level than when it is above the target level. A simple characterization of this set of relationships is as follows:

$$\pi = \pi^e + b(y - y*)$$

$$\pi^e = A(L)\pi, \quad \pi > \pi^T$$

$$\pi^e = \pi^T, \quad \pi \leq \pi^T.$$

An alternative representation might link expected inflation to current and past rates of inflation when excess demand is positive and there is upward pressure on inflation, while expected inflation is related to the target rate of inflation when excess demand is negative and there is downward pressure on inflation. Whatever the exact specification of the model, it raises the possibility that the augmented Phillips curve holds at certain times while the older Phillips curve, without augmentation, holds at others, at least temporarily.[50]

What might cause this type of behavior, with rates of inflation below the price stability target less likely to lead to downward revisions of long-run inflation expectations than rates of inflation above the price stability target are to lead to upward revisions of expectations? Partly, it is a reflection of the history of the postwar period with its long experience of price increases but virtually none of price declines. Partly, it is based on an interpretation of the incentives facing the central bank. As formulated explicitly in the time-inconsistency models of the Barro-Gordon type, central banks may have an incentive to raise inflation above expected inflation to try to achieve extra output over the short run. There are no such incentives on the downside since a rate of inflation below expectations is associated with economic slack. Hence, there is no reason to interpret a rate of inflation below the announced target as indicative of a desire by the authorities to push inflation below the target.

What is the role in the policy framework of movements of the current rate of inflation?

As was evident in the earlier discussion, it is the effect of shocks to the forecast of inflation relative to the target for inflation that is the crucial determinant of the need for central bank action. Movements of the current rate of inflation play two roles within this policy framework.

First, movements of current inflation relative to the bands can provide a useful communications opportunity to explain central bank actions. Central to this role is the interpretation and explanation of the source of shocks, particularly whether they are likely to be transitory or more long-lasting, and their implications for the future path of inflation. If, for example, a rise in the measured rate of inflation is associated with a shock that is likely to have only temporary effects on inflation and is so perceived by the public, only a relatively modest central bank action would be needed in response. However, if the shock leads to an increase in the momentum of inflation that is expected to persist and to affect future rates of inflation, firm action should be taken even if inflation is still within the band.

The other key role of the actual outcome of inflation is as a check both on the model being used explicitly or implicitly to forecast inflation, and on the interpretation of shocks. A sequence of over- or under-predictions of inflation would indicate either that one or more of the key relationships on which policy is based, say that between the pattern of demand and inflation, is incorrectly specified, perhaps because capacity has been incorrectly estimated, or that the forecasters had interpreted the shocks incorrectly (for example, underestimating the persistence of a demand shock) and had therefore arrived at an incorrect assessment of the effect of the shock on inflation and/or inflation expectations.[51]

How can monetary policy be eased when interest rates are close to zero?

One of the criticisms of the policy goal of achieving price stability is that it rules out using negative real interest rates to provide stimulus to the economy at a time of weakness.[52] The implication of this line of argument is that targeting a positive rate of inflation is superior to price stability because of the added flexibility the possibility of having negative real rates gives the policymaker.

An important point worth noting in the context of this argument is that the achievement of price stability is likely to lead to a lessening in the amplitude of the business cycle fluctuations, since in the postwar period deep recessions (of the sort that might call for negative real rates) have typically been preceded by periods of strong inflation pressure that resulted in significant distortions in spending behavior, which, in turn, affected the subsequent downturn. In the absence of such inflationary distortions, the downturns are likely to be much milder. Hence, there is less likelihood of the need for a period of negative real interest rates. And the empirical work examining how the economy would have functioned if there had been no possibility of negative real interest rates indicates that there would have been only a small deterioration in overall economic performance.[53]

Moreover, while there is a floor of zero to nominal short-term rates, a near-zero nominal rate may still imply a real interest rate appreciably below its equilibrium value,[54] and hence, the interest rate channel can still be used to provide some stimulus to the economy.[55] In addition, for those who believe in more direct links between money and/or credit and spending,[56] central bank actions can be expansionary even when interest rate declines are limited because rates are close to zero. Also, in a flexible exchange rate world monetary conditions can be eased through both interest rate and exchange rate movements. Even if there is only limited easing possible via the interest rate, there can still be a depreciation of the currency at a time of economic weakness and downward pressure on the rate of inflation.[57]

Differences between targeting on monetary aggregates and targeting on inflation

While the nature of the policy process described above appears on the surface to be significantly different from that in countries using monetary aggregates as an intermediate target, I would argue that the differences are smaller than would appear on the surface. What is the role of an intermediate target? It is a variable that is closely linked with the final target of monetary policy and is affected by changes in the central bank's instrument (that is, the short-term interest rate). In the case of Germany and Switzerland today and in the case of many other countries that targeted monetary aggregates in earlier years, the final target was clearly the rate of inflation,[58] and the centrality of the monetary aggregates derived from their ability to serve as a leading indicator of inflation.[59] When this link broke down in many countries, monetary aggregates fell into disfavor as an intermediate target, although in some of these countries they were retained as information variables.

Since the value of the monetary aggregate as an intermediate target is the result of its link to inflation, it is not surprising that central banks respond to the movement in such an aggregate only when they believe that it is signaling future movements in inflation. And in circumstances where other information suggests that movements of the aggregate are not precursors of future inflation developments, even central banks targeting on the aggregates appear unwilling to adjust interest rates in response to movements in the monetary aggregate target.[60] Implicitly (or perhaps explicitly) they are making a forecast of inflation and responding to it. Put another way, even central banks targeting monetary aggregates do not adjust interest rates in an automatic or mechanical way when these aggregates grow too rapidly or too slowly. They clearly interpret the effect these movements have on future inflation in light of other information regarding financial and real side developments, such as indications of financial innovations, and so forth.

This is not to say that there are no differences between targeting inflation directly, and targeting monetary aggregates directly and inflation indirectly. The weight given to the aggregates as an indicator of inflation is clearly greater in the latter than in the former, the growth of the aggregates may have a direct effect on inflation expectations in those countries targeting on the aggregates, and there may be a different response to supply shocks.

It might also appear that decisions regarding the magnitude of policy actions are much simpler for countries that rely on monetary aggregates than for those that focus directly or indirectly on inflation. Movements of monetary aggregates above or below their targets lead to changes in short-term rates (based on the estimated relationships between changes in interest rates and changes in the monetary aggregates) designed to bring them back to their target. The approach thus seems to rely simply on the effect of interest rate changes on the monetary aggregates, and not on the entire transmission mechanism. But the perceived simplicity of this process is more apparent than real. First, as just discussed, there is typically no automaticity of reaction to movements in monetary aggregates; rather, there is an interpretation of whether the movements are driven by demand and price movements or by financial shocks (such as innovations). Second, a continuing assessment of the usefulness of the aggregates as a leading indicator of inflation is needed. Third, especially in the case of broader aggregates, the relationship between interest rate movements and the growth of aggregates occurs in large part through the effect of the interest rate changes on output and prices, so that knowledge of the transmission process may still be needed. Fourth, judgment is needed on the speed with which the monetary aggregate is brought back to its target. Fifth, in the case of a narrow aggregate target with high interest rate elasticity the interest rate movements needed to bring the aggregates back to target may not be sufficient to rein in inflationary or disinflationary pressures.[61] It is thus not evident that any less judgment is needed or used in adjusting interest rates in countries whose policy is based on monetary aggregate targets than in those focusing on inflation or price targets.

In sum, there is less difference between targeting on monetary aggregates and inflation-control targeting than appears on the surface.

Transparency and communications

Throughout this paper, there have been a large number of references to credibility, and to the implications of a greater or lesser degree of credibility on the actions that a central bank would have to take to achieve its target for inflation or price stability. In particular, the relevance of credibility was noted in the ability of the central bank to respond to demand shocks somewhat less quickly in circumstances when it is not sure whether they are temporary or persistent (the room for maneuver argument), the ability not to respond to supply shocks that have an effect only on the price level, the ability to bring inflation back to its target gradually when it has strayed from its target, and the ability to take easing action without creating doubts about the commitment of the authorities to the price stability target.

Given the significant benefits of credibility, how can the central bank improve its credibility and what can it do to lessen the negative effects of a lack of complete credibility? The only certain way of achieving credibility is a long period of success in maintaining a very low rate of inflation. And, as has often been noted, credibility is fragile and can be weakened by an apparent reversal of the commitment to the policy goal of low inflation or price stability. That said, there are certain things that can be done to enhance credibility, some by the central bank, others by authorities outside the central bank.

Fiscal problems can result in a concern by markets about the potential for monetization of the debt, lessening the credibility of the monetary authorities and resulting in a higher expected rate of inflation and a higher inflation uncertainty premium. Indeed, with serious fiscal problems there is the potential for a vicious circle, in which increases in international interest rates are expected to lead to increases in domestic rates, which, in turn, would cause a deterioration of the fiscal situation.[62] With the resulting rise in risk premiums, domestic interest rates could well rise more than international rates, even through domestic economic and inflation conditions do not warrant tighter monetary conditions.[63] Thus, in countries with serious fiscal problems, the credibility of the monetary authorities can be enhanced by an improvement by the government of its deficit and/or debt position. Similarly, political or constitutional difficulties (for example, weak governments unable to take needed fiscal action, or concerns about the future breakup of a country) can result in higher risk premia and a greater concern that inflation will be used to try to extricate a country from its debt burden, and they can therefore exacerbate a situation in which the monetary authorities are lacking in credibility. Any lessening of these difficulties might therefore lead to an improvement in the credibility of the monetary authorities.

Changes in institutional arrangements that clarify the mandate of the central bank and/or increase its independence can be of considerable assistance in building up credibility (and reducing risk premia). New Zealand has been a leader in this respect, with the central bank receiving both a clear mandate to achieve price stability (the definition of which is determined in an agreement between the Governor and the Minister of Finance) and the instrument independence to achieve that goal. In formal terms, these institutional changes can be seen as one way in which central banks can pre-commit to the achievement of price stability and can be sheltered from any political pressure on their day-to-day operating tactics to achieve that goal.

One important way in which the central bank can itself take the initiative to increase credibility or at least to mitigate the potentially negative effects of an absence of credibility is by increasing transparency of its objectives and actions.[64] By being clearer and more explicit about its goals, methods of operations, and interpretation of economic developments, the central bank can increase the understanding by the market and the public of its objectives and its tactical actions, and reduce the likelihood of an unfavorable response to its actions. Transparency can thus be thought of as a bridge to credibility, where the latter is not yet built up, or as a support to credibility where it already exists.

There are a number of aspects of transparency that need to be addressed. Consider, first, transparency about the objective of price stability. This can help longer-term savers and investors plan their behavior on the basis of the commitment by the central bank to stable prices in the long run.[65] Clear explanations by the central bank of the benefits of price stability will also help build public support for the objective. In addition, it is essential to have a clear statement of objectives if one expects markets to understand the policy actions being taken.

While a publicly-announced longer-term objective of price stability (or very low inflation) is the centerpiece of the policy strategy, it can be very useful to make the policy objective more concrete. This is the role of the targets for inflation or for the growth rate of monetary aggregates, particularly on the way to price stability. The central bank can then build up credibility by achieving its announced targets. It is also helpful to maintain a band for price changes even when price stability is achieved, both to maintain the accountability of the central bank, and to give some indication of the types of inflation outcomes that are most likely to lead the central bank to take action. In this context, it is worth repeating that a discussion in advance of how the central bank will react to various contingencies will have the benefit of helping the public and markets to understand the thinking of the central bank, and will reduce the likelihood of a misinterpretation of the actions of the central bank (or lack of action) when one of the contingencies occurs. For example, as discussed earlier, an assertion in advance that the central bank would accommodate the first round or price level effects of a rise in a sales taxes or VAT but not the second round effects, or wage-price spiral, would forewarn the market and public that there would be one year in which growth in the overall CPI would rise above the target (although other measures such as the CPI less food, energy and indirect taxes would be largely unaffected by the tax change), while policy action would be taken if the initial price effect fed into a wage-price spiral.

Transparency with respect to the views of the monetary authorities regarding the transmission mechanism and the economic situation is likely to result in the market having a better understanding of the tactics which the central bank is using and why it is taking action to change the benchmark rate of interest. Indeed, in cases where markets are in full agreement with the central bank's interpretation of economic and inflation developments and in which they understand the tactics being employed, money market rates are likely to move in advance of the adjustment of the benchmark rate on which the central bank operates, as the markets correctly anticipate action by the authorities. For example, the release of surprisingly weak inflation or output data indicates that future inflation would likely be lower than previously anticipated, that an easing of monetary conditions would be appropriate, and that a decline in the benchmark rate is likely to be forthcoming. In these circumstances, one would expect to see in response to the newly released data, a decline in money market interest rates and possibly in interest rates further out the maturity spectrum, as well perhaps as some depreciation of the currency, as markets act in anticipation of a decline in the benchmark rate. This type of response facilitates policy actions by signaling that the market agrees with the central bank interpretation of economic developments and the need for some easing to achieve the targets (without loss of credibility).

Recently, many central banks have issued periodic reports on inflation or on monetary policy to explain their actions in the recent past and to indicate some of the factors likely to play a role in their future actions. Speeches by senior officials and testimony in Congress or Parliament can also play an important role in this regard, although a situation in which different officials provide differing interpretations of economic developments may be confusing to the markets.

In Canada, in addition to the above measures, there have recently been a number of changes in operating tactics aimed at helping markets to understand central bank tactics and actions. These include: the use of a narrow band for the benchmark 1-day rate to signal the range desired by the central bank for this rate;[66] the linking of bank rate to the top of the band for the 1-day rate rather than to the 91-day treasury bill rate in order to lessen the confusion arising from two sometimes conflicting signals of the policy stance of the bank; and the issue of a press release when the band and bank rate are changed, explaining the reasons for the change. The outcome, in my view, has been a much better understanding by the markets of the central bank actions, a more favorable backdrop against which to take action, and less likelihood of an unfavorable reaction by the market to a change since it is less likely to be a surprise to them.

In sum, transparency and more open communications can be very helpful in building up credibility and in obtaining the desired outcome from policy actions. In the end, however, it is the achievement of price stability or the pre-announced desired path for inflation that will be the key to the development of credibility.

Author's Note: I am indebted to a number of my colleagues at the Bank of Canada for comments and criticisms of earlier drafts of this paper. Any remaining errors are, of course, my own responsibility.

Endnotes

[1]See Leiderman and Svensson (1995) or Haldane (1995a) for discussions of inflation targeting and the experience of a number of countries that have adopted inflation targets as the goal of policy. For a discussion of the Canadian experience, see Freedman (1995a).

[2]For a comparison of the implications of the two concepts, see Fillion and Tetlow (1994) and Haldane and Salmon (1995).

[3]Alchian and Klein (1973), Goodhart (1995).

[4]Asset prices should, however, be treated as an important information variable, because of their reflection of market expectations of future economic developments and their direct effect on future aggregate demand (for example, the possible effect of a stock market boom on housing and durables purchases).

[5]Whether the authorities choose to use the ordinary CPI or some other measure such as the trimmed mean will depend both on the properties of the latter and the ability to explain its movements to the public.

[6]See, for example, Gordon (1993), Crawford (1993), and Yates (1995).

[7]The Bureau of Labor Statistics estimate of bias for the U.S. CPI is 0.6 percentage points. For a different view, see the report by the Boskin committee (1995). The bias in the CPI in the United States may be higher than that in many other countries because of the formula bias in the U.S. measure.

[8]Note that these two arguments are mutually inconsistent, with the former focusing on the effects on the economy of declining prices and wages, and the latter focusing on the possibility that the economy will be unable to generate declines in prices and wages.

[9]The recent Japanese experience with mildly declining prices was associated with considerable weakness in the economy but not a serious depression.

[10]If the target were based on a price level rather than a rate of inflation, this argument would be even stronger since a period of declining prices would be expected to be followed by a period of rising prices.

[11]See also Yates (1995).

[12]See also McLaughlin (1994). For contrary views, see Akerlof, Dickens, and Perry (1996) and Fortin (1996).

[13]In Canada, there is fragmentary evidence of some increase in the relative importance of variable pay schemes (bonuses, and so forth) as opposed to increases in base wage rates. If sustained, this development would be a practical example of institutional changes toward greater wage flexibility.

[14]For ease of exposition, throughout this paper I refer to the very short-term rate of interest as either the instrument of monetary policy (rather than as the operational target of policy, a more accurate term in many countries) or as the benchmark rate of interest. In fact, the actual

instrument in many countries is the change in the central bank balance sheet that results in the change in the very short-term rate of interest.

[15]Svensson (1996).

[16]If the inflation outcome differs from that which had been projected, there might have to be modifications in the model of the economy underlying the forecast or in the linkages presumed to hold between interest rates and the rate of inflation.

[17]I use the term persistent (or long-lasting) rather than permanent because very few shocks are truly permanent, and the effects for policy purposes are similar whether the shock lasts, say, three years or a much longer time.

[18]In this simplified model, the only source of lags comes from expectations. More complex models would allow for other sources of lags and dynamics, for example, contracts lasting more than one time period.

[19]In rational or partly rational expectations models, expected inflation will be linked entirely or in part to the model forecast of future inflation.

[20]The band may be centered on a zero rate of inflation or on a non-zero rate of inflation.

[21]See Taylor (1993).

[22]These can be thought of as past easing or tightening still "in the pipeline."

[23]In the explanation of how monetary policy would operate on the path to price stability, it was indicated that a series of tax changes would be treated differently from an occasional change, with the former necessitating an offsetting change in the trend rate of growth of core inflation (CPI excluding food, energy, and the effect of indirect taxes) so that the trend in the overall CPI would not be affected by the continuing series of tax changes. A similar distinction is made between transitory and trend differences between core inflation and food and energy price inflation. Whether these provisos should carry over to a world in which price stability has been achieved would depend on the credibility of the price stability target and whether inflation expectations would adjust to higher measured inflation caused by a series of tax or food and energy price changes.

[24]Their ability to make this distinction may be assisted by the treatment of taxes in the definition of inflation for operational purposes and by a communications exercise that indicates that the central bank will accommodate the first-round effects on the price level of the sales tax change but not any second-round effects leading to a wage-price spiral.

[25]Thus, for example, if the overall CPI target growth were 1 percent, food and energy prices had a trend growth of 3 percent, and food and energy comprised 20 percent of the CPI basket, the operational target of CPI excluding food and energy would have to be set at 0.5 percent.

[26]Another factor in many cases was an overvaluation of the currency.

[27]Indeed, many importers were not able to pass through all of the direct effect of the depreciation to their customers.

[28]A change in real interest rates can have a lasting effect on the mortgage cost component of

housing, but this would be a once-and-for-all change in the price level, not an ongoing effect on the rate of inflation.

[29]See Crawford and Kasumovich (1996) on inflation variability in Canada.

[30]Haldane (1995b), Duguay and Poloz (1994), Longworth and Freedman (1995).

[31]And the Bank of England even publishes confidence bands around its inflation forecast.

[32]The distinction between the fundamental factors and the transitory factors affecting inflation is an organizing principle in the semi-annual *Monetary Policy Report* issued by the Bank of Canada.

[33]Recent developments in the United States attest to this observation.

[34]In some models both factors play a role, although the level of excess demand is more important than its rate of growth. The term "speed limit effect" is sometimes applied to the effect of the rate of growth of output on inflation.

[35]This argument would not carry over to an environment in which price inflation was rigid in the downward direction and the inflation rate was near zero.

[36]See Armour and others (1996). All these relationships can be thought of either as causal or as simple empirical regularities without a theoretic explanation.

[37]Breedon (1995), Svensson (1993, 1994), Côté, Jacob, Nelmes, and Whittingham (1996).

[38]In other countries indexed debt is issued only at a small number of maturities. Only in the United Kingdom is there sufficient breadth of issues to permit estimates of expected inflation over various future time periods.

[39]It is thus not surprising that in Canada survey results of expected inflation are consistently lower than estimates from the differences between interest rates on conventional debt and on indexed debt. Similarly, in the United Kingdom, this measure of inflation expectations consistently overpredicts inflation outcomes.

[40]See, for example, Ireland (1996).

[41]Söderlind (1995).

[42]Svensson (1993).

[43]Thiessen (1995).

[44]See Brainard (1967) on the effect of uncertainty on the size of the action that the authorities should take.

[45]As noted in Freedman (1994), the monetary conditions index concept is most useful in the period between formal projection exercises. Moreover, while the real monetary conditions index (based on the real interest rate and the real value of the currency) is the theoretically appropriate construct, much more use is made of the nominal index because of the practical difficulties of constructing the real index in the short run.

[46]Of course, whether the easing occurs through an interest rate decline or through a currency depreciation will have implications for the component of aggregate demand that will be affected, as well as the time path for the rate of inflation.

[47]Certain kinds of shocks affect both desired monetary conditions and actual monetary conditions. Thus, for example, a terms of trade improvement would require a tightening in desired monetary conditions because it is expansionary, but also typically results in tighter actual monetary conditions since it leads to an appreciation of the exchange rate. For more details, see Freedman (1995b).

[48]There is even the possibility of instrument instability in certain cases. See, for example, Holbrook (1972).

[49]Zelmer (1996).

[50]If inflation persistently remains below the target, eventually expectations would begin to adjust to actual inflation and the rigid link between expected inflation and target inflation would break down.

[51]See Longworth and Freedman (1995).

[52]Summers (1991).

[53]Fuhrer and Madigan (1994).

[54]It is worth noting that the equilibrium real interest rate has probably increased in response to the elimination of restrictions in financial markets.

[55]Of course, in a period of deflation, the floor to real interest rates would not be zero but would equal the rate of deflation. This reinforces the importance of avoiding periods of ongoing deflation.

[56]See, for example, Gertler and Gilchrist (1993) for a discussion of the role of the credit channel in the transmission mechanism.

[57]Of course, in circumstances where governments are not overly constrained by their debt position, an easing in fiscal policy can also help provide stimulus to the economy.

[58]Of course, the really ultimate target is improvement in the standard of living in the country, and price stability is the means whereby monetary policy contributes to that ultimate goal.

[59]This property may derive from a causal relationship or simply reflect an empirical regularity.

[60]This is analogous to the Poole (1970) analysis of financial shocks versus real shocks.

[61]Thiessen (1983).

[62]This effect is strongest when the debt outstanding is concentrated in shorter-term issues.

[63]Conversely, at times of falling international interest rates, the potential improvement in the fiscal situation could lead to a greater decline in domestic rates than in international rates.

[64]Thiessen (1995), Blinder (1996).

[65]Support by the government for the announced goal can also be helpful in convincing the public that the objective is more likely to be met.

[66]In the future (after the introduction of a large-value payment system) the central bank will also signal its preferred position within the band for the 1-day rate.

References

Akerlof, G.A., W.T. Dickens, and G.L. Perry. "The Macroeconomics of Low Inflation," *Brookings Papers on Economic Activity,* (1), (1996), pp. 1-59.

Alchian, A.A., and B. Klein. "On a Correct Measure of Inflation," *Journal of Money, Credit and Banking,* 5 (1, Part 1), (1973), pp. 173-91.

Armour, J., J. Atta-Mensah, W. Engert, and S. Hendry. *A Distant-Early-Warning Model of Inflation Based on M1 Disequilibria,* Working Paper 96-5. Ottawa: Bank of Canada, 1996.

Bank of Canada. "Targets for Reducing Inflation," *Bank of Canada Review,* (March 1991), pp. 3-15.

Blinder, A.S. *The Federal Reserve in the Nation's Service.* Paper presented at Princeton University, April 1996.

Boskin, M.J. "Toward a More Accurate Measure of the Cost of Living," *Interim Report to the Senate Finance Committee from the Advisory Commission to Study the Consumer Price Index,* September 15, 1995.

Brainard, W.C. "Uncertainty and the Effectiveness of Policy," *American Economic Review,* 57(2), (1967), pp. 411-25.

Breedon, F. "Bond Prices and Market Expectations of Inflation," *Bank of England Quarterly Bulletin,* (May 1995), pp. 160-65.

Card, D., and D. Hyslop. "Does Inflation 'Grease the Wheels' of the Labor Market?" *NBER Working Paper no. 5538,* April 1996.

Côté, A., J. Jacob, J. Nelmes, and M. Whittingham. "Inflation Expectations and Real Return Bonds," *Bank of Canada Review,* (Summer 1996), pp. 41-53.

Crawford, A. *Measurement Biases in the Canadian CPI,* Technical Report 64. Ottawa: Bank of Canada, 1993.

___________, and C. Dupasquier. "Can Inflation Serve as a Lubricant for Market Equilibrium?" in *Economic Behaviour and Policy Choice under Price Stability.* Ottawa: Bank of Canada, 1994, pp. 49-80.

___________, and M. Kasumovich. *Does Inflation Uncertainty Vary with the Level of Inflation*? Working Paper 96-9. Ottawa: Bank of Canada, 1996.

Duguay, P., and S. Poloz. "The Role of Economic Projections in Canadian Monetary Policy Formulation," *Canadian Public Policy,* 20(2), (1994), pp. 189-99.

Fillion, J-F, and R. Tetlow. "Zero Inflation or Price-Level Targeting: Some Answers from Stochastic Simulations on a Small Open-Economy Macro Model," in *Economic Behaviour and Policy Choice under Price Stability.* Ottawa: Bank of Canada, 1994, pp. 129-66.

Fortin, P. "The Great Canadian Slump," *Canadian Journal of Economics,* 29(4), (1996), forthcoming.

Freedman, C. "The Use of Indicators and of the Monetary Conditions Index in Canada," in T.J.T. Baliño and C. Cottarelli, eds., *Frameworks for Monetary Stability.* Washington, D.C.: International Monetary Fund, 1994, pp. 458-76.

___________. "The Canadian Experience with Targets for Reducing and Controlling Inflation," in L. Leiderman and L.E.O. Svensson, eds., *Inflation Targets.* London: Centre for

Economic Policy Research, 1995a, pp. 19-31.
__________. "The Role of Monetary Conditions and the Monetary Conditions Index in Canada," *Bank of Canada Review,* (Autumn 1995b), pp. 53-9.
Fuhrer, J., and B. Madigan. *Monetary Policy When Interest Rates are Bounded at Zero,* Working Paper 94-1. Federal Reserve Bank of Boston, 1994.
Gertler, M., and S. Gilchrist. "The Role of Credit Market Imperfections in the Monetary Transmission Mechanism: Arguments and Evidence," *Scandinavian Journal of Economics,* 95(1), (1993), pp. 43-64.
Goodhart, C.A.E. "Price Stability and Financial Fragility," in K. Sawamoto, F. Nakajima, and H. Taguchi, eds., *Financial Stability in a Changing Environment.* London: The Macmillan Press, 1995, pp. 439-97.
Gordon, R. J. "Measuring the Aggregate Price Level: Implications for Economic Performance and Policy," in K. Shigehara, ed., *Price Stabilization in the 1990s.* London: The Macmillan Press, 1993, pp. 233-68.
Haldane, A.G., ed. *Targeting Inflation.* Bank of England, 1995a.
__________. "Introduction," in A.G. Haldane, ed., *Targeting Inflation.* Bank of England, (1995b), pp. 1-12.
__________. and C.K. Salmon. "Three Issues on Inflation Targets," in A.G. Haldane, ed., *Targeting Inflation.* Bank of England, (1995), pp. 170-201.
Holbrook, R.S. "Optimal Economic Policy and the Problem of Instrument Instability," *American Economic Review,* 62 (1), (1972), pp. 57-65.
Ireland, P.N. "Long-Term Interest Rates and Inflation: A Fisherian Approach," Federal Reserve Bank of Richmond *Economic Quarterly.* 82(1), (1996), pp. 21-35.
Lebow, D.E., J.M. Roberts, and D.J. Stockton. *Economic Performance Under Price Stability,* Working Paper 125. Board of Governors of the Federal Reserve System, 1992.
Leiderman, L., and L.E.O. Svensson, eds. *Inflation Targets.* London: Centre for Economic Policy Research, 1995.
Longworth, D., and C. Freedman. "The Role of the Staff Economic Projection in Conducting Canadian Monetary Policy," in A.G. Haldane, ed., *Targeting Inflation.* Bank of England, (1995), pp. 101-12.
McLaughlin, K.J. "Rigid Wages?" *Journal of Monetary Economics,* 34(3), (1994), pp. 383-414.
Poole, W. "Optimal Choice of Monetary Policy Instruments in a Simple Stochastic Macro Model," *Quarterly Journal of Economics,* 84(2), (1970), pp. 197-216.
Söderlind, P. *Forward Interest Rates as Indicators of Inflation Expectations,* CEPR Discussion Paper no. 1313, (December 1995).
Summers, L. "How Should Long-Term Monetary Policy Be Determined?" *Journal of Money, Credit and Banking,* 23 (3, Part 2), (1991), pp. 625-31.
Svensson, L.E.O. *Term, Inflation and Foreign Exchange Risk Premia: A Unified Treatment,* NBER Working Paper no. 4544, (November 1993).
__________. *Monetary Policy with Flexible Exchange Rates and Forward Interest Rates as Indicators,* NBER Working Paper no. 4633, (January 1994).
__________. *Inflation Forecast Targeting: Implementing and Monitoring Inflation Targets,* 1996, mimeo.
Taylor, J.B. "Discretion Versus Policy Rules in Practice," *Carnegie-Rochester Conference Series on Public Policy,* 39, (December 1993), pp. 195-214.
Thiessen, G.G. "The Canadian Experience with Monetary Targeting," in P. Meek, ed., *Central Bank Views on Monetary Targeting.* Federal Reserve Bank of New York, (1983), pp. 100-4.
__________. "Uncertainty and the Transmission of Monetary Policy in Canada—The HERMES-Glendon Lecture," *Bank of Canada Review,* (Summer 1995), pp. 3-21.
Yates, A. "On the Design of Inflation Targets," in A.G. Haldane, ed., *Targeting Inflation.* Bank of England, (1995), pp. 135-69.

Zelmer, M. "Strategies Versus Tactics for Monetary Policy Operations," in *Money Markets and Central Bank Operations*. Proceedings of a conference held at the Bank of Canada, 1996, forthcoming.

Commentary: What Operating Procedures Should Be Adopted to Maintain Price Stability?—Practical Issues

Otmar Issing

With his paper, Charles Freedman provides an impressive overview of the most important practical issues relating to the maintenance of price stability in a monetary framework with direct inflation targets. His lucid analysis ranges from the choice of the appropriate price index to the potential benefits of greater transparency about the objectives and actions of monetary policy.

Charles Freedman invites us in his paper to consider whether the maintenance of low rates of inflation requires a different monetary policy strategy from the one needed to combat high or rising rates of inflation. The topicality of this subject derives from the fact that, since the beginning of the 1990s, inflation has declined sharply all over the world. For example, the rate of inflation in the ten major industrial countries averaged 2.2 percent both in 1994 and in 1995. For 1996 and 1997, too, the Organization for Economic Cooperation and Development (OECD) expects moderate, or further diminishing, growth rates of consumer prices in its member countries; the forecasts for the OECD countries, excluding Turkey and Mexico, predict less than 2 percent per year in each case (measured against the rate of change in the GDP deflator).[1] With the exception of 1986, when the sharp decline in oil prices had a restraining effect on the rise in consumer prices all over the world, the rates of inflation are thus at their lowest level for more than thirty years, and in some countries, they have reached a level which is generally equated with price stability.

In the United States, the rate of inflation has fallen from more than 5 percent in 1990 to approximately 3 percent; the same applies to the average price increase in the fifteen member states of the European Union. In Canada, just as in Germany, the rate of inflation is at present below 2 percent, and no new rise seems likely in the foreseeable future. It is true that in some countries a similarly low price increase could be observed for some time, for example, in Germany in 1967-68 and then again in 1986-88. What is new is that the decreasing, or low, rates of inflation have not been limited in the past few years to a few industrial countries, but, instead, it is obviously a global phenomenon. This trend has prompted some commentators to designate inflation as an "extinct volcano" and to announce the beginning of the "zero era." Some are already talking about the "death of inflation," and even the danger of a global deflation is being mooted.[2] In Germany, the new school, which asserts that "inflation is dead," calls up memories of the vision of the former Minister of Economics Karl Schiller, who as early as 1968 announced: "Inflation is dead, as dead as a rusty nail."

However, experience since then has shown that the combating of inflation can by no means be considered a problem which has been finally solved or may even be relativized again. We should never be too sure that the mistakes of the past will not be repeated; and this applies all the more to a central bank. On the other hand, we can at least hope that the problems which were associated with the high rates of inflation were so dramatic that they will not be easily forgotten.

There are many reasons for the trend toward slower price increases in the past few years, but monetary policy is clearly the most important one; conversely, it must take the blame for mistakes committed in earlier years. In this context, the breakneck speed of inflation rates in many countries in the 1970s was not least attributable to the attempt to use an expansionary monetary policy to overcome the negative effects on employment of the oil price shocks. When, however, inflation in the OECD countries accelerated to more than 12 percent in the mid-1970s and failed to decline perceptibly toward the end of the decade, the perception spread that high inflation rates were obviously not capable of solving the growing employment problems. Once it was realized that inflation is basically a monetary phenomenon and that the influence of monetary policy on employment lasts only as long as the expected inflation trend differs from the actual rate of inflation, it became imperative to concentrate monetary policy once again on its core task. As a result, a growing willingness to regain price stability could be observed in the 1980s.

Concurrently with the appreciation that monetary policy should concentrate on solving the inflation problem, it became increasingly clear that the success of that policy is greatly dependent on institutional arrangements. Particularly the independence of the central bank—which had not been a major topic of academic discussion for a long time either—has since become the nucleus of a positive and normative theory of inflation. The fact that there is a close connection between the independence of the central bank and success in the field of combating inflation can be justified convincingly not only in theory. Empirical evidence is conclusive, too: numerous studies have shown that, as the degree of autonomy of a central bank increases, the average rate of inflation and its fluctuations decrease, as a rule. At the same time, the fact that high and volatile inflation rates are associated with high costs for the overall economy and that stable prices are conducive to the long-term growth process are, in my opinion, two of the established findings of our discipline.[3] However, far less research has been devoted to the "excess burden" or "sacrifice ratio" in the case of a no-more-than-moderate pace of monetary erosion. Is the result to be expected here really worth the effort?

This question might well be answered in the affirmative, bearing in mind especially the sometimes complex interplay between inflation and the tax and transfer system and the ensuing distortionary effects. If one follows the cost-benefit analysis undertaken by Martin Feldstein for the United States, which is also interesting from a methodological point of view, the potential benefit of the transition from a low rate of inflation to price stability is by no means a *quantité négligeable*.[4] Even if, like Feldstein, one takes due account of the costs of transition, the positive welfare effect will materialize every year and, on a present value analysis, dominate the temporary output losses.

Experience of inflation in the past has prompted some countries to commit their central banks statutorily to pursuing the objective of price stability, and to grant them a high degree of independence in doing this. Other countries have tried to prove the stability-orientation of their monetary policy by announcing official objectives and by ensuring greater transparency in terms of the decisonmaking criteria they apply. Charles Freedman has just presented the Canadian model to us. The Bank of England, too, has made major efforts in that direction.[5]

The position of the central banks vis-à-vis their respective governments has also been strengthened in the past few years by the fact that, as a result of the increasing liberalization of the capital markets, monetary policy in the major industrial countries has been subjected more and more to the critical observation by the international financial markets. Investors from all over the world are closely watching each national economic policy-related decision. The increasing "expectation bias" of the financial markets has meant that a discretionary departure from a stability-oriented course is penalized more quickly and more sharply by capital outflows and rising interest rates. The mere suspicion that the control of inflation is to be sacrificed in favor of other objectives can lead to a massive loss in confidence. The resulting risk premiums push up interest rates at the long end of the market and thus frustrate the original intention of pursuing an employment-oriented monetary policy.

To put it in a nutshell:

- The financial markets have become an important ally for implementing a stability-oriented monetary policy.

- In cases where convictions as to the central task of monetary policy are still of a faltering nature, the globalized financial markets take over the function of a merciless disciplinarian.

One might even go so far as to say that the high inflation rates of the past destroyed the very basis of the existence of inflation by drawing the attention of the financial markets to the dangers of an easier monetary policy. Inflation committed suicide, as it were. However, the wolf always comes when you stop crying, "Wolf." In fact, things are not going so well in our economies that we do not have be afraid of the temptation to solve problems through inflation becoming irresistible again. The fact that at present there is virtual agreement on the importance of stable money is, therefore, no guarantee for ensuring that the pendulum will not swing the other way again in future. If, for example, public debt, which in many countries threatens to get out of hand, cannot be restrained, the inflation tax could once again be regarded as a simple and politically "cheap" means for solving the debt problem. Keeping watch and warning against the dangers of a new shifting of priorities, therefore, remain a permanent task of the central banks.

Even though the underlying conditions for maintaining the price stability achieved seem to be favorable at present, a stability-oriented policy cannot, therefore, be taken for granted. In this context, I should like to draw your attention to three key questions concerning monetary policy.

—How can confidence be created in the stability orientation of the central bank through the latter's self-commitment?

—What is the appropriate monetary policy strategy—not least in view of the first question?

—How can this strategy be best implemented in practice?

In view of the increased sensitivity of the financial markets, the central bank has to gear its approach toward anchoring market participants' expectations about inflation as far as possible to the low level achieved at present. Fostering the belief that price stability is in the interest of the central bank itself and in the interest of those responsible for its monetary policy (the key words *independence* and *statutory commitment to price stability* spring to mind here) and achieving as much transparency as possible in the monetary policy decisionmaking process are important requirements here. Only if the confidence of the markets in the permanence of the price stability achieved can be ensured, can society fully profit from the positive welfare effects of an existing high degree of price stability. Failing this, expectations about inflation, and thus longer-term interest rates, will continue to contain no-confidence premiums, which, in turn, will have a negative effect on investment and real growth, and thus jeopardize the acceptability of a monetary policy geared toward price stability.

But even if the central bank is clearly committed to the final objective of price stability, announcing a correspondingly low inflation target, as an anchor for inflationary expectations, is hardly sufficient. Instead, the central bank has not only to announce the final objective but also has to disclose the policy rules and to convince the public that the decisionmaking criteria used are suitable for maintaining over the long term the degree of price level stability already achieved. In view of the length of time required before monetary policy impulses eventually affect demand and prices, all central banks have to depend in their decisionmaking on indicators or intermediate variables, which signal incipient inflation dangers as early and as reliably as possible.

In this context, a number of central banks have placed increased emphasis on inflation forecasts and their discussion in public. As we have heard from Charles Freedman, such inflation forecasts can be interpreted as an intermediate objective on the road to price stability. Doubtless, an explicit discussion of inflation targets and inflation expectations alone is an important step toward more transparency. This applies particularly to those central banks whose policy—for whatever reasons—was previously geared less clearly to price stability. In addition, the fact that under that approach all relevant information is evaluated by the central bank will be considered attractive. On the other hand, we have to assume, as before, that our knowledge of inflationary processes is very incomplete. It is, therefore, likely that it is not only the results of inflation forecasts which will remain controversial but also the ideas of what are the appropriate forecasting procedures. Providing for transparency will, therefore, always remain an ambitious task.

A monetary policy which is based on a multitude of more or less equivalent indicators and the resulting inflation assessment is, however, more difficult to fathom for the markets and the other economic agents than a strategy which concentrates on pursuing an intermediate objective. Those central banks which have direct inflation targets are aware of the fact that they have to counteract the impression of arbitrariness inherent in an approach of looking at everything by stepping up their efforts at more transparency. Even if the central bank publishes its assessment of future price perspectives regularly and in detail, however, the transparency of a policy rule which is based on inflation forecasts will probably be lower than in the case of a monetary policy which focuses on an intermediate monetary objective.

I agree, in principle, with Charles Freedman when he says that the differences between monetary targeting and direct inflation targeting will presumably be lower, in practice, than might initially be assumed on the basis of the theoretical discussion. Both approaches are ultimately geared toward the final objective of lower inflation rates and are based, for the assessment of future inflation dangers, on a multitude of financial and real economic indicators. But the most important difference probably consists in the different weights attached to the individual indicators. It is true that in its decision-making the Bundesbank takes into consideration the entire monetary policy environment, but it attaches particular importance to the growth of the money stock, which is reflected in the derivation and the announcement of the monetary targets.

Monetary targets not only increase the transparency of the policy rule; they also promote a clear definition of economic policy responsibilities: by setting the monetary target, the central bank assumes responsibility for the inflation trend, but not for fiscal or wage policy decisions which lead to a one-off shift in the price level or have a short-term impact on the current rate of inflation. By contrast, the higher priority attached to price forecasts and to the final objective under a direct inflation targeting approach runs the risk that monetary policy will become involved in the general economic policy decisionmaking process, and this might make it more difficult to defend its independence.

In contrast to the Bank of Canada, the Bundesbank has remained faithful for more than two decades to its concept of deriving monetary targets, announcing them, and pursuing them. No one would claim that there have been no difficulties in maintaining this strategy. The annual target has been missed nearly every other year. However, even in those years, the monetary targets have proved to be successful as important points of reference, if only because we have been forced publicly to justify deviations from the target by putting forward convincing arguments. On the other hand, this has protected us from the danger of accepting failures to meet the target too easily. I would even go as far as to say that this is not only attributable to the comparatively good result with respect to the final objective, namely, price stability. It is also the strategy and its implementation which have helped to establish the reputation of the Bundesbank's monetary policy.

In the Bundesbank we have always endeavored to make the monetary targets somewhat less abstract and to demonstrate the link between monetary growth and our price notions to the public. We established this link when we derived our targets. It was simple and at the same time flexible, and helped us to influence expectation formation in the economy in accordance with our objectives.

In the 1970s and in the first half of the 1980s, when the inflation rates were still far above our own targets and when it was imperative to regain price stability step by step, we initially based our monetary targets on the so-called unavoidable price increase rates. With these objectives, we were able to reduce monetary growth rates gradually. When in the second half of the 1980s price stability had been achieved, we chose our monetary targets in a way to ensure that they were compatible with annual price increases of no more than 2 percent.

Even though the Bundesbank has not always stated explicitly which inflation measure it considered the most appropriate one, it has tended to prefer a broad definition of that measure: if there are no major price shocks, the GDP deflator, for example, may well be an acceptable choice. However, periods with high import price rises, such as we experienced in connection with the oil price shocks, require additional considerations in that respect. If inflation rates overshoot this critical ceiling, we have to take the distorting and growth-impeding effects of price rises so seriously that we cannot accept them over the long term. All in all, the changeover from a policy of regaining price stability to a policy of maintaining a high degree of price stability within the framework of our concept has been possible without posing real problems.

The situation became more difficult when, in the wake of German reunification and the strong expansionary impulses associated with this, prices in Germany at the beginning of the 1990s rose more sharply for some time. Although it was foreseeable that this inflationary impulse would not disappear immediately, we did not assume higher price increase rates when we derived our targets. In other words, our monetary targets were very ambitious at that time. One might even say too ambitious. We thus quite intentionally tolerated ex ante overshootings of the target, which actually materialized then. As a result, our record of target achievement has necessarily suffered. On the other hand, through the target and its derivation we could make it clear that we were not prepared to accommodate higher price rises permanently in monetary terms. We thus, in fact, succeeded in keeping expectations about inflation in check. Neither in the foreign exchange markets nor in the capital markets have there been manifestations of no confidence in our policy. This was extremely important at a time when fiscal deficits rose sharply and when we had to regain price stability relatively quickly and without incurring excessive real economic costs.

This success was, of course, also due to the fact that the Bundesbank had previously shown how serious it takes its obligation to ensure stable prices. I can, therefore, only underline the *leitmotif* of Charles Freedman's paper, namely that credibility is of utmost importance. For us, monetary targets and their derivation were important for making our intentions regarding stability clear to the public. On the other hand, if we had abandoned the strategy of monetary targeting at the very time the situation was extremely difficult, this would presumably have caused devastating psychological damage. Monetary policymakers would then have had to react all the more restrictively in order to make it clear that they would never give monetary stability a lower priority, even if only temporarily.

Finally, with respect to implementation, our current monetary policy is not significantly different from that in periods of higher price rise rates—or, where it does differ, this is not due to the changed price situation. This is another advantage of a monetary targeting strategy. It would presumably be more problematic if, for example, we had adopted a strategy which depends more on finding the correct "real" rate of interest, since uncertainties concerning expectations about inflation would then be of key importance.

Endnotes

[1]See *OECD Economic Outlook*, No. 59 (June 1996), p. 7.

[2]See, for example, R. Bootle, *The Death of Inflation—Surviving and Thriving in the Zero Era*, (London, 1996).

[3]See also the recent study by J. Barro, "Inflation and Economic Growth," *Quarterly Bulletin*, Vol. 35, No. 2 (Bank of England, 1995), pp. 166-75.

[4]See Feldstein, M., "The Costs and Benefits of Going from Low Inflation to Price Stability," (NBER Working Paper 5469, 1996).

[5]See C. B. Briault, A. G. Haldane, and M. A. King, *Independence and Accountability*, (October 1995), mimeo.

Commentary: What Operating Procedures Should Be Adopted to Maintain Price Stability?—Practical Issues

Donald L. Kohn

Chuck Freedman has done quite a good job describing the analytical framework for how a modern central bank conducts monetary policy. The general process he describes—analyzing the forces affecting the economy, making a forecast (explicit or implicit) based on that analysis, adjusting a short-term interest rate to align the forecast better with objectives, modifying the forecast and the short-term rate in response to incoming data—applies in most key respects to the United States and, I suspect, many other central banks as well. Of course, the United States differs from Chuck's pattern in one important respect—the policy process is not focused on achieving a numerical inflation target over a specified period. I thought I would begin my comments with some thoughts about this difference.

One clear lesson from the late 1960s and 1970s, as the Bretton Woods system broke down, was that central banks needed new constraints on the longer-run inflationary consequences of their actions. When policy focused on output and employment, inflation rates became unanchored—shifting with each shock that hit the economy—and tended to move higher. Over the last decade, many countries have adopted inflation targets as the apparatus to provide longer-run discipline.

In the United States, long-run discipline on monetary policy has been provided not by numerical targets but the firm focus of an independent central bank on reducing inflation over the long run, so as to eventually reach price stability—as specified in the Federal Reserve Act. This long-run focus has been especially important in two types of circumstances. When inflation has threatened to pick up, as in 1988 and 1994, it has triggered vigorous firming. And when the economy has been weak, as in the early 1990s, it has fostered attention to long-run inflation expectations, which has helped to discipline easing and avoid a subsequent overshooting of aggregate demand. The less quantitative and time-specific objective of the Federal Reserve has given it considerable flexibility in responding to unexpected developments, enabling it to smooth the path of output and vary the pace of progress toward price stability as circumstances seemed to dictate. The results largely speak for themselves. Inflation has been brought down to a low level, with only one mild recession since 1982.

Although in concept, short-run flexibility and long-run discipline are fully compatible, in practice, approaches to policy end up striking a balance between them. Quantitative inflation targeting shifts the emphasis toward long-run discipline. There are a number of reasons why this might be desirable. In many countries, flexibility produced high and erratic inflation rates. As compared to a less quantitative objective, inflation targets should result in more certain progress toward long-run inflation goals and less tendency toward backsliding once those goals are reached. In this regard, an important attribute of those targets is their effect on the government that agrees to them. That government is forced to recognize low inflation or price stability as the appropriate long-term goal of monetary policy, and should be constrained from pressuring or retaliating against a central bank striving to achieve it. In addition, the clarity of inflation targets enhances accountability and can help markets to act in ways that reinforce the intentions of the central bank.

Inflation targets come in many flavors, but the tradeoff, as I noted, was the possible loss of some flexibility—especially in those regimes that tie specific inflation outcomes to specific time periods—and I have some concerns in this regard. I suspect, for example, that some inflation targets might not be flexible enough to allow a central bank to follow a Taylor-rule type of regime, where the long-run intention is explicit but the time it takes to get there is contingent on economic circumstances. In addition, one valuable use of flexibility is the potential for moving policy in directions that may seem counterintuitive to the general public under inflation targets. The Federal Reserve eased when inflation was moving higher in the last half of 1989 and early 1990 and again in mid-1995. To be sure, such actions might have been justified by reference to inflation forecasts, but one wonders whether these easings, which turned out to be well-advised, wouldn't have been more difficult with explicit inflation targets. Given the lags in the effects of policy, it is not surprising that inflation forecasts loom so large in Chuck's description of the policy process under inflation targets. Moreover, as he argues, because the central bank is being judged against specific outcomes, its response, or lack of response, to misses in the target under various circumstances needs to be specified in advance.

All monetary policy involves forecasts in one degree or another, but some forms of inflation targeting would seem to imply considerable weight on an inherently uncertain and imprecise projection and associated contingencies. We know that forecasts will be wrong and contingencies will arise in ways that are unanticipated. Central banks that are using forecasts know this, of course. And those that publish their forecasts, like the Bank of England, can emphasize the uncertainty, as it has done through the use of probability distributions. But the Bank's very efforts in this regard suggest difficulty in communicating the appropriate role for the forecast in policy, and even internally, policymakers may lose sight of the wide confidence bands around any forecast. The risk is that the central bank will be less able to react in a timely way to shifts in aggregate demand. In the early 1990s, private forecasters and Federal Reserve policymakers persistently projected more inflation than occurred. Although policymakers' forecasts played some role in their decisions, the impact might have been larger and the scope for easing to cushion shortfalls in demand somewhat less if policy had been tied explicitly to these projections.

The interaction of announcements of inflation targets and outcomes with central bank credibility was an important subtheme in

Chuck's paper. The credibility of low inflation is important. In particular, as Chuck notes, it buys what he calls "room for maneuver"—the opportunity for the central bank to assess the emerging situation and gauge its policy response without engendering major shifts in inflation expectations. Given the inevitable misses from inflation targets, it's natural to worry about credibility, or at least central bank reputation, in such a regime, and to design announcements to protect it.

As Chuck is well aware, however, empirical evidence that central bank announcements have broad effects on credibility is sparse, at best. Our experience in the United States may not be entirely relevant, but it has been that expectations of inflation wax and wane very gradually in response to experience over extended periods. Good behavior may be rewarded with inflation expectations that become slightly less sensitive to recent experience, so that temporary supply shocks are less threatening, but the changes occur quite slowly, and I suspect have little to do with Federal Reserve statements on seeking price stability. I would guess this applies to inflation targets and announcements as well. Announcements may very well condition behavior in financial markets, and these effects can be important, but they are less likely to carry over into product or labor markets where they count most for economic performance.

My second general topic is whether the monetary policy process ought to be modified when economies are operating close to or at price stability. Price stability differs from moderate inflation by bringing into greater play possible constraints around "zero." Chuck lists the concerns: To the extent there are downward rigidities of wages and prices at zero, Phillips curves will be non-linear and sacrifice ratios may rise as price stability is approached; because nominal interest rates are bounded at zero, monetary policy may be constrained in its ability to reduce real interest rates; and because price stability implies that the prices of some goods and services will be declining, asset prices may fall more frequently, with effects on the financial system.

Our recent experience in the United States supports Chuck's tendency to downplay the importance of these problems. As inflation has retreated to the lowest level in 30 years, we have not seen evidence that nominal wage and price rigidities have, in effect, raised nonaccelerating-inflation-rates of unemployment (NAIRUs); indeed, the surprises have been on the side of lower NAIRUs and higher levels of output than might be expected. The asset deflation and financial fragility issues we have dealt with occurred at inflation rates of 4 to 5 percent in the late 1980s, not at the 2.5 to 3 percent rates of the mid-1990s. Because asset prices build in expected inflation, widespread declines will occur primarily when inflation—at whatever level—falls short of these expectations, especially if the cause is a run-up in real interest rates. Swings in asset prices ought to be considerably damped if policy successfully and predictably holds inflation at very low or nonexistent levels.

But we can't dismiss these concerns about operating near price stability altogether. One possible response would be to aim for an average inflation rate a shade above price stability, and this seems to be the approach of many countries. But there are other strategies that may enable central banks to pursue true price stability, if research and analysis show some costs from even very low inflation. One would be to seek further reductions in inflation very gradually, to enable expectations to adjust and institutions in labor and product markets to adapt in ways that facilitate downward movements in labor compensation and prices. This also would give central banks a chance to look for signs that wage and price rigidities were beginning to impede economic performance. Financial markets might benefit as well from a very slow approach to price stability. If there is a tendency for asset price declines to be more widespread at price stability, such an approach would allow lenders to recognize potential problems and recalibrate loan standards, such as loan-to-value ratios and cash-flow requirements, for the new environment.

Another policy adaptation might make the zero floor on nominal interest rates less formidable. It is delayed or hesitant policy action that results in insufficient scope to reduce real rates when shocks turn out to be large and persistent, putting in motion deflationary processes. To guard against this, central banks operating near price stability perhaps should be willing to act especially forcefully and quickly when they suspect downward demand shocks. Of course, the danger with such a tactic would be a possible tendency toward inflation; that is, responding more quickly to downward than to upward shocks would tend to give rise to an economy operating above its potential if shocks were symmetrically distributed. The central bank would need to compensate with other biases on the tightening side—for example, being especially quick to reverse easings that turned out to be unnecessary and being ready to tighten substantially in response to upward shocks that it had waited to confirm.

Other government policies may also need to be adapted to support a monetary policy focused on price stability. For example, the elimination of structural fiscal deficits would seem even more urgent so as to free fiscal policy for use as a countercyclical instrument in the event monetary policy confronts the zero interest rate constraint. In this context, however, eliminating the deficit using a rigid balanced budget constraint that short-circuited not only discretionary but automatic countercyclical properties of fiscal policy would only tend to reinforce the argument for aiming at a little inflation. The United States has undertaken significant deregulation in many industries over the last twenty years, and it seems likely that we have removed most artificial barriers to declines in prices and wages that would inadvertently become binding when some prices should be falling at overall price stability. Nonetheless, we need to be sure of this, and I suspect regulatory constraints on downward movements in prices and wages are an even more important issue in other countries. In addition, financial supervisory policies may need to be modified to take account of the fact that inflation will not be available to ameliorate the problems of debtors. Taken together these policies should help reduce some of the concerns that might be associated with price stability and strengthen the hand of the monetary authority in containing and eliminating inflation.

A final issue associated with policies at price stability is staying there—avoiding backsliding. Public support for price stability may erode as unpleasant episodes of inflation recede further into history, adding to demands to run the economy at higher levels. If business cycles are damped when inflation is contained, as they have been in the United States, trends in the growth of output come into sharper focus. When the trend has slowed, there has been a tendency to look first to the institution that has a lot to do with the cyclical performance of the economy. The credibility of low inflation will only add to the pressures. Credible low inflation may look like a favorable supply shock; output can run higher for longer with muted inflation consequences if people expect inflation to return to previous low levels. It will be hard to distinguish between true favorable shocks, which may be exploitable for additional output, and credibility, which can not without inflationary consequences. Even legally mandated inflation objectives may not be a sufficient bulwark against public opinion that perceives considerable gains and little cost from boosting the economy.

I don't see any easy answers to this problem. Central banks and economists will need to continue to remind the public and their elected representatives of the limits of the power of the central bank to augment growth, and the adverse consequences of trying to do so.

Finally, I would like to turn to an explanation of "opportunism."[1] This subject is not directly related to Chuck's paper because opportunism is a description of a strategy to get to price stability rather than an aspect of operating there. But it has been the subject of much comment at this conference, and I thought it would be useful to clarify some attributes of this strategy.

At the outset, it is very important to recognize that the opportunistic strategy is not official Federal Reserve policy. Members of the Federal Open Market Committee (FOMC) do not necessarily agree on what strategy should be used for getting to price stability. Opportunism is one way people observing Federal Reserve actions in recent years have described what they have seen.

One distinguishing characteristic of the opportunistic approach is that it involves different modes of behavior on the part of the central bank depending on the prevailing level of inflation. When inflation is high, an opportunistic policymaker would actively seek to bring it down. The period of 1979 to 1982 is an example of this sort of situation. Inflation in 1979 was clearly too high, and the Federal Reserve fought it, opening an output gap. On the other hand, when inflation is already low or moderate, the opportunistic policymaker does not take active measures to reduce it further. Once inflation had fallen into the 3.5 to 4.5 percent range in the mid-1980s, people observing the Federal Reserve thought they could not detect steps to lower it more.

There are certain actions the central bank is prepared to take when inflation is moderate, under this strategy. First, it leans very hard against increases in inflation. Examples of this in recent years would include the tightenings of 1984, 1988-89, and 1994. In these cases when inflation threatened to exceed its previous range, the Federal Reserve firmed policy to prevent the uptick or bring inflation back into the range again. Chairman Greenspan's Humphrey-Hawkins testimony of February 1990 explained the Federal Reserve's intentions in that episode. Inflation, in fact, had broken out of the previous range, and the Federal Reserve was going to bring it back down—to take out the increase in inflation that had occurred in 1989 and early 1990.

Second, when an output gap unexpectedly opens up under conditions of moderate inflation, through positive supply, or negative demand shocks, the opportunistic central bank moves to close that output gap, but not to overshoot. As a consequence, such shocks produce a period in which output is below potential and inflation falls toward price stability.

Opportunistic strategy is distinguished from a deliberate disinflation strategy under conditions of moderate inflation. Under both strategies, central banks would attempt to reduce high inflation. But, in contrast to the opportunistic strategy, the deliberate strategy would be at least midly restrictive even when inflation is only moderate, maintaining a small output gap until price stability is reached.

Two further points about the differences between these two strategies: On the one hand, in practice, the difference between them tends not to be very substantial. In fact, it has been very hard for observers to distinguish whether the Federal Reserve has been pursuing an opportunistic or a deliberate policy. For example, John Taylor looked at the Federal Reserve's actions over the 1987-93 period and thought that they fit his rule, which is a deliberate disinflationary policy strategy. In the Taylor rule, whenever inflation is above the goal—in his formulation the long-term goal is 2 percent—policy is on the restrictive side unless a significant output gap already exists. Other people looked at the same policy actions over the same period and saw the Federal Reserve operating in an opportunistic fashion. In theory, the deliberate strategy would be slightly more restrictive than the opportunistic policy at moderate inflation rates, but in actual operations, this difference might be so small it would be hard to detect.

But on the other hand, there is a real issue here. If in fact price stability is the right goal for policy because we think economies operate better without inflation, why not simply go ahead and pursue that goal? Even if you are above it by a small amount, why wait—as the opportunist would—to take the inflation down from a moderate rate to price stability? This is the genuine question to be asked when talking about opportunism. What are the underlying costs and benefits of taking the longer time that opportunism is likely to entail in getting to price stability?

One of the difficulties in evaluating this question, and one reason why a central bank might not move very decisively to go from low or moderate inflation to price stability, is we are still not very clear about the costs and benefits of that last little bit of disinflation. There are costs—principally the output gap that must be incurred to reduce inflation. There are benefits as well and we are making progress in identifying those benefits; Marty Feldstein's paper on the distortions caused by inflation interactions with the tax system identified a benefit of going to price stability. I think most of us feel that, on balance, it is likely that the benefits exceed the costs of going from moderate inflation to price stability. But the case for reducing moderate inflation is not as clear-cut as for reducing high inflation. As a consequence, public opinion polls, like those Stan Fischer was citing, indicate that support is not strong for reducing inflation from moderate levels.

So there are genuine issues here about going from moderate inflation to price stability. The public's utility functions—how it values, or ought to value, the extra decline in inflation versus the output lost in getting there—is where the discussion should be, and is the crux of the opportunism versus deliberate policy choice.

Author's Note: The views expressed are solely my own and do not necessarily reflect the views of the Board or any other members of its staff.

Endnote

[1]For a full exposition see Orphanides and Wilcox, "An Opportunistic Approach to Disinflation," FEDS working paper 96-24, 1996.

General Discussion:
What Operating Procedures Should Be Adopted to Maintain Price Stability—Practical Issues

Chairman: Andrew Crockett

Mr. Crockett: Thank you, Don. I propose what we do now is perhaps eat into ten minutes or so of the coffee break, which gives us almost fifteen minutes for observations from the floor. I will try to favor those who have not had a chance to express their views before. With the panel's permission, I will ask them to reply only if there are very important points so that we have the benefit of as much as possible from the floor. Lars Svensson, I know, had asked to make a point—which breaks my rule not to ask people who have spoken before. But, Lars first.

Mr. Svensson: Needless to say, I am in full agreement with Chuck's framework. I find his paper full of useful observations and good advice. I have a question, though. Can one summarize what you say as a general rule that when shocks arrive or there is a change in expectations or anything, one should basically look at how the two-year inflation forecast is affected and then take the necessary action? Is that a brief summary of your paper?

Then, another point: I think the framework that Chuck lays out and the framework that I agree very much with, has an additional potential—namely, to improve the quality of the monetary policy debate within the media. Often it is rather populistic, unfortunately. But in principle with this framework, one can distinguish debate about the targets, about the model, about the information available, about assumptions made, and about the resulting forecasts. If you can separate these points, then you can perhaps debate on a somewhat higher level than is often the case.

Finally, again the opportunistic approach to disinflation. If you look up "opportunistic" in a dictionary it means "without regard to principles." In general, a standard framework with reasonable loss functions and objectives like those that have been laid out in the papers of Stan Fischer, Mervyn King, John Taylor, and Chuck Freedman give no support whatsoever for the opportunistic approach. What you need is a steady leaning toward the long-run target. That is what the standard framework and reasonable preferences support.

Mr. Crockett: Mr. Lieberman.

Mr. Lieberman: That was an excellent paper by Chuck Freedman, and the comments by Don Kohn anticipated some of my comment. I thought there were some interesting and critical issues raised. If forecasts of inflation are crucial in formulating policies, as Chuck and Don and the entire previous session discussed, those of us who make a living forecasting understand how tenuous that can be. And forecasting inflation also can be very counterproductive for a central bank. Consider a very simple hypothetical case of where the unemployment rate is roughly at the NAIRU or perhaps below it, growth is above trend (above potential), and inflation is near the upper end of the central bank's target or market expectations; then a central bank head who projects a slowdown in activity can have a big impact on market expectations—especially if the central bank enjoys a lot of credibility. That would encourage the market to drive up bond prices and interest rates down, and a drop in interest rates might then be inconsistent with the projected slowdown in activity. In that case, you would get a counterproductive result of where expectations of moderating growth and continued good inflation performance actually contribute to stronger economic activity and an unfavorable outcome of higher inflation. The implications of that kind of a framework are four: (1) Central bank credibility is dependent upon forecast accuracy; (2) market expectations can be very misleading—in other words, you can fool all of the people some of the time, and as a result, can be counterproductive; (3) as the Chairman's comments yesterday suggested, there is a substantial role for expectations in the formulation of policy, but if the market expects inflation to be well-behaved, that can be problematical—after all, forecasts can be wrong, including the central bank's forecasts; (4) if forecasts are used, then, by definition, policy should consistently try to be preemptive.

Mr. Crockett: Thank you. Larry Summers.

Mr. Summers: An observation on opportunistic disinflation. I suspect efforts to model this analytically will be more fruitful if, instead of focusing on what loss function justifies it, instead focus on the learning behavior of economic agents. And what is really being captured is that you are at a point where you do not want to inflate because you will lose credibility, but there is no need to disinflate. And being seen to be consciously affecting inflation is very much damaging to a central bank's credibility. I also wanted to just touch on this zero nominal interest rate floor and to argue that it really does require considerable further study and thinking. If we all succeed in bringing down budget deficits in a way we hope to, equilibrium real interest rates will presumably fall and will therefore make the zero interest rate floor a more relevant issue in the future than in the past. Second, I think there are low nominal interest rate effects that do not figure in our models. One of the important sources of resistance in Japan to lower interest rates was that there were a lot of people who lived on the income from their bonds and were not very impressed with a 0.5 percent nominal yield. And as long as there is a distinction between income and eating into principal, the level of nominal interest rates will make a difference. Similarly, to reflect another concern, those who borrow in order to finance speculative positions, I suspect, pay rather more attention to the nominal interest rate than to the underlying rate of inflation in the country in which they are borrowing. For that reason also, nominal interest rates of a one-quarter or a one-half percent understandably raise legitimate concerns. Last, just to stress the point, the issue is not whether you need negative real interest rates. If price stability is being targeted with zero inflation, then half the time there will be negative inflation. At that point, it is not possible to get to a zero real interest rate, even if the nominal interest rate is lowered to zero. And, as Chuck Freedman and I have discussed, the open economy aspects of this problem require a good deal more consideration.

Mr. Crockett: Mickey Levy.

Mr. Levy: This has to do with forecasting and targeting. As we know, several central banks do have explicit inflation targets and the Federal Reserve does not. However, twice a year, in its semi-annual report to the Congress and the Humphrey-Hawkins testimony, the Federal Reserve provides its central tendency forecasts for real GDP growth, nominal GDP growth, the CPI, and the unemployment rate. What I have found going back since its inception about fifteen years ago is an extraordinarily close correlation between changes in the federal funds rate and deviations of actual performance from these Fed central tendency forecasts. This correlation holds symmetrically: the federal funds rate rises when real and nominal growth are above the Fed's central tendency forecasts and falls when these variables are below the central tendency forecasts. In the last couple years, we have experienced a relatively stable rate of inflation. The Federal Reserve's central tendency forecasts have actually done a very good job of forecasting actual inflation. Accordingly, all of the changes in the federal funds rate have been associated with periods when nominal and real GDP deviated from the Fed's central tendency forecasts. Market interest rates move accordingly. That is why the market seems to move so much on a lot of these measures of real performance. Now, one issue is that the Fed's central tendency forecast of inflation has been stuck around 2.75 to 3 percent. Does the Fed plan on lowering it? This is important insofar as the Fed's central tendency forecasts provide a lot of information about the Fed's comfort range, if not its target. Secondly, I think the way the Federal Reserve conveys information about the inflation process is extraordinarily important. I know there is a lot of discussion now about what is potential growth and what is the NAIRU. One of the problems with identifying real growth and the unemployment rate as the sources of rising inflation is that it conveys misleading information to financial markets and the public, and complicates the Fed's pursuit of price stability.

Mr. Crockett: Allen Sinai.

Mr. Sinai: A couple of questions for you, Chuck, on your excellent paper that deals candidly and explicitly with key topics of the conference. It was a terrific paper. You say that, typically, the focus has been on the core rate, excluding food and energy. Did you mean this to be Canada only, or do you include central banks in the United States and other places where inflation targeting is going on? The "core" notion, I believe, came from the severe shocks of the 1970s and 1980s where there were clear exogenous shocks to the inflationary process. But these two components are really a significant part of prices and the inflationary process in the normal course of events. So, yet another question. Should not a central bank differ in its assessment of a target inflation rate where the CPI is used in the tracking of its progress? Should we be looking at food and energy prices in terms of whether they are endogenous to that situation or exogenous shocks, such as in the 1970s and 1980s? And a related observation to the choice of the inflation measure: A lot of attention is paid to the core rate in markets, mainly because of the belief that the central bank pays attention to it in its policymaking. If the central bank were to announce its inflation guide was the chain-weighted GDP deflator, say in the United States, regardless of what the Humphrey-Hawkins testimony requires, then markets would not react to the core CPI hardly at all. Long-term bond yields would react to the current chain-weighted GDP deflator measure in the United States—which is substantially different from the CPI. Long-term bond yields would probably go down significantly right away. And there is a second comment and question on the issue of wage rigidity where you cite evidence, but you don't cite the Akerlof, Dickens, and Perry paper—where they found evidence that there is not downward wage rigidity. You do not mention that. Anecdotally, I think there is support of what you say, that we have massive re-engineering in the United States, massive substitutability of new vintage labor for old vintage labor, which carries with it lower wages and wage compensation and in many cases higher productivity. And that has been a very significant part of the low wage inflation in the United States, not just job insecurity which has been frequently cited as the reason for low wage inflation for a long time.

Mr. Crockett: Last, and if he can promise to keep within 60 seconds, Peter Kenen.

Mr. Kenen: Let me revert very quickly to the debate about zero and negative real rates and raise this question. If an inflation rate of 2 percent satisfies what we probably must now call the Volcker/Greenspan test that the inflation rate does not substantially affect economic behavior, then for all practical purposes, the real and nominal rates are the same. In which case I see no advantage in having the scope to get the measured real rate down to, say, minus 2. It seems to me, the issue between 2 percent inflation and zero inflation is the set of issues raised by Akerlof, Dickens, and Perry concerning the costs in real terms of moving lower and staying lower and concerns about measurement error. The extra flexibility that one has at 2 percent versus zero in terms of the real rate, it seems to me, is nil if indeed 2 percent is too low to affect economic behavior.

Mr. Crockett: Thank you very much. I will give Chuck Freedman just a very brief period of time to respond to the major points that were raised. Some of the specific questions, I think, could be taken up bilaterally. Chuck.

Mr. Freedman: Thank you very much. In response to the comment by Lars Svensson, I think the notion of shocks affecting the two-year or one-and-a-half-year out forecast is a good way of looking at it. I would want to emphasize the point, though, that it is not mechanistic. I hope I did not leave the impression that when we talk about a forecast, it is what comes out of a model. There is a lot of judgment that comes in. That is why central bank governors are paid what they are. In a sense, at the end, those decisions are the tough ones. What is the forecast of inflation now? What kind of bands are there in terms of uncertainty? Should we be acting? Are there too many risks, etcetera, etcetera? So I think with that qualification I agree with the way you phrase it. In fact, I would add one further question: Should the forecast be published? Some central banks do publish—Don Brash, of course, at the Reserve Bank of New Zealand and the Bank of England—most all the rest do not. And there is an interesting question as to whether it should be published. I'll just mention that core versus total CPI is a very important point. We use the core as the operational measure. We make it very clear if the core diverges in any trend fashion from the overall, it is the overall that counts. I think that is important for the credibility of the policy—if food and energy prices result in wiggles in the CPI they are not taken into account in policy. But if, for example, food and energy prices were growing substantially faster in the way of trend, they would have to be taken into account in policy; and then the target for the core CPI would be below the target for the overall CPI. I do mention Akerlof, Dickens, and Perry in the newest version of my paper. I had not received it when I wrote the first version. It raises interesting issues, but I think in a sense this becomes a very empirical point, as we have heard throughout this conference. Finally, I guess I would take a bit of issue with Don Kohn regarding the question of whether you can have more or less flexibility in response to inflation moving up, when you have an explicit target. I would argue you probably have more flexibility if you have an explicit target, because then you can explain to people that you think these are transitory upward movements of inflation, but that you are still adhering to the target, and the trend will soon turn down. If you do not have an explicit target, there is always the risk that people will be interpreting policy as moving away from the overall goal. But I think that is a debatable point.

Mr. Crockett: Thank you. Don Kohn, briefly.

Mr. Kohn: In regard to Lars, I entirely agree that the standard framework does not produce opportunism, and I am not sure opportunism is right. But I think we need to be clear as economists whether that standard framework, which is so tractable in our models and operates in such nice ways, is a real representation of the public's preferences.

Overview

Andrew Crockett

When coming to a conference such as this, in which a group consisting largely of central bankers addresses the issue of price stability, the first question it is natural to ask is: how much room will there be for discussion and debate? But as usual, the Federal Reserve Bank of Kansas City has picked a topic where behind the scenes there is an interesting intellectual debate. There are some very tricky questions: how do you get to price stability? How do you judge when you have arrived? And when you are there, how do you stay there? And while many central banks, particularly in the industrial world, have succeeded in reducing the public's concern about inflation, this does not, by any means, dismiss the inherent interest or the policy importance of those three questions.

Let me say something about each of the questions, starting with the basic one that has come up in a number of the papers. How do you know when you have arrived at price stability? Put another way, what rate of inflation corresponds to the classic definition of Alan Greenspan and Paul Volcker of price stability as a situation in which inflation is no longer a factor in day-to-day economic decisionmaking?

I found it interesting how much consensus there seemed to be in yesterday's sessions regarding two of Stanley Fischer's propositions. First, industrialized countries that have already attained single-digit inflation should target a rate of inflation in the range of

1 to 3 percent. Second, the objective should be defined in terms of the inflation rate, not in terms of the price level. Those two propositions received somewhat more critical questioning today and they are issues that will be with us for a while. Personally, I tend to agree with Fischer's position. But there is clearly scope for debate.

On the one hand, some argue that genuine price stability (zero inflation) brings significant economic advantages. I am sure Marty Feldstein will speak in a moment about the findings in his paper in this respect. On the other hand, there are also views favoring a rate of inflation higher than 1 to 3 percent. As Otmar Issing reminded us this morning, there are plenty of people, not perhaps in this room, who are prepared to cite evidence that somewhat higher rates of inflation do not seem to have significant long-run adverse effects, and have short-run attractions, at least from a political standpoint. I am not among that group, but I think we would delude ourselves if we thought those views would not be expressed. So I see pressures being brought to bear from both sides on the consensus of a 1 to 3 percent inflation target that seems to be widely accepted here.

In that context, another point that I found interesting was Larry Summers' observation that price stability has to be something that sits comfortably with public opinion. I think Larry said, "If central banks' objectives do not appear reasonable or achievable to public opinion, then it is going to be very hard to maintain credibility in them and in the central banks." That raises the question of whether public opinion regarding price stability is immutable or whether a process of education might change it, especially if the public is persuaded by economic arguments that are tilted in one direction or the other. David Mullins' comments went along those lines.

Let me now turn to the second question: how to get inflation down when it is clearly too high? The precise definition of a price stability objective in a country that has already achieved low inflation is a far cry from the concerns that we heard yesterday about the problem of lowering inflation in formerly high-inflation countries. In yesterday's presentations there was a strong consensus that part of the process involves using the exchange rate as an anchor to bring down expectations. There was also agreement that fiscal policy—the budget—is key. If the budget is not in a satisfactory state, then it is going to be very difficult to lower inflation from high levels.

What I found less conclusively answered in our discussions about reducing inflation was how to take the "last step" from satisfactory progress to genuine price stability. This is not a new problem. Many countries have had the problem and very few have satisfactorily taken that last step—too few to draw any credible lessons. After inflation has been down to the 10 to 20 percent range, or even under 10 percent, how do you go to the 1 to 3 percent level? It is clear to me that at some stage most countries will have to loosen the exchange rate anchor and find a domestic anchor. But how to do that is obviously a very difficult process. To mix the metaphor, if you stay on the horse too long you are liable to get thrown and find yourself in a worse situation, or at least in a more bruised situation, than if you dismount at an appropriate stage and find another and more satisfactory horse to carry you the rest of the way to price stability. That is my solution for countries starting from high inflation.

There is a parallel, but different, question for countries that start from moderate inflation as the industrial countries did in the 1980s and brought inflation down to where we are now, the 2 to 4 percent level. These countries have almost, but not quite, reached their long-run objective. The issues they face is the debate that we heard alluded to this morning in Donald Kohn's remarks about "opportunistic disinflation." How do you take that last step when you are almost at price stability? The central banks concerned are not prepared to accept the existing inflation rate as fully satisfactory on a permanent basis and yet they are not prepared to pay the price, in terms of lost output, to take the last step to full price stability. I see the opportunistic disinflation debate a little bit in that context. How do you carry public opinion with you in the best fashion, when you are taking a step that you believe is economically desirable but where there is not an enormous amount of public support?

The last of the three questions is: how do you stay at price stability once you get there? One of the points that was strongly made, and I certainly agree with it, was this: if central banks can build up credibility in their long-run pursuit of a reasonable and acceptable definition of price stability, then they will have given themselves some room to maneuver to respond to disturbances (supply shocks) that in the short run may carry the inflation rate away from the long-run objective. This concept of building up credibility in order to increase room for maneuver in responding to shocks was not seriously questioned in our discussions. I don't question it myself. I think increased credibility of central banks makes it easier for them to respond to disturbances in a way that improves the tradeoff between output and inflation. There is not an enormous amount of empirical support for this proposition, however. Indeed, there are empirical papers that suggest that the notion of credibility improving the sacrifice ratio is very hard to substantiate. That is an area where I would like to see additional research because I have a rather profound conviction (perhaps not surprising from somebody living in Basle and coming from a central bank) that there is enormous benefit from credibility. This is not simply because it is nice to be believed and to have a good reputation, but because credibility can improve the economic tradeoffs that central banks have to deal with.

I hope I have succeeded in suggesting that the issues raised in this conference are not simply esoteric ones of interest to central bankers, but genuine policy concerns that are crucial to the goal of preserving a stable and well-functioning monetary environment.

Overview

Martin Feldstein

Today's low rate of inflation and the current debate about focusing monetary policy on the goal of price stability stand in sharp contrast to the economic situation and the professional debate of twenty years ago. Inflation in the United States was then twice what it is now and on a path toward four times the current rate. Economists underestimated the impact of demand, speaking instead of cost-push inflation and emphasizing the role of trade unions, monopoly businesses, and oil price shocks. Monetary policy's role was viewed as very limited, a vestige of the Keynesian tradition that emphasized the impotence of monetary policy during the depression. The long-run Phillips curve was still the dominant view, offering a permanently lower unemployment rate in exchange for accepting a higher rate of inflation. Economists provided no serious rationale for reducing inflation, focusing their case against inflation on the distorting effect of inflation on the demand for narrow money balances, an argument that the defenders of the existing inflation could derisively dismiss as an attempt to economize on the shoe leather costs of frequent trips to the bank. Some even turned this argument on its head, advocating a higher rate of inflation as a way of encouraging households to substitute real capital for money balances.

Why have things changed so radically in two decades? Why do the Federal Reserve, the public, and our elected officials accept price stability as the appropriate goal of monetary policy? And why has monetary policy brought us so close to achieving that goal?

In the United States, the public reacted to the pain caused by the increase in inflation that pushed interest rates up sharply at the end of the 1970s. The higher interest rates hurt small businesses and farmers who had to borrow at variable interest rates, reduced the home-buying ability for the millions of individuals who saw the monthly mortgage payments slip out of reach, and pushed many small banks and thrift companies into insolvency.

By 1980, the U.S. inflation rate had reached a double-digit level. The public feared that inflation was out of control and might spiral higher and higher. These concerns and the damaging effects of inflation that had already been sustained provided political support for the painful contractionary policies needed to reduce inflation.

But the shift to an anti-inflationary monetary policy was also the effect of the intellectual revolution that had taken place. The economics profession rejected the notion of a long-run Phillips curve. The consensus shifted to the view, advocated in 1968 by Milton Friedman, that there is no long-run tradeoff between unemployment and inflation. The economics profession also recognized the power of monetary policy to reduce inflation by moving along a short-run Phillips curve. Although the case for low inflation was never well articulated, today no one advocates raising inflation from 3 percent to 5 percent in order to reduce unemployment.

But what of the future? When the economy is next in recession, will there be support among the politicians and the economics profession for increasing inflation in order to speed the return to full employment? More generally, will (and should) the Federal Reserve and other central banks take the steps needed to shift from low inflation to price stability?

I believe that price stability should be the goal of monetary policy and that it should be achieved in the United States within the next four years. More precisely, the goal should be an inflation rate of not more than 1 or 2 percent. This rate would equate the measured rate of increase of the consumer price index (CPI) with the estimated bias in the rate of inflation. At an inflation rate of between 1 and 2 percent, the purchasing power of the dollar would be preserved. I think that a case could also be made for going further to a zero measured inflation rate even though that implies a rising purchasing power of the dollar.

I will begin by discussing the gain that would result from going from low inflation to price stability. I will then consider the arguments that have been advanced for accepting a higher inflation rate and will explain why I think those arguments are wrong. Finally, I will turn to the question of timing and consider the issue of when and how fast the Federal Reserve should move to price stability.

The case for price stability

Although there is strong evidence that very high rates of inflation reduce the rate of economic growth, there is no persuasive evidence that growth would be faster with full price stability than it would be at a low single-digit inflation rate. Why then should we regard price stability as a desirable goal?

Many reasons have been adduced for reducing an already low rate of inflation. Price stability is desirable because it is easier to maintain (that is, it requires less deflation) in the face of inflationary shocks than even a moderate rate of inflation because the public has more confidence in a central bank that has achieved price stability. Price stability also aids those individuals who have difficulty in long-term financial planning in an environment of uncertain or rising prices. I shall not comment on these reasons or try to quantify them.

My own thinking and research about the benefits of price stability have focused on the effect of inflation on the allocation of resources and, therefore, on the level of real income. The most important such effect is the interaction of taxes and inflation. Let me explain.[1]

Our system of taxing capital income would distort the allocation of resources even if there were complete price stability. Two of the most important such distortions are the bias in favor of current consumption (rather than retirement consumption or other postponed consumption) and the bias in favor of investments in owner-occupied housing rather than other uses of capital. Because of the way that our personal income tax and our corporate income tax work, these distortions are exacerbated by inflation. At a 3 percent rate of inflation, the biases in favor of current consumption and in favor of owner-occupied housing are bigger than they would be at a 1 percent rate of inflation.

How important is this effect of inflation? My detailed calculations indicate that the interaction of taxes and inflation has a very large effect. Looking just at the impact on the household sector—that is, ignoring the effects on the structure of business investment and the international allocation of investment—I have estimated that reducing the inflation rate by two percentage points (for example, from 3 percent inflation to 1 percent inflation) would raise the level of real GDP by 1 percent. This is a permanent effect. GDP would be higher by 1 percent each year in the future as long as the inflation rate remained at its lower level.[2]

The technical analysis that leads to this conclusion is presented in Feldstein (1996). The calculations do not assume a large responsiveness of savings to net-of-tax interest rates. Even with the extreme assumption that changes in the real net-of-tax interest rate do not change saving at all, a two-percentage-point reduction of inflation would permanently raise the level of real GDP by two-thirds of 1 percent.[3]

The case against price stability

Four arguments against going from low inflation to price stability have been presented in the economics literature and discussed at this meeting. Although there may be some validity in each of them, I do not believe that either singly or collectively they outweigh the tax-inflation case for going to price stability or even to a lower inflation rate.

Mismeasurement of inflation

There is widespread agreement that increases in the CPI overstate the true rise in the cost of living. This overstatement is generally believed to be between 1 percent and 2 percent a year.

This implies that the inflation rate should nevertheless be reduced from the current level of about 3 percent to between 1 percent and 2 percent to maintain the purchasing power of the dollar.

But the tax argument provides a case for going beyond the inflation rate that corresponds to the constant purchasing power of income. A lower measured inflation rate would reduce the deadweight loss of the tax system and increase the level of real income.

More generally, even if a constant purchasing power of money is regarded as the primary goal of monetary policy (rather than using negative inflation to reduce tax distortions), the tax-inflation analysis implies that the appropriate response to uncertainty about the correct measure of inflation is to take the risk of having too little inflation rather than too much inflation.

Short-run cost of disinflation

Economists recognize (although central banks do not always admit) that reducing the permanent rate of inflation requires a temporary loss of output. Estimates of the short-run Phillips curve imply that reducing the inflation rate by two percentage points involves an output loss over time equal to five percentage points of GDP, for example, a shortfall of GDP below what it would otherwise be of 2.5 percent for two years.

Although this is a large and serious cost and involves significant hardship for some of those who become unemployed or remain unemployed in the process of disinflation, the 5 percent of GDP one-time cost is small when compared to a permanent increase in real income equal to 1 percent of the rising level of GDP year after year.

This comparison makes a very strong case for reducing inflation from the current 3 percent rate of CPI increase to a 1 percent CPI inflation rate or less.

A long-run Phillips curve at low inflation

The notion of a long-run Phillips curve linking unemployment and wage increases has been rejected on both empirical and theoretical grounds. A large volume of empirical literature has established that there is no long-run tradeoff between the rate of unemployment and the rate of increase of money wages. This empirical finding was anticipated by theoretical analyses that emphasized that such a relation could only persist if employers and employees failed to distinguish between nominal wage increases and real inflation-adjusted wage increases.

The evidence based on past economic experience cannot speak unambiguously to what might happen at very low inflation rates. When the inflation rate is (say) 4 percent, an individual who gets a nominal wage increase of 1 percent has a real wage decrease of 3 percent. To achieve that same real wage decrease when inflation is only 1 percent would require that nominal wages fall by 2 percent. Although the real wage decrease is the same in both cases, it is argued by some that it would be much harder to achieve if it required nominal wages to decline. If cyclical fluctuations require some real wages to be reduced temporarily but nominal wage reductions are hard to achieve, price stability or very low inflation may lead to a higher level of unemployment. In short, a reluctance to accept negative nominal wage changes may create a long-run Phillips curve at low levels of unemployment.[4]

Although the proponents of this view can point to the difficulty of achieving negative wage changes in the past, such evidence is all based on the experience in an economy with inflation rates of 4 percent or more. In that context, a fall in nominal wages corresponds to a very large real wage decline of more than 4 percent. In a very different inflation environment, in which the inflation rate has been approximately zero for a long period of time, the difficulty of negative changes may be substantially less. I find it unlikely that such money illusion would be a permanent factor of the economy.

There are, moreover, opportunities to reduce an individual's compensation without reducing the individual's money wage rate. One way would be to reduce fringe benefits, including changes in such things as post-retirement medical care, employer pension contributions, health plan features, and so forth. Such changes could actually achieve long-term reductions in the real cost of employment. The ability to make short-term reductions in employment costs can be enhanced by shifting to greater reliance on variable compensation with bonus payments that can fluctuate with business conditions.

Even if experience were to indicate that price stability was accompanied by some increase in unemployment, the resulting loss would have to be balanced against the very substantial gain that results from lower inflation through the tax-inflation interaction.

Of course, if future experience were to show that price stability did lead to an increase in unemployment of a magnitude that outweighs the price stability gains from the inflation-tax interaction, a shift to an expansionary monetary policy could raise the rate of inflation and reduce the level of unemployment. But until the evidence of such a rise in unemployment is clearly perceived, it seems quite inappropriate not to seek the quite certain gains that would follow lower inflation because of a fear that doing so might impose costs that must now be regarded as uncertain.

Impaired effectiveness of monetary policy

Price stability makes it difficult for the Federal Reserve to achieve a large reduction in the real rate of interest during a cyclical downturn because the nominal interest rate must be greater than zero. When inflation is normally 4 percent and the short-term interest rate is normally 6 percent, the Fed can reduce the real interest rate from 2 percent to minus 2 percent by cutting the nominal rate to 2 percent. It is impossible to get such a reduction in the real interest rate if the nominal rate starts at only 2 percent.

The inability to achieve a sharp decline in short-term interest rates does not mean that monetary policy is ineffective in recession. Expansionary monetary policy may be able to reduce long-term interest rates and to raise the price of equities, two aspects of the cost of funds that may be more important than short-term interest rates. Expansionary monetary policy may also be able to increase domestic demand by unsterilized exchange rate intervention.

Moreover, in the context of a fixed short-term interest rate (a liquidity trap in Keynesian terminology), the automatic fiscal stabilizers like unemployment insurance become more effective.

Even if recoveries from deflationary shocks are slower when prices are stable, the GDP losses in those recession years have to be balanced against the gain of price stability that comes from the tax-inflation interaction. A higher real annual income of 1 percent every year could easily outweigh the GDP losses of slower recovery from the occasional recessions.

Once again, this is a hypothetical problem that has not been observed in practice because the economy has not existed with price stability at any time in the past half-century. If the problem turns out to be a real one in practice, the rate of inflation could be raised. But until the problem is realized in practice, it seems unwise to sacrifice the potential gain from lower inflation because of a fear of the hypothetical impact of low inflation on the efficacy of monetary policy.

Timing of disinflation

Whatever the agreed long-term goal for inflation, there are questions of how fast the central bank should seek to achieve its desired level of inflation and under what conditions, if any, it should not act at all. These questions of timing are critical issues in the design of explicit rules for monetary policy and cannot be avoided even with less formal guidelines. The recent discussion about "opportunistic disinflation" (the notion that the Fed should wait until there is a spontaneous recession rather than raise interest rates to reduce demand) is an important example of the question of when the Federal Reserve might prefer inaction to action.

Appropriate timing depends on two factors, a technical one and a political one. Economists generally emphasize the technical consideration of the speed of adjustment of the expectations of private sector decisionmakers. The faster that those expectations adjust, the less costly in terms of lost output is any given degree of monetary tightening and, therefore, the more rapidly that monetary policy should disinflate. I agree with that analysis but believe that to understand monetary policy we must also look at the political context.

Central banks are ultimately subject to political control. The Federal Reserve is a statutory institution, created by the Congress and accountable to the Congress. From time to time, the Congress threatens to change the composition of the Federal Open Market Committee (FOMC) and the process by which its members are appointed and confirmed.

As a result, the Federal Reserve cannot do things that the public and the relevant elected officials strongly disapprove. Two examples will illustrate this and bring us to the current situation.

The disinflation of 1981-83

Between July 1980 and January 1981, Paul Volcker and his colleagues pushed the federal funds rate from 9 percent to more than 19 percent, precipitating a recession that began in July 1981. The Federal Reserve was able to raise interest rates so sharply because there was very strong public support for disinflation from the double-digit inflation rates that occurred in 1979 and 1980. But although inflation fell to 7.7 percent in the second half of 1981 and to 6.6 percent in the first half of 1982, the Fed kept the fed funds rate at an average of 15.5 percent in the second half of 1981 and at 14.3 percent in the first half of 1982. These very high real rates drove the unemployment rate to over 10 percent in the second half of 1982. This very deep recession was sufficient to cut the rate of inflation down to only 1.2 percent in the second half of 1982 and to 3.8 percent for 1983 as a whole.

The extremely high real interest rates in 1982 (an average fed funds rate of 12.3 percent for the year as a whole and a CPI increase of 3.9 percent implied a real fed funds rate of 8.4 percent) can be seen as a decision by the Federal Reserve to seize the moment when there was still political support in order to bring the inflation rate down sharply.[5] It is doubtful that a more gradual policy that reduced inflation to the same 3.8 percent over several more years would have been politically viable.[6]

The current situation

Consider, finally, the current situation in August 1996. The core rate of measured CPI inflation is between 2.5 percent and 3 percent. The real federal funds rate is about 2.5 percent. Why not disinflate further now if, as Chairman Greenspan frequently states, the Fed's goal is price stability?

The FOMC members can see that money wages are rising more rapidly than a year ago, that the unemployment rate and capacity utilization are well beyond recently experienced levels at which inflation accelerates, and that real output is growing rapidly. I think there is a strong technical case now for increasing the interest rate in order to prevent a rise in inflation and to reduce the existing inflation toward price stability.

But there is no public or political support now for such tightening. Inflation has remained low, with the core CPI rising at a steady rate of less than 3 percent for several quarters. Although monetary policy should reflect inflationary pressures and forecasts of future inflation, it would be difficult to argue that the inflation will soon be rising after more than six months in which most economists have been surprised by the lack of an increase in inflation.

If there were a real danger of a sharp rise in inflation, the Fed might move even without public support. But with little such risk now, the

Fed has chosen to conserve its political capital—waiting for a time when there is clear evidence of rising inflation before it increases the fed funds rate.

But that day is likely to come. I hope that when it does, the Fed will act firmly and that doing so will provide the occasion for what the Fed may then call an opportunistic disinflation to true price stability.

Endnotes

[1]This discussion of the interaction of inflation and taxes is based on the research reported in Feldstein (1996) and the papers cited therein.

[2]Note that going from 1 percent inflation to minus 1 percent inflation (that is, to actual deflation) would produce an additional real income gain from the inflation-tax interaction that is almost as large as the real income gain that would come from decreasing inflation from 3 percent to 1 percent.

[3]The gain from reduced inflation is the reduction of the deadweight loss in the intertemporal allocation of income and in the allocation of capital between housing and other uses. The magnitude of the gain from lower inflation is not the small "triangle" of traditional welfare analysis because inflation exacerbates an existing deadweight loss, causing a much larger "trapezoid."

[4]This argument has recently been developed by Akerlof, Dickens, and Perry (1996).

[5]One indication of just how high rates were in 1982 is that the federal funds rate was five percentage points higher than the level predicted by John Taylor's interest rate "rule" as calibrated to the Greenspan years.

[6]The back-to-back recessions that began in January 1980 and ended in November 1982 with only a six-month gap in between, meant a period of downturn of nearly three years and thus, nearly three times as long as the typical postwar recession.

References

Akerlof, George, William Dickens, and George Perry. "The Macroeconomics of Low Inflation," *Brookings Papers on Economic Activity,* 1996.

Feldstein, Martin. "The Costs and Benefits of Going from Low Inflation to Price Stability," *NBER Working Paper 5469*, forthcoming in C. Romer and D. Romer, eds., *Monetary Policy and Inflation.* Chicago: University of Chicago Press, 1996.

Overview

Jean-Claude Trichet

Thank you, Mr. Chairman. First of all let me say how impressive it is to be before such a distinguished audience. With the permission of Alan Greenspan, I would like to remind everyone about a response he made once in the U.S. Senate, according to the report we received in Paris. Alan was testifying before a Senate hearing and after he spoke, a senator responded, "Then Alan, I understand that you are very likely to increase (or decrease) rates in the year to come." And the quoted answer Alan gave was, "Senator, if you think you understood what I just said, I probably made a mistake somewhere."

Let me say a few words about the French experience seen from three particular angles: first, our experience in bringing down inflation during the 1980s; second, central bank independence which, for the last three years, has been a particularly telling experience for us; third, our experience with monetary targeting, which is important here. And after having been as concise as possible on these three matters, I would like, as did the Chairman, to express my personal views on what kind of lessons can be drawn from this extraordinary colloquium.

First, our experience in bringing down inflation. In France over the last seven years, we have brought inflation down from about 9 percent to around 2 percent. What I consider absolutely key in this process, which became a regular process year after year, was that as we diminished inflation each year we gained confidence in the efficiency of the process. We based it on a set of economic policy operational tools. First of all, of course, was our monetary policy. In our perspective, monetary policy was based upon two intermediate targets. We first set nominal money targets based upon appropriate monetary aggregates. We also considered our belonging to a multilateral framework, the exchange rate mechanism (ERM), as being important to that process. In our European perspective, these two tools were mutually re-enforcing and were extremely helpful from the monetary policy standpoint for embarking on this disinflationary process.

But *monetary policy* actions alone, of course, could not suffice. We also embarked on an *appropriate fiscal policy* over that time. I would say that we pursued a tighter fiscal policy from 1983 until 1988. So, over that five-year period, our tightening of fiscal policy mutually re-enforced our monetary policy. In our case, and I think it is important to be reminded of this, we also attached great importance to revenue and wage policies. We had some sort of *a priori* vision of the wages developments, which has proven extremely useful in our disinflation process. I think it would be a mistake not to mention that as fully part of the process. On top of that, we implemented a number of structural reforms of major importance, including price liberalization, exchange control liberalization, credit liberalization, privatization, and so forth. I think these structural reforms were the fourth policy element, which was undoubtedly key in that process.

We observed that this recipe was working and we could tell very early in the process that we could get where we wanted to go. We don't suggest, of course, that this is a universal model that could be applied everywhere. But it might be interesting to analyze it in the perspective of this colloquium.

The second point I would like to make relates to the independence of the central bank. I understand that at one end of the spectrum of the analysis of this problem, some believe there is a similarity between independence and transparency. They believe both could be considered close substitutes. There might be a hint on the fact that central bank independence is not necessarily the most important question or even an accurate question. Others insist that instrument independence is sufficient because they believe there are several ways to design central bank incentives to achieve the optimal policy—a policy that would timely respond to shocks while maintaining long-run price stability. I think that others are claiming that instrument and goal independence should be the norm. In our experience, we have a lot of both instrument and goal independence. The law states the Bank of France shall formulate and implement monetary policy with the aim of ensuring price stability. It is more or less the same wording that is in the Maastricht Treaty as it regards the overall goal of the future European System of Central Banks (ESCB) and European Central Bank (ECB). From our perspective, we consider this formulation to be a good one because ensuring price stability is the goal. I would say practically that there is as much independence of monetary policy embodied in working out the right formulation on the goal on one hand and the right implementation on the other.

I would insist that in our case today, and not only during the disinflationary process, we are basing our monetary policy on two intermediate indicators. One indicator was domestic and based on monetary aggregates targeting, and the other was the participation in a multilateral exchange rate mechanism. Today, we still consider it worth continuing on this path even after we have worked out an appropriate level of low inflation. The formulation of our present monetary policy is threefold. First, the monetary policy council of the Bank of France provides a target figure on inflation because we think doing so is important for anchoring expectations of economic agents. Measured consumer price index (CPI) must remain at or less than 2 percent. For us that is the ultimate goal and we mention it as part of our monetary policy. But we don't consider it as directly targeted. To reach that ultimate goal we have two intermediate targets that we formulate in the following fashion. We monitor the appropriate monetary aggregates, which in our case remains M3, even though it is highly volatile. We target a 5 percent growth for

M3 in the medium run. This figure of 5 percent is based on an inflation rate of 2 percent or less and a GDP in volume terms of 2.5 to 3 percent. For the medium run, we also look at other indicators such as M1, M2, and total domestic debt. In particular we consider domestic debt as an important additional indicator, which is, to my knowledge, also the case in the Fed's perspective. We believe that we must look over all these indicators. Nevertheless, we consider monetary aggregate targeting key in a medium-term perspective. We also pursue a second intermediate target, which is a stable external value of the currency in relation to the most credible currencies in the exchange rate mechanism. That is the way we formulate our policy.

Now let me tell you about something we insist very much on, and that is the medium-term perspective. We can see that growth of M3 appears to be highly volatile, due, in part, to financial deregulation which has spread all over the world, particularly in Europe and in my country, to tax regulation. Therefore, the medium-term perspective of monitoring M3 seems to be of extreme importance. We would not like to annually target M3 because we think it would be difficult to fit exactly with the volatility of this aggregate.

Now that I have talked about the French experience, let me say a few words about provisional conclusions that I would draw from this stimulating colloquium. I think there is a large consensus on the following five points.

First, there is wide agreement on the remarks that Alan Greenspan made regarding the definition of price stability—a situation where inflation is not taken into account in the decisions of economic agents. I totally agree with this definition, as I believe many others do.

Second, there is support that inflation is a very complex phenomenon and its measurement is extremely complicated. In a number of countries there is a belief that the underlying true inflation rate is less than the measured CPI. I think we are going to have to live with this situation, one which is probably triggered by very rapid technological changes. Nevertheless, I don't think we should depart from our present measurements. And what is important is to ensure that there is consistency in the measurements of inflation across countries so that the comparison between the various economies remain valid, whether or not there is a systematic bias in all economies. By the way, we cannot help mentioning that if there was an important bias between real inflation and apparent inflation it would also mean that real growth in volume terms was much more important than apparent growth.

Third, there is strong consensus that there are no "monetary free lunches." I must confess, Martin (Feldstein), that your presentation was agreeable music to the ears of a central banker. I think there is real consensus that there are no magical solutions. One of the authors clearly warned in his paper to beware of magical solutions. I totally agree with that, as I assume most of us do.

The fourth point is very important from the perspective of a central banker, and I think there was also a consensus on it. It is that sound and credible medium- and long-term objectives are absolutely necessary. I believe this is the case irrespective of whether direct inflation targeting, inflation targeting, or monetary targeting is pursued. In any case, we have to run sound and credible policies not only in the short run but in the medium and long run. Credibility in the medium and long run is of the essence in our own central banking concepts. If we are not credible in the medium and long term, the benefits of what we are doing in the short term are lost in a very large part. As practitioners, we are influencing medium- and long-term rates only if we are credible in the medium and long term. I think some of the volatility we see at the long end of the yield curve, in this economy and elsewhere, is something which is intriguing and probably highly challenging in the perspective of this concept of long-term credibility.

I would also like to say that one of the provisional lessons I've drawn from what I heard here is that modesty is also of the essence. I would say this is true both in central banking and in academic circles when analyzing central banking. Reality is a permanently challenging tool. Reality is changing not only because technological trends are absolutely vibrant, but also because they have triggered this moving reality by changing the behavior of economic agents. I'm struck that we have to permanently cope with various changes of behaviors. It may be one of the reasons why we permanently invent new theories and discuss a lot of various theories. We as practitioners have to try to make sense out of the reality we have in front of us, and which is permanently changing. We are not living in a world where we can know in advance what the likely reactions of our citizens will be. Again, this is a permanent challenge.

I would like also to make a few general points about the concept of transparency. I put myself in between the two schools that I have observed here—those who say total transparency is absolutely of the essence and those who argue for a very large degree of discretion. Alan (Greenspan) in his response to the senator gave the best illustration of the latter, that a central bank must keep some degree of "mystery." To reconcile the two schools you have to be extremely transparent and visible as regards your medium- and long-term goals, but you have to retain a large deal of unpredictability in your short-term actions. This seems to be very important regarding financial markets. If you are totally visible and mechanistically predictable, I don't think you're necessarily doing a good job, given the present state of the world and with the financial markets the way they are. I would like to use the metaphor of sailing. When you sail from North America to Europe in some kind of trans-Atlantic race, you know where you're going, say, from Quebec to St. Malo. You know you're going to St. Malo. That is very clear, you are extremely visible in your goal, and you try to get to this harbor as soon as possible. But, of course, you are not totally predictable on a day-to-day basis. I mean, the wind is not totally predictable, the sea is not totally predictable, and you have to cope with a lot of problems in your ship and so forth. Again, a large degree of predictability in the long- and medium-term goals and a good deal of unpredictability in the short-term actions are the right blend in my eyes.

Now I would like to say a few words about the reasons why strict rules for the use of instruments should be viewed with some reserve.

I see the merit of the concepts that have been raised here and I see the benefit of analyzing those models, but I don't think that a mechanistic approach would be good.

Regarding inflation versus price level: From the practitioners' point of view, the price level concept is a difficult level to cope with and I would suggest looking at yearly inflation and not the price level.

I would also like to reflect on the issue of the external side of the coin. The open economy aspects of our economies seem to be a little bit under-assessed in a large number of analyses. Part of it is because we are in the United States, where the size of the economy permits a lot of the analysis to somewhat disregard the open economy aspect. But from the perspective of a country like France where the size of GDP is big, but not that big, one-fourth the size of the United States, the fact that we have an open economy is important. In France, the medium- and long-term rates are absolutely key for monetary policy action, not only the short-term rates. Again, in an open world where the arbitrage between investments at all maturities is made permanently by the financial markets, it is absolutely key that you account for your long-term credibility—not only from the perspective of domestic agents but also from the perspective of global investors. They can choose between these investments without any kind of restrictions. I would like to mention to the professors here that there might be a lot of very interesting subjects in reflecting on this interaction. The United States, Japan, Germany, France, the United Kingdom, and all the other countries are under arbitrage. We have to take that into account.

I'm not surprising anyone by telling you that I prefer monetary aggregate targeting to direct inflation targeting for a lot of reasons. One reason, which I think was mentioned by Mr. Issing, is that it fits better with the independence of the central bank. Direct inflation targeting is a concept that necessitates a discussion with the executive to reach an agreement. Monetary aggregates targeting is fully in the hands of the central bank. I think that is one of the reasons why monetary aggregate targeting will likely be adopted by the ECB.

I would like to conclude by saying that what is true for the Bank of France and for our monetary policy is totally true for the future ESCB and ECB. Long-term credibility of the ECB and ESCB is absolutely key. Already our ten-year interest rates are incorporating two and one-half years of the French franc and seven and one-half years of the new future European currency. I assume the same is true of German interest rates. The ECB and the ESCB will have the legacy of the track records and credibility of key European central banks. These are banks that global investors know pretty well. In the case of Europe, monetary stability and credibility can be illustrated by one very simple point. Seven countries have not realigned their currencies one vis-à-vis the others for nine and one-half years. And these seven countries represent about 170 million inhabitants. So you already have an enormous core in Europe backing the credibility of the future ESCB and future ECB.

General Discussion:
Overview Panel

Chairman: Andrew Crockett

Mr. Crockett: Thank you very much, Jean-Claude. Very interesting observations and comments from both of our presenters. So, I think we should ask the Kansas City Fed if we could trespass just a few minutes into the luncheon in order to have as many reactions as possible. Ric Mishkin.

Mr. Mishkin: I want to make two points. The first one is a point that Marty Feldstein raised, but I want to add to it because it is extremely important. Monetary policy can be effective when interest rates hit at floor zero. There are two reasons why I think this is true. One is that if you look at the literature on the monetary transmission mechanisms, one of the things you realize is that, despite the fact that as central bankers we focus on short-term interbank interest rates as our policy tool, many other asset prices are extremely important in terms of how monetary policy affects the economy. Hence it is very possible to pursue expansionary monetary policy even when the interest rate floor hits zero. I will not go into detail on this point, but I have written a paper for a conference at the Bank of France which goes into this issue. The other thing that should be mentioned is there is a lot of evidence which shows that the recovery from the Great Depression in the United States was one in which expansionary monetary policy was able to stimulate the economy even though short-term interest rates had hit a floor of zero. Therefore, I think this issue of worrying about hitting a floor of zero is not one that should worry us in terms of pursuing price stability.

The second issue I want to raise is that it is very important to recognize that a good inflation target is two-sided. Many people think that inflation targets are only to prevent high inflation. However, just as importantly, and maybe even more importantly, good inflation targeting prevents deflation. Indeed, preventing deflation is something that is extremely important in terms of making sure that we do not have serious economic contractions. I think the example of Japan recently illustrates that inflation targeting would have been helpful for them. They actually ended up with deflation. It was very clear that, even though the measured inflation was around zero, or a little bit less, true inflation was, in fact, negative. So, indeed, one of the things you can do to prevent serious contractions or even worse, prevent situations that get you into a financial crisis as a result of a deflationary episode, is to have an inflation target, and make it very clear that not only is it bad to go above the inflation target, but it is also bad, and maybe even worse, to go below the target. Thinking of inflation targets as indicating that monetary authorities are only going to be tough and wring inflation out of the economy is a misperception of inflation targets.

Mr. Crockett: Thank you. In order to let the maximum number of people make a point, I ask that you not only be brief but also make only one point rather than multiple points, so that you can focus on the main one. Jacob.

Mr. Frenkel: I would like to add a footnote to Marty's very interesting calculations and the comparison between the permanent gain from lower inflation compared with a transitory course of the disinflation. I think this presumes that you can actually stay permanently at medium or low inflation. If one presumes that even that hypothesis is questionable, and if you assume to aim at 3 to 4 percent inflation, you are bound to raise it down the road; then I would say that the appropriate calculations should include the cost of disinflation itself—for the same reason that the calculations of enjoying drinking should include the cost of the hangover.

Mr. Crockett: Yes.

Mr. Stiglitz: Since there weren't that many hands up, let me make a couple of brief points. One issue that has not been talked about very much during this conference is that it is natural for central bankers to focus on aggregate variables like output and inflation. But the people who bear the cost of disinflation, the people who bear unemployment, are often different from the people who are the bond holders and may bear the benefits from a lowering rate of inflation. There are distribution consequences of a number of the policies that are implicit in the discussion here that ought to be borne in mind, particularly by central bankers. The second point is that Marty's calculation of the distortion associated with taxes—the tax system, as we all know, is very complicated and we do not want to go into the whole detail—but one point is that on other aspects of our depreciation policies, we do not have true economic depreciation, we have accelerated depreciation relative to true economic depreciation. Under quite plausible assumptions, the distortion caused by our accelerated depreciation system relative to true economic depreciation increases as we get the inflation rate down from 2 percent to 1 percent to zero percent. A third point I would like to make quickly is that in terms of the overall strategies of policies, the framework that Svensson put forward is the appropriate way of thinking about this. One of the key issues on this focuses on the uncertainty of policymakers—they simply do not know what the NAIRU is or what the response times are. The key empirical issue, given this uncertainty, has to do with the cost of the errors and the cost of correcting the errors. Most of the models that people have been using have basically used linear assumptions, where the cost of disinflation is the same as the cost of inflation. There is some recent empirical work that suggests that the cost of disinflation may be substantially less than the cost of inflation. So that if you make an error, and allow the economy for a short period of time to have a slightly higher rate of inflation because you have misestimated the NAIRU, the cost of correcting that error may be very low. So taking that nominal error into account is very important in designing optimal policy. Finally, let me just comment on Ric's comment about the importance of avoiding deflation. In an economy in which there are nonindexed contracts, many of the costs that he describes are also costs that are associated with rapid disinflation, that is to say, bringing down inflation below the rates that were expected at the time the contracts were made. And that argues for a gradualist policy of adjustment.

Mr. Crockett: Scott Pardee.

Mr. Pardee: There has been no discussion whatsoever of the international dimension of monetary policy from the U.S. point of view. It is puzzling, because we have had whole sessions on exchange rate issues in the past. I guess the only answer to that is that perhaps we have had great success, both in the monetary policy of the United States in recent years in stabilizing the dollar as well as the current policy of the U.S. Treasury—that a strong dollar is in the national interest.

Mr. Crockett: Thank you. Elena.

Ms. Kohutikova: I would like to make two points. I'll try to be very brief. I am from the National Bank of Slovakia, and I would like to mention some remarks regarding the credibility of the central bank. I would like to say that the credibility of the central bank is crucial for the countries which have started the transformation process. I think the credibility and independence of the central bank was the main reason for the successful inflation rate development in Slovakia. As a lot of you already know, we started from a high inflation rate and a large devaluation expectation, but we were successful in bringing down year-on-year inflation from 25.1 percent at the end of 1993 to 5.5 percent at the end of July this year. And I think it was because of two reasons. First, the central bank started to build credibility as its first goal, and persuaded the public, firms, and also foreign investors that the bank would be able to keep inflation under control. Second, it was done in a stable exchange rate environment, which means a stable exchange rate policy during the time. Now there is the question of the forecasting. If we would like to continue to maintain our credibility, we have to influence expectations over the future. And we would like to start to do medium-term forecasting as was mentioned here—that means two years' forecasting—to provide our credibility. Now, should we be satisfied with an inflation rate between 5 to 6 percent for the next year and allow the economy to follow the restructuring process and for privatization to take place? Or should we be more ambitious and continue to reduce the inflation rate? Various economists have said that an inflation rate between 5 to 6 percent in transformation countries is very low. And, some economists think we should increase the inflation rate to 8 or 9 percent to help the economy grow. Another group of economists say we should keep inflation at our current level for the next three to five years to finish the transformation process. The central bank would like to continue reducing inflation until it reaches levels of developed countries by the end of the century. I do not want an answer to this problem. I would like only to say that whatever the inflation rate you chose for medium-term forecasting for monetary targets, forecasting could present a very big risk for the short-term credibility of the central bank, because of the lag of information and long-term statistical data. On the other hand, in my opinion, it is necessary to do it and to influence the expectations in a positive way.

Mr. Crockett: Thank you. I think you can probably say that most of those in this room agree with the group of economists that you cite at the central bank. Could we make our comments very brief now, because we are running over. I would like to give Marty and Jean-Claude an opportunity to comment at the end.

Mr. Barnes: There has not been much discussion about the role of asset prices in this process of moving to price stability. Clearly, inflation was very destructive for financial markets in the 1970s, and the move to disinflation was very positive for financial markets. We have seen that the bullish disinflation process can create speculative bubbles from time to time in asset prices. I was just wondering—is asset price inflation a side show for central bankers in the move to price stability? Or is the potential instability caused by these speculative bubbles something that we should be thinking about in this process?

Mr. Crockett: Thank you. John Berry.

Mr. Berry: I have a question for Marty. Would you achieve potentially the same results without the 5 percent loss of GDP simply by changing the tax laws directly, perhaps by eliminating the mortgage interest deduction that homeowners have or at least limiting that very severely, or perhaps by indexing the basis in capital gains or making some other type of change in the tax law?

Mr. Crockett: Let us draw it to a close now. We have had a number of questions. Can I ask Marty to give a brief response?

Mr. Feldstein: I will try to be brief. With respect to the issue Joe Stiglitz raised about the distortions on the corporate side, the work that I reported on is going to be extended. We will look in that research at the corporate side and also at the impact of inflation on international capital flows, and we will see whether that increases or decreases the dead-weight loss. With respect to John Berry's question, if you scrap the tax system, as we know it, completely and replace it with some kind of a consumption tax, in principle you could get rid of these problems. But if you work within the corporate income tax and personal income tax system, if you try to get around it by indexing, then I think the short answer is you cannot. As I said in my prepared remarks, I used to be a strong believer in indexing the tax laws. And, in a world in which there are stocks and bonds and that is about all, it is not hard to think about how to do that. Once you begin to think about the products that some of the smart people in this room and elsewhere create, then it becomes very hard to think about how you would index. Think about a convertible bond. Do you treat it like an equity or do you treat it like a bond, with respect to indexing? Doesn't that depend on whether it is in the money, or out of the money? It just becomes a very difficult problem. In the paper that made these other calculations, I devote some considerable space to explaining why I think you cannot get around this by indexing.

Mr. Crockett: Thank you. Jean-Claude.

Mr. Trichet: Two remarks. The first one concerns the question of whether or not targeting should be taking into account the two reverse aspects, or whether inflation is too high or too low. In reflecting on that, I would say that dilemma is an additional argument in favor of a monetary targeting strategy. And the question stands even more in the absence of precise knowledge of what inflation really is. If you do not know exactly what inflation really is, you do not know either what GDP growth in volume terms really is, even if you have an accurate perception of nominal GDP. It seems to me that this makes an additional element again to try to monitor monetary aggregates, in a way where you have some kind of automatic compensation between the possibility of making mistakes on inflation or making mistakes in the other areas. Furthermore, when inflation is obviously low and GDP is obviously low, then you have very low nominal evolutions; in such circumstances, the growth of monetary aggregates and of GDP in volume terms is low. So you are, I would say, on the safe side. And it seems to me that it might be again an additional argument in favor of this monetary strategy. As we get speculative bubbles, it seems to me—and I am speaking under the control of all central bankers present—that it is precisely part of central banking tasks to avoid bubbles in general, which does not necessarily please markets, but is undoubtedly part of the responsibility of the central bankers. Bearing in mind medium- and long-term interests have to be compared to short-term interests, that is a permanent arbitrage that the central banks have to make even if it is quite difficult to weigh the arguments.

Mr. Crockett: Thank you very much, Jean-Claude. Well, that now brings to an end the formal part of the conference.

I know Tom Hoenig wants to say something to us. But before he does, and recognizing, of course, that we still have lunch, dinner, and the afternoon ahead of us, I would like, on behalf of all of us here, to say a few words of thanks to our hosts—the Kansas City Fed. Over the past twenty years or so that it has existed, the Jackson Hole Conference has become, I think, the premier bonding experience for central bankers during the course of the year. And it is that because of an extraordinary combination of factors. First and foremost, I think, is the foresight with which the Kansas City Fed has selected fascinating subjects to discuss and the wide range of experience that it has brought together in the participants in the conference. Of course, I would not want to diminish the importance of the surroundings in which we undertake these discussions. I know all of us who come on a regular or occasional basis look forward enormously to meeting old friends, to discussing stimulating subjects, to enjoying the wonderful environment of the Grand Tetons and the Jackson Lake Lodge. I would like lastly to say a special word of thanks not just to the two Toms—Tom Hoenig and Tom Davis, who do a remarkable job of putting on this conference—but, of course, to all of their staff, because we all know that a conference like this does not get organized without an enormous amount of staff work. We see the tip of the iceberg, I suspect. A lot more goes into it. And I think we should remember those too. Lastly, and especially, we know that this is the last occasion that Tom Davis will be here in his present capacity. I am sure it will not be the last occasion that we have the opportunity to see him among us. And I would like particularly to say "thank you" to Tom Davis for everything he has done over the years for this conference, but more generally, a very warm "thank you" to all of our hosts, Tom Hoenig and all his colleagues at the Kansas City Fed. Thank you very much.

The Contributors

Donald T. Brash, *Governor, Reserve Bank of New Zealand*

Mr. Brash was appointed to his present position in September 1988. Earlier, he had served with the World Bank in Washington, D.C., as chief executive of Broadbank, the New Zealand Kiwifruit Authority, and the First Bank group. He is a former member of the New Zealand Monetary and Economic Council and the Committee of Inquiry into Inflation Accounting; chairman of the Economic Monitoring Group; a Foundation member of the New Zealand Planning Council; chairman of the advisory panel on the Goods and Services Tax; and chairman of four subsequent consultive committees on taxation reform on behalf of the New Zealand government.

Domingo Cavallo, *Former Minister of Economy and Public Works, Republic of Argentina*

Mr. Cavallo served in his ministry position from 1991 until his resignation in July 1996. He had been Minister of Foreign Relations for the previous two years, and National Deputy for the Province of Córdoba for two years before that. Earlier, he was president of the Central Bank of Argentina, undersecretary of the Argentine Ministry of Internal Affairs, vice president and director of the Bank of Córdoba, and undersecretary of development for that province. Mr. Cavallo also taught at the National and Catholic Universities of Córdoba and won scholarships for post-graduate study to Harvard University. He has been a member of the World Bank Research Observer Editorial Board since 1987.

Andrew Crockett, *General Manager, Bank for International Settlements*

Mr. Crockett assumed his present position in January 1994, after four years at the Bank of England where he was an executive director, responsible for international affairs. In that capacity, he served as a member of the Monetary Committee of the European Union, Alternate Governor of the International Monetary Fund (IMF) for the United Kingdom, and a member, and subsequently chairman, of Working Party 3 of the Organization for Economic Cooperation and Development. He is a member of the Group of Thirty. Mr. Crockett began his career with the Bank of England, and from 1972-89 was a staff member of the IMF, serving in various posts including chief of the Special Studies Department, assistant director of the Middle Eastern Department, and deputy director of the Research Department.

Rudiger Dornbusch, *Professor, Massachusetts Institute of Technology*

Mr. Dornbusch is the Ford International Professor of Economics at MIT, where he has taught since 1975. A research associate of the National Bureau of Economic Research, he also serves on the Panel for Economic Activity at the Brookings Institution, the Advisory Board of the Institute for International Economics, and the Academic Panel of the Federal Reserve Bank of New York. He has been a consultant to the International Monetary Fund, the United Nations, and the World Bank. He has written extensively on exchange rate and currency problems, inflation, stabilization, and trade policy, and has a monthly column in *Business Week*. Among other honors, he is a fellow of the American Academy of Arts and Sciences and of the Econometric Society.

Martin Feldstein, *President, National Bureau of Economic Research*

Mr. Feldstein is the George F. Baker Professor of Economics at Harvard University as well as president of NBER, a private, non-profit research organization. From 1982 through 1984, Mr. Feldstein was chairman of President Reagan's Council of Economic Advisers. He is a fellow of the Econometric Society and the National

Association of Business Economists and a member of the American Philosophical Society, the Trilateral Commission, the Council on Foreign Relations, and the American Academy of Arts and Sciences. The recipient of several honorary degrees, he is also a director of several corporations, an economic adviser to businesses in the United States and abroad, and a regular contributor to the *Wall Street Journal*.

Stanley Fischer, *First Deputy Managing Director, International Monetary Fund*

Mr. Fischer, a member of the Massachusetts Institute of Technology faculty since 1973, became deputy director of the International Monetary Fund in September 1994. He was vice president for development economics and chief economist at the World Bank from 1988 to 1990, and has consulted for the U.S. State Department, the U.S. Treasury, the IMF, the Bank of Israel, and the Central Bank of Venezuela. The author, co-author, or editor of a number of books, including several basic economics textbooks, and widely published in professional journals, Mr. Fischer is the current editor of the *NBER Macroeconomic Annual.*

Charles Freedman, *Deputy Governor, Bank of Canada*

Mr. Freedman was appointed to his present post in 1988. His main responsibilities relate to the design of monetary policy, issues regarding financial institutions, and clearing and settlement systems. Prior to joining the Research Department of the Bank of Canada in 1974, he taught at the University of Minnesota and was a research consultant for the bank. In 1978, he became deputy chief of the Department of Monetary and Financial Analysis, and chief, a year later. He was appointed adviser to the governor in 1984. During 1989-90, he was the Clifford Clark visiting economist at the Department of Finance. Mr. Freedman is a member of both the Canadian and American Economics Associations.

Jacob Frenkel, *Governor, Bank of Israel*

Mr. Frenkel was named governor of the Bank of Israel in 1991 and reappointed to a second five-year term in 1996. He was economic counselor and director of research at the International Monetary

Fund from 1987 to 1991, and the David Rockefeller Professor of International Economics at the University of Chicago from 1973 to 1990. He is a member of the G-7 Council, the Advisory Committee of the Institute for International Economics, and the Group of Thirty. He is also a research associate of the National Bureau of Economic Research, a fellow of the Econometric Society, and a foreign honorary member of the American Academy of Arts and Sciences. His many books and articles focus on the areas of international economics and macroeconomics.

Alan Greenspan, *Chairman, Board of Governors of the Federal Reserve System*
Mr. Greenspan was appointed in 1996 to a third four-year term as chairman of the Federal Reserve Board. Previously, he was chairman and president of the New York consulting firm of Townsend-Greenspan & Co., chairman of President Ford's Council of Economic Advisers, chairman of the National Commission on Social Security Reform, and a member of President Reagan's Economic Policy Advisory Board. He was also senior adviser to the Brookings Institution's Panel on Economic Activity, consultant to the Congressional Budget Office, and president of the National Association of Business Economists.

Otmar Issing, *Member of the Directorate, Deutsche Bundesbank*
Mr. Issing became a member of the board of the Deutsche Bundesbank and a member of the policymaking Central Bank Council in 1990. He is in charge of the Bundesbank's Economic Research and Statistical Departments. From 1988 to 1990, he was a member of the German Council of Economic Experts. Previously, he had been professor of economics at the Universities of Nuremberg and Würtzburg and in 1991, became an elected member of the Academy of Sciences and Literature in Mainz. Apart from his numerous contributions to professional journals and collected volumes, Mr. Issing has written a number of books, including two leading textbooks in monetary economics.

Mervyn King, *Chief Economist and Executive Director, Bank of England*

Mr. King accepted his present position in March 1991, a year after becoming a non-executive director of the Bank of England. After teaching posts at Cambridge and Birmingham Universities, and visiting professorships at Harvard University and Massachusetts Institute of Technology, Mr. King joined the faculty of the London School of Economics in 1984, and was the first director of the LSE Financial Markets Group. His recent research has been on economic growth, business cycles, and the volatility of financial markets. Mr. King is a fellow of The British Academy, a member of Academia Europaea, and a past president of the European Economic Association.

Donald L. Kohn, *Director, Division of Monetary Affairs, Board of Governors of the Federal Reserve System*

Mr. Kohn was named to his present position in October 1987, after having served twelve years at the Board as an economist in the Government Finance Section, chief of the Capital Markets Section, associate director and deputy director in the Division of Research and Statistics, and deputy director in the Office of the Staff Director for Monetary and Financial Policy. His current duties include coordinating staff resources for analysis of monetary policy and associated issues. He began his career with the Federal Reserve as a financial economist at the Federal Reserve Bank of Kansas City from 1970 to 1975.

Bennett T. McCallum, *Professor, Carnegie-Mellon University*

Mr. McCallum is the H.J. Heinz Professor of Economics in the Graduate School of Industrial Administration at Carnegie-Mellon University. The author of several textbooks and numerous papers on monetary economics, macroeconomics, and econometrics, he also serves on the editorial boards of several journals. Mr. McCallum is a research associate of the National Bureau of Economic Research, a research adviser at the Federal Reserve Bank of Richmond, and a fellow of the Econometric Society. In the past six years, he has been a visiting scholar at the International Monetary Fund, the Bank of Japan, the Bank of England, and the Reserve Bank of New Zealand.

David W. Mullins, Jr., *Principal, Long-Term Capital Management, L.P.*
Mr. Mullins is a principal, co-founder, and limited partner in Long-Term Capital Management, an investment management firm. A member of the Board of Governors of the Federal Reserve System from 1990 to 1994, he was vice chairman from 1991 to 1994. He was assistant secretary of the U.S. Treasury for domestic finance for two years prior to his Fed service. From 1974 through 1988, he taught at Harvard University's Graduate School of Business Administration. Mr. Mullins has published widely on financial economics and has consulted for numerous firms and governmental agencies. After the 1987 stock market crash, he served as associate director of the Presidential Task Force on Market Mechanisms (better known as the Brady Commission).

Lawrence Summers, *Deputy Secretary of the U.S. Treasury*
Mr. Summers began his current position in August 1995. For the previous two years, he was undersecretary of the Treasury for international affairs. From 1991 to 1993, he was vice president of development economics and chief economist at the World Bank. Mr. Summers taught at the Massachusetts Institute of Technology from 1979 to 1982 and was a domestic policy economist on the President's Council of Economic Advisers in 1982-83. He joined the Harvard University faculty in 1983. He has written extensively on economic analysis and policy, edited the series *Tax Policy and the Economy*, and, from 1984 to 1990, was editor of the *Quarterly Journal of Economics.*

Lars E.O. Svensson, *Professor, Institute for International Economic Studies*
Mr. Svensson joined the faculty of Stockholm University's institute in 1984. He is also a research associate of the National Bureau of Economic Research, a research fellow of the Center of Economic Policy Research in London, a fellow of the Econometric Society, a member of the Royal Swedish Academy of Sciences, a member of the Nobel Prize for Economics Committee, and a member of Academia Europaea. He has written extensively on monetary economics and monetary policy, exchange rate theory and policy, and general international macroeconomics. He consults regularly for several

international, U.S., and Swedish agencies and serves as an adviser to the Bank of Sweden.

John B. Taylor, *Professor, Stanford University*
Mr. Taylor is the Mary and Robert Raymond Professor of Economics at Stanford and director of the Center for Economic Policy Research. Before joining the Stanford faculty in 1984, he taught economics at Princeton and Columbia Universities and was a senior staff economist on the Council of Economic Advisers. He was a member of that council from 1989 to 1991. Now an adviser to the Congressional Budget Office and an honorary adviser to the Bank of Japan, Mr. Taylor is a fellow of the American Academy of Arts and Sciences and the Econometric Society and a research associate at the National Bureau of Economic Research. His most recent book is *Economics*, an introductory textbook for college students.

Gordon Thiessen, *Governor, Bank of Canada*
Mr. Thiessen was appointed to his present position in February 1994. During his seven-year term, he also chairs the bank's board of directors. He joined the Bank of Canada in 1963, working in both the research and monetary and financial analysis departments. From 1973 to 1975, he was a visiting economist at the Reserve Bank of Australia, then returned to the Bank of Canada where he served successively as adviser to the governor, deputy governor, and senior deputy governor. He has been a director of the bank and a member of the executive committee since 1987.

Josef Tosovsky, *Governor, Czech National Bank*
Mr. Tosovsky was named to his current post in 1993. He joined the State Bank of Czechoslovakia (the central bank of the former Czechoslovakia) in 1973, working in various capacities and undertaking foreign assignments in Britain, France, and other western countries. He became president of the bank in 1989. As governor of the Czech National Bank, he represents the Czech Republic in the International Monetary Fund, the World Bank, and the EBRD. A member of the Scientific Board of the Prague School of Economics, he has been honored for his work in economic transformation. In 1994, he received only the second European Banker of the Year award.

Jean-Claude Trichet, *Governor, Bank of France*
Mr. Trichet accepted his present position in 1993, after a long career in service to the French government. In 1978, he became economic adviser to the Minister for Economic Affairs and Finance and adviser to French President D'Estaing. He moved to the French Treasury in 1981 and served as head of the Office for Development Aid, deputy director of Bilateral Affairs, head of International Affairs, and chief-of-staff to the Minister of Economic Affairs, Finance, and Privatization. He was named undersecretary of the Treasury in 1987, a post he held until moving to the central bank. Mr. Trichet has been decorated by a number of foreign nations and by France, which awarded him the National Legion of Honor.

The Participants

JAMES ALEY
Fortune Magazine

ÖMER ALTAY
General Manager
Foreign Relations Department
Central Bank of Turkey

WAYNE ANGELL
Senior Managing Director
and Chief Economist
Bear Stearns & Co., Inc.

STEPHEN H. AXILROD
Economic Consultant
New York, New York

URBAN BÄCKSTRÖM
Governor
Bank of Sweden

ARMANDO BAQUEIRO
Director of International
Institutions and Agreements
Bank of Mexico

MARTIN H. BARNES
The Bank Credit Analyst
Research Group

STEVEN BECKNER
Market News Service

JACK H. BEEBE
Senior Vice President and
Director of Research
Federal Reserve Bank
of San Francisco

C. FRED BERGSTEN
Director
Institute for International
Economics

RICHARD B. BERNER
Executive Vice President
and Chief Economist
Mellon Bank

JOHN BERRY
Washington Post

SÜKRÜ BINAY
Vice Governor
Central Bank of Turkey

CAREN BOHAN
Reuters America, Inc.

ROGER E. BRINNER
Executive Director
and Chief Economist
DRI/McGraw-Hill

J. ALFRED BROADDUS, JR.
President
Federal Reserve Bank
of Richmond

LYNN E. BROWNE
Senior Vice President and
Director of Research
Federal Reserve Bank
of Boston

ANTONIO CASAS-GONZALEZ
President
Central Bank of Venezuela

ROBERT H. CHANDROSS
Senior Vice President and
Chief Economist
Republic National Bank
of New York

ROBERT CHOTE
Financial Times

GERALD CORRIGAN
Chairman
International Advisers
Goldman Sachs and Company

JOSEPH R. COYNE
Assistant to the Board
Board of Governors of the
Federal Reserve System

J. DEWEY DAANE
Professor Emeritus
Owen Graduate School
of Management
Vanderbilt University

DANIEL DAIANU
Chief Economist
National Bank of Romania

MICHAEL R. DARBY
Professor
Anderson Graduate School
of Management
University of California-
Los Angeles

THOMAS E. DAVIS
Senior Vice President
and Director of Research
Federal Reserve Bank
of Kansas City

ROBERT A. DENNIS
Assistant Director
Macroeconomic Analysis
Congressional Budget Office

ANTONIO DE SOUSA
Governor
Bank of Portugal

RIMMER de VRIES
Consultant
J.P. Morgan and Company

WILLIAM G. DEWALD
Senior Vice President
Federal Reserve Bank
of St. Louis

MARK R. DRABENSTOTT
Vice President and Economist
Federal Reserve Bank
of Kansas City

ROBERT H. DUGGER
Director
Tudor Investment Corporation

ROBERT A. EISENBEIS
Senior Vice President and
Director of Research
Federal Reserve Bank
of Atlanta

ZIAD FARIZ
Governor and Chairman
Central Bank of Jordan

LUBOMIR FILIPOV
Governor
National Bank of Bulgaria

PETER R. FISHER
Executive Vice President
Markets Group
Federal Reserve Bank
of New York

WILLIAM F. FORD
Professor
Middle Tennessee State
University

MARY ANN GADZIALA
Associate Director
U.S. Securities and
Exchange Commission

LEONHARD GLESKE
Former Member of the
Directorate
Deutsche Bundesbank

MORRIS GOLDSTEIN
Senior Fellow
Institute for International
Economics

ABNER GOLDSTINE
Senior Vice President
Capital Research and
Management Company

MARVIN S. GOODFRIEND
Senior Vice President
and Director of Research
Federal Reserve Bank
of Richmond

LYLE GRAMLEY
Consulting Economist
Mortgage Bankers Association of America

STEPHEN GRENVILLE
Assistant Governor
Reserve Bank of Australia

HANNA GRONKIEWICZ-WALTZ
President
National Bank of Poland

JACK GUYNN
President
Federal Reserve Bank of Atlanta

CRAIG S. HAKKIO
Vice President and Economist
Federal Reserve Bank of Kansas City

DAVID D. HALE
Senior Vice President and Chief Economist
Zurich Kemper Investments, Inc.

H. ROBERT HELLER
President
International Payments Institute

DALE W. HENDERSON
Associate Director
Division of International Finance
Board of Governors of the Federal Reserve System

STEINGRIMUR HERMANNSSON
Governor
Central Bank of Iceland

PHILIPP HILDEBRAND
Director, London Office
Moore Capital Management

THOMAS M. HOENIG
President
Federal Reserve Bank of Kansas City

STUART G. HOFFMAN
Senior Vice President and Chief Economist
PNC Bank Corporation

W. LEE HOSKINS
Chairman and CEO
Huntington National Bank

WILLIAM C. HUNTER
Senior Vice President and Director of Research
Federal Reserve Bank of Chicago

CHENGYUE JIAO
Representative in the Americas
People's Bank of China

DONALD J. JOHNSTON
Secretary General
Organization for Economic
Cooperation and Development

JERRY L. JORDAN
President
Federal Reserve Bank
of Cleveland

JOHN P. JUDD
Vice President and Associate
Director of Research
Federal Reserve Bank
of San Francisco

GEORGE KAHN
Assistant Vice President
and Economist
Federal Reserve Bank
of Kansas City

HENRY KAUFMAN
President
Henry Kaufman &
Company, Inc.

EDWARD W. KELLEY, JR.
Governor
Board of Governors of the
Federal Reserve System

PETER KENEN
Professor
Princeton University

MICHAEL KERAN
Senior Vice President and
Chief Economist
SeaBridge Capital
Management Company

ELENA KOHUTIKOVA
Chief Executive Director
National Bank of Slovakia

J. KONING
Director Secretary
De Nederlandsche Bank N.V.

ÁLMOS KOVÁCS
Deputy President
National Bank of Hungary

CATHY KRISTIANSEN
Knight-Ridder Financial News

LAWRENCE KUDLOW
Economic Counsel
A.B. Laffer, V.A. Canto
and Associates

IWAO KURODA
Director
Institute for Monetary and
Economic Studies
Bank of Japan

KYUNG-JAE LEE
Auditor
Bank of Korea

MICKEY D. LEVY
Chief Economist
Nationsbanc Capital
Markets, Inc.

CHARLES LIEBERMAN
Chief Economist and
Managing Director
Chase Securities, Inc.

DAVID E. LINDSEY
Deputy Director
Division of Monetary Affairs
Board of Governors of the
Federal Reserve System

JOHN LIPSKY
Chief Economist
Salomon Brothers, Inc.

JOHN MAKIN
Principal
Caxton Corporation

PADRAIG McGOWAN
Director General
Central Bank of Ireland

MICHAEL McKEE
Bloomberg Business News

ROBERT D. McTEER, JR.
President
Federal Reserve Bank
of Dallas

PETER G. MERZ
Director
Head of the Legal Service
Swiss National Bank

LAURENCE H. MEYER
Governor
Board of Governors of the
Federal Reserve System

CATHY E. MINEHAN
President
Federal Reserve Bank
of Boston

FREDERIC MISHKIN
Executive Vice President and
Director of Research
Federal Reserve Bank
of New York

KIRSTEN MORDHORST
Director
Danmarks Nationalbank

MICHAEL H. MOSKOW
President
Federal Reserve Bank
of Chicago

ALKIMAR R. MOURA
Director
Central Bank of Brazil

WILLIAM MURRAY
AP-Dow Jones News Services

LUCAS D. PAPADEMOS
Governor
Bank of Greece

SCOTT E. PARDEE
Senior Adviser
Yamaichi International (America) Inc.

ROBERT T. PARRY
President
Federal Reserve Bank of San Francisco

JONATHAN PETERSON
Los Angeles Times

SUSAN M. PHILLIPS
Governor
Board of Governors of the Federal Reserve System

FRANK A. POTENZIANI
Trustee
M & T Trust

GUY QUADEN
Executive Director
National Bank of Belgium

ALICE M. RIVLIN
Vice Chairman
Board of Governors of the Federal Reserve System

NORMAN ROBERTSON
Carnegie-Mellon University

SALVATORE ROSSI
Senior Manager
Research Department
Bank of Italy

ROBERTO SALINAS-LEON
Executive Director
Center for Free Enterprise Research

HAROUTIUN SAMUELIAN
Vice Governor
Bank of Lebanon

LEONARD SANTOW
Managing Director
Griggs and Santow, Inc.

AUREL SCHUBERT
Manager of International Economic Analysis
Central Bank of Austria

KUMIHARU SHIGEHARA
Head of the Department of Economics and Statistics
Organization for Economic Cooperation and Development

ALLEN SINAI
Chief Economist and
Managing Director
Lehman Brothers

VLADIMIR N.
SMENKOVSKIY
Director of Research
Central Bank of the
Russian Federation

MARK SNIDERMAN
Senior Vice President and
Director of Research
Federal Reserve Bank
of Cleveland

JON A. SOLHEIM
Director
Bank of Norway

RICHARD STEVENSON
New York Times

JOSEPH E. STIGLITZ
Chairman
Council of Economic Advisers

DAVID J. STOCKTON
Deputy Director, Division of
Research and Statistics
Board of Governors of the
Federal Reserve System

YOSHIO SUZUKI
Chief Counselor
Nomura Research
Institute, Ltd.

ALTIN TANKU
Chief Officer
Balance of Payments Sector
Monetary Policy and
Operation Department
Bank of Albania

MIGUEL URRUTIA
Governor
Central Bank of Colombia

MATTI VANHALA
Member of the Board
Bank of Finland

STUART E. WEINER
Vice President and Economist
Federal Reserve Bank
of Kansas City

JOHN WILKE
Wall Street Journal

ALBERT M. WOJNILOWER
Senior Economic Adviser
Clipper Asset Management

JAMES D. WOLFENSOHN
President
The World Bank